Ecstasy and Intimacy

ECSTASY AND INTIMACY

When the Holy Spirit Meets the Human Spirit

Edith M. Humphrey

WILLIAM B. EERDMANS PUBLISHING COMPANY
GRAND RAPIDS, MICHIGAN / CAMBRIDGE, U.K.

Wm. B. Eerdmans Publishing Co.

255 Jefferson Ave. S.E., Grand Rapids, Michigan 49503 /

P.O. Box 163, Cambridge CB3 9PU U.K.

www.eerdmans.com

Printed in the United States of America

10 09 08 07 06   7 6 5 4 3 2 1

Library of Congress Cataloging-in-Publication Data

Humphrey, Edith McEwan.

Ecstasy and intimacy: recovering the Trinitarian shape of Christian spirituality /

Edith M. Humphrey.

p.   cm.

Includes bibliographical references (p.).

ISBN-10: 0-8028-3147-8 / ISBN-13: 978-0-8028-3147-7 (pbk.: alk. paper)

1. Spirituality 2. Holy Spirit. 3. Trinity.   I. Title.

BV4501.3.H857   2006

248 — dc22

2005054129

In memory of Andrew McEwan (1924–2005),
my father and mentor,
and in gratitude to Maxym Lysack,
my spiritual father

Contents

CONTENTS

Foreword

I find *Ecstasy and Intimacy* both fresh and refreshing — an outstanding new voice in the field of Christian spirituality, which is in need of fresh voices. At present much of the writing in the field merely hangs on the coattails of current enthusiasms, exploiting them in cheap ways. The landscape is so cluttered with these subjectivist and narcissist exploitations that the word itself, *spirituality*, has lost any ascertainable meaning in either church or world. But there is also a great deal of academic interest in the subject. That has been better served than the popular — but the writings for the most part are directed to the academy, where they do much good, but not among the pastors and congregations who most need them. This is the situation in which I find Dr. Humphrey's work so timely.

Countering popularized, generic spirituality, she insists and demonstrates that theology is an essential and integrated feature of all spirituality. Popular spirituality at present is virtually devoid of theology — moralism and gnosticism between them have emptied spirituality of theology. But it is back in full here: Incarnation and the Trinity insistently and graciously take their place as the context in which all spirituality is both understood and lived. She grounds that spirituality in the work of the Spirit at work with our spirits, bringing about lives of embodied obedience and faith. The realities of Trinity and Incarnation are everywhere in evidence throughout these pages and provide both structure and content.

On the academic front, none of the concerns of scholarship are slighted. All of them are interpreted and presented in an integrated and coherent way: biblical exegesis gives its defining witness, theological doctrines maintain their integrity and respect, and the representative leaders

ix

and writers in the history of spirituality (and this is conspicuously achieved) are inclusive of East and West; the spiritual theologians of Eastern Orthodoxy and those of western Catholicism and Protestantism become, under her pen, members and witnesses of common life in the Spirit, in Christ.

I find it a remarkable achievement: a serious work on spiritual theology that is accessible to congregations and their pastors; a competent scholarly treatment of spiritual theology that combines intellectual vigor with the life of prayer for students and their professors in classrooms. It is a much needed "bridge book" at a time when interest in spirituality is high and competent, mature wisdom is low.

EUGENE H. PETERSON
Professor Emeritus of Spiritual Theology
Regent College, Vancouver, B.C.

Preface

This is not a "how to" book on the Christian walk with the Holy Spirit. There are many helpful aids of that sort that have been written by brothers and sisters throughout the ages, by those who have experienced the sort of intimacy with the Lord for which we all yearn. My aim here is more modest. This is a *study* of "Christian spirituality," intended to clarify what is meant by this term, and to hold out the astonishing potential of Christian intimacy with God, witnessed to by Scripture and the ongoing tradition of the Church in West and East. The work emerges from retreats, classes, and personal query, and is offered to my friends in Christ in order to shine a small light into this age of confusion. It is intended not as an idiosyncratic or "novel" approach to the faith, but is strong only insofar as it truthfully represents the common mind of Christ's body, the Church, past and present. I am therefore enormously grateful to the many students, pastors, priests, family members and friends who have challenged me in my living, thinking and praying, and given this study whatever depth it may possess. In particular, I want to thank Bessie McEwan, Ellen Little, Debra Wilson, Andrew Purves, Charles Partee, Eugene Peterson, and Matthew Bell, who have read all the manuscript, or portions of it, and given invaluable responses.

I am convinced that today's Christian community especially would benefit from a phrase now usually relegated to the footnotes of Luke's Gospel (because it does not meet scholarly tests for "best readings" in evaluating our ancient manuscripts of the New Testament). I refer to Jesus' verbal reprimand of two disciples who were dismayed by the spirit of their age, and wanted to "correct" their contemporaries in no uncertain terms. To them (in older versions such as the King James) Jesus exclaims, "Ye know not what manner of spirit ye are of!" (9:55). A traditional French translation, the *Louis Segond*, puts it this way: *Vous ne savez de quel esprit vous êtes animés* ("You do not know by which spirit you are enlivened!").

We, too, have reason to be dismayed by the darkness and ambiguities of our day, and may well find ourselves disoriented so that we mistake "the Spirit" who gives us life. We need, in every way, to be formed and informed by the love, light, and life of the true God — and this most deliberately in an age that seems intent to do it "my way." The following eleven chapters, divided into an introduction, three "triads" of three chapters each, and a conclusion, may be used by one reader or by a group studying together. Each section is followed by short readings to aid in further meditation (so that study is graced by prayer), by suggestions for further study, and by questions for further discussion. All biblical quotations, except where I offer my own translation, are taken from the Revised Standard Version. Section II B, which contains a select survey of "spiritual theologians" through the ages, may either be "tasted" only in part and returned to later, or given a good deal more time at the first reading than the other chapters. Though the readings in this section are by no means comprehensive, the material is intense and varied! It is therefore important not to be wearied by the feast represented there, but rather to read what is manageable, and to take the necessary time (whether all at once, or bit by bit) to truly gain from these insights of our older siblings in Christ.

It is my prayer that this investigation into the human spirit and the Holy Spirit will intrigue those who read it to move further into the Christian tradition of authentic spirituality. A deep love for the biblical writings and for the Christian spiritual theologians is sure to strengthen our identity in Christ, our fellowship with the Triune God, our communion with each other, and our lively testimony to those who are not yet part of the Christian family. As St. Seraphim of Sarov challenges us, "Acquire the Spirit of peace and a multitude around you will be saved." Together, as the body of Christ, we are meant to know the "Spirit" of whom we partake, that One who enlivens us and by whom we live with open faces until finally the Father brings us, transformed, into his new creation.

Almighty God, Your Son our Savior Jesus Christ is the light of the world. May your people, illumined by your word and sacraments, shine with the radiance of his glory, that he may be known, worshipped, and obeyed to the ends of the earth. Accept all we offer you this day and make us new in him, who is Lord forever, and lives and reigns with you and the Holy Spirit unto all ages, Amen.

Feast of the Transfiguration, 2004

The Holy Spirit and the Spirit of the Age:
Discerning the Difference

At some point in the past twenty years, North Americans crossed a Rubicon. Perhaps we were unaware of it at the time, but it is now apparent that there has been a great divide, a sea change in our thinking, which has affected both academy and church. When I was an undergraduate, the emphasis in class was completely upon "objectivity," "neutral observation," "proving one's point." Now the spotlight is upon "my story," "my response," and "celebrating diversity." Not so long ago our universities valued the "scientific" study of religion; now no one blinks at hiring those who practice eclectic and imaginative spiritualities, and "engagement" is valued alongside "sound scholarship." The average undergraduate today might consider the scruples of New Testament scholar Rudolf Bultmann incomprehensible: he said "We cannot use electric lights and radios, and, in the event of illness, avail ourselves of modern medicine and clinical means and at the same time believe in the spirit and wonder world of the New Testament" (*New Testament and Mythology*, p. 4).

"Why not?" many of those under twenty will wonder. It is clear that, whatever objections to Christianity may be found in our age, fewer and fewer critics harp on the contradictions between faith and science. An uneasy covenant seems to have been forged, as "holistic" thinking has come into vogue. Today, many organizations not only hold seminars and workshops, they go "on retreat." Alternative therapies, including the laying on of hands, are applied to cancer patients in secular treatment centers. In my home country of Canada, the Québec government has at last capitulated to secularity and abolished the distinction between Protestant and Catholic school boards. However, because this structural change was effected so recently, the outcries from a spiritually-conscious public obliged each board to offer a spectrum of religious and moral values programs in each school to suit the palates of Protestants, Catholics, and others. Students browse the Internet and the self-help shelves as well as the collections of university libraries. Indeed, spirituality is back in fashion! Type "spirituality" into any Internet search engine and you will find websites with headings that are incredibly varied:

> Spirituality for Today
> Women's Spirituality Book List
> The Spirited Walker: Fitness Walking for Clarity, Balance and Spiritual
>   Connection
> Medical Intuition
> Jesuit Spirituality
> Native American Spirituality
> Transgender Spirituality
> Spirit Tools for a New Age (pyramids, wands, daggers, and
>   pendulums)
> Spirituality and Health
> Spirituality and Living Longer
> The Inner Self Magazine: Spirituality as Opposed to Religion
> Spirituality in the Workplace
> Sex and Spirituality: Frequently Asked Questions
> Apply Spiritual Ideas in Practical Ways!
> Spirituality Book — the Invisible Path to Success
> Psychotherapy and Spirituality
> The Spirituality of Wine (by Canadian author Tom Harper)
> The Spiritual Walk of the Labyrinth
> (. . . and last but not least) Male Spirituality

Some of these may sound so bizarre to those of us in the Christian tradition that we may be tempted to dismiss them. Such a dismissal is not wise, however, if we take our warning from the second and third centuries, when Gnosticism made its inroads into the Church, and if we look at the eclecticism apparent in some theological schools, or the current influential theologies that are increasingly marked by non-Christian ideals. We might think, for example, of the strong emphasis some contemporary spiritualities place upon empowerment, or of the notion that mystical experiences take us beyond doctrine to the "real thing" where all religions, including Christianity, merely aim.

At the same time, however, we must remember that utter Reality (that is, God himself) and true power (that is, his mercy and justice) are seen in the One who has made himself known to us. In coming to be God-with-us, the Word of God disclosed to us (as far as we are able to bear it) the mystery and glory of the Three-In-One and One-In-Three — Father, Son, and Holy Spirit. Not only that, but because of what God has done in Jesus, we have been given the Spirit, who guides us into the truth, love, and unity of the One whose face we long to see. In Christ, our spirits respond to this Spirit, who is united with the Father and Son forever.

Perhaps the reader is reeling at the switch from social commentary to traditional theological language! If so, this study is offered as an aid in joining together what many consider to be the "real world" with the world that is *real*. After all, our mode of living in the world is intricately connected with our understanding of reality, and especially our understanding of God, the One who defines what it is to be real. Though this is written with my brothers and sisters of the Christian household in mind, I invite any who are interested in spirituality to consider (from the perspective of the ancient creeds and the living Christian faith) the shape that human life, guided by God's Spirit, might take. A look back into the Christian family history tells us that it is not simply the "systematic theologians" like John Calvin, Karl Barth, and Helmut Thielicke, who have concentrated upon the conjoined truths of the Incarnation and the Trinity. Rather, this focus is also kept in a determined manner in the memoirs, letters, prayers, and lives of those who have been intimate with God, going as far back as the writers of the New Testament. Our spirituality, if it is truly Christian, must be focused on the incarnate God who has revealed to us the mystery of the Trinity.

Why is it that the Trinity is so very important to the spiritual life? We could begin at the very center of things, contemplating the great wonder of the Triune God, in which the Persons of Father, Son, and Holy Spirit commune in utter love, freely "going out" to one another in their ineffable interrelationships as they commune with and glorify each other. As we hear the voices of those who have been closest to the Lord, we will discover that the inner communion of the Trinity, though veiled in its essence to us, can be described in terms of what human beings call *ecstasy*. (The word itself comes from the Greek, where "*Ek-static*" means, quite literally, "standing outside" oneself; it thus refers to the abandonment of self as one goes out to the other.) It is that ecstatic movement which, it seems, enables the mysterious *intimacy* shared between the Divine Persons. Or, perhaps it is the other way around — does their shared intimacy allow for their ecstatic freedom? Intimacy and ecstasy, at any rate, are mutual states, each nourishing or attending the other.

But the inner-relationship of the Triune God is a notoriously difficult place to start. So let us instead consider what we have learned about this God through his dealings with us. As Christians, we celebrate and proclaim the "ecstasy" of God the Son, his going out to us, and standing with us. The good news is that God himself has visited us, dramatically and decisively, in the One who is God-with-us. Jesus, our Lord, has been baptized into the deepest elements of our world, has lived our life perfectly, has died our death righteously, has conquered that death in resurrection, and has ascended to the Father, taking up human flesh in triumph and glory. As a result of these particular events, the Holy Spirit has also come to dwell intimately with God's people, working out the reconciliation that has already been accomplished in Christ.

The great pattern of life, then, is the ecstasy and intimacy of God himself, who went out of the self to the extreme point, and so dwells among us in an intimacy that we can hardly imagine. Simultaneously as the Holy Spirit dwells among his own, we are told that the life of believers is hidden with the ascended Christ (Colossians 3:3), who bears our very selves upon himself, as the Jewish high priest wore the names of Israel's tribes upon his vestures, and who ceaselessly pleads for us before the throne of God. The mystery of the Incarnation is that God has assumed human nature, taking it up into himself so that it may be both healed and glorified. In the person of Jesus, we see the location of a great mystery, where human being and God the Son meet together, conjoined without any compromise of either humanity or deity. So it is that, by the ecstasy of God in the Son, and the strengthening life of that other "sent" One, the Holy Spirit, we fallen human creatures come to understand and to possess the very stuff of life. Healing begins as we go out of ourselves, immersed in the death of Jesus in baptism. Ongoing healing and transformation takes place as we are joined with him and with each other, in ever-increasing intimacy, in the Eucharist and the life of the Church. God's own rhythm of ecstasy and intimacy find an echo in the communal life of his people, and so we are both reclaimed and reformed.

One does not have to understand all the intricacies of trinitarian life to grasp this. The delight of intimacy and ecstasy is seen, for example, by the unschooled but spiritually informed Julian of Norwich. In rapture, she proclaimed,

> God the blessed Trinity . . . joined and united us to himself, and through this union we are kept as pure and as noble as we were created. By the power of that same precious union we love our Creator and delight in him, praise him and thank him and endlessly rejoice in him. And this is the work which is constantly performed in every soul which will be saved, and this is the godly will. . . . (*Showings*, chapter 58)

We yearn, do we not, to knit together the fabric of living and thinking that has often been unraveled, or cut apart? Through the study of Scripture, theologians, and great spiritual teachers, we will consider what is authentic to Christian spirituality, and how an understanding of this is both crucial and life-giving in an age of flux and confusion. Christians cannot, after all, call something "spiritual" *just* because it gives us a sense of awe, or because it brings us into community with others, or into touch with ourselves — though it is quite likely that those things, persons, and experiences that have such an effect upon us have a connection to God's Spirit to which they or we may be oblivious! Because the Trinity is the source of all love, light, and reality, however, our spiritual life can never be divorced from the tangible, wondrous picture of Jesus, perfect God and perfect Man: he is God in the flesh, the last and second Adam. Any health, any growth we experience comes from him, whether we are aware of this or not: but the conscious cultivation of the life that God has in mind for us is connected to our full celebration and concentration upon this mystery of God's ecstasy and intimacy, portrayed in Jesus the Christ.

Today many confuse "spirituality" with "experience" — the unintentional result being that they actually worship human esoteric moments or points of wonder, without apprehending the fuller reality that God has in store for us. We must not place that One, from whom are all things, and in whom all things converge, in a subordinate position. A study of those who have been intimate with Christ in past ages indicates that when the Spirit speaks, he directs us towards the unique and revolutionary Incarnation of God the Son. It may not always be easy to discern the difference between the worship of experience and the worship of that

One from whom all experience flows. Though we are Christians, we are in a fallen and confused world; moreover, in the twenty-first century, we inhabit a world unpracticed in the disciplines that form the mind and life of Christ. We may *feel* spiritual, but we need to watch the checks and balances that have been given to us — the story of Scripture, the witness of the Church through the ages, and the voice of the entire communion today. Careful listening to how the Spirit has led Christians throughout the ages may surprise us. We may well discover that our age and even our ecclesial community have become tone-deaf to some of the most basic spiritual truths. Surely this is why members of churches and denominations across the board find themselves embattled over whether new measures taken by some groups represent "a Holy Spirit moment" or a departure from the "faith once given." In a day that is so intrigued with spirituality as a means to authentic living, we need to recover an understanding of the Third Person of the Trinity, and what this means for us in practical, as well as theological terms. Not that practicality and theology are to be sharply distinguished! For what we know about God is the foundation for what we know about ourselves and our world.

Jesus is quoted in the Gospel of Matthew as saying that "a scribe trained for the kingdom of God is like a householder who brings out of his treasure room what is new, and what is old" (Matt. 13:52). Jesus' words were well heeded by the seventeenth-century priest and poet George Herbert, whose poem "Ungratefullnesse" calls attention to the great mysteries unveiled in the salvation story:

> Thou hast but two rare cabinets full of treasure,
> The *Trinity,* and *Incarnation:*
> Thou hast unlockt them both,
> And made them jewels to betroth
> The work of thy creation
> Unto thy self in everlasting pleasure.

This poem reminds us of the two rare gifts that the holy God has bestowed upon us, his much-beloved creation — the "unlocked treasures" of the Trinity and the Incarnation. He has shown us these great mysteries as promises of things to come; he has, in the unveiled secrets of the Trinity and the Incarnation, shown us something about his own nature (wonder of wonders!) and about ours.

How is it, then, that so many remain unimpressed about these great treasures? Well, it has, perhaps, always been this way. As human beings, we are prone to the destructive attitude of ungratefulness. Theologians have looked back to the story of the Fall in Eden, and have seen the first sin of humanity to be arrogance, overweening pride, disobedience, and so on. But all these things are secondary, aren't they? In Romans, Paul tells us that the very first sin is lack of gratitude — our inability to accept the Good Creator and the good creation as God had given it, and to give thanks (1:21). That primal sin continues today as many turn away from the very One who aims to make them free, and as many try to construct their own world around them, rather than taking reality, as God has given it, from his hands.

In the last two hundred years we have seen many scholars attacking these two great treasures of Christianity, Trinity and Incarnation. They have been unable to appreciate the greatness of these mysteries, and because of this lack of gratitude, have misrepresented and belittled them. All this has taken place in the Church, at the same time as there has been an interesting drama of reversal in the secular world — first, a dismissal of anything "spiritual" and so not scientific, and finally a popular revolt, so that society in general is now engaging in an undiscriminating love-affair with anything spiritual. The world has, in the past generation, looked everywhere but to the Christian tradition for an understanding of the spirit. But it is just when God's people come face-to-face with the mystery of the Triune God, and fall on their faces before God's own great humility, astounded at that ecstatic action in which God became human for our sakes — it is at these moments that we find our own meaning and our own healing. It is in gazing at him that we find our own place and start on the way to health.

Perhaps the problem is that we have, as a Christian family, frequently relegated our understanding of the spirit and the Holy Spirit to a locked cabinet labeled "Correct Doctrine." We know they are there, but we never feel compelled to bring them out. Yet the Epistle of James tells us that if our faith is simply an agreement of the mind, it is not a living faith — "you believe that God is one; you do well. Even the demons believe — and shudder!" (James 2:19). It is not enough, in other words, to have correct doctrine — to say, for example, that we believe the Apostles' and Nicene Creeds in an intellectual sense. Nor should we use doctrines to place ourselves above others whose understanding is not complete. No, our glimpse into the wonders of the Triune God, and the Incarnation, should do more than feed our brains, or make us feel good about ourselves — it should change us!

The spring before I left Canada to teach at a seminary in Pittsburgh, I had two significant experiences. The first was when as a guest speaker I visited a large mainline church not of my own Anglican tradition. This was a church filled with believing Christians — I knew many of them personally. Yet throughout the entire service, I was surprised to discover that the trinitarian name of Father, Son, and Holy Spirit was only invoked once, and then in a modified formula that, responding to the concerns of feminism, did not speak of Father and Son. In the absence of hearing God's proper name, I realized that the invocation of the Triune God has become part of the air that I breathe: I missed the name "Father, Son, and Spirit" with an intensity that almost hurt. I wanted to cry out to my friends, "I know that you love this God: call out his name!"

That same week I had the joy of taking a friend of mine, a former Jehovah's Witness, to Evening Prayer. The Jehovah's Witnesses strictly prohibit their members from worshiping at Christian churches, and so for years after she left that religion it was difficult for her even to enter a church building. But the time came when she felt brave enough to do so. She and I had talked a great deal about Jesus and about the Scriptures; in many ways she knew "what to expect." But as we sat through the service, I was struck, for the first time, with the number of times that God the Father, Son, and Holy Spirit was named. Almost, I was uncomfortable for her, for the Jehovah's Witnesses teach that the Trinity is an idolatrous doctrine, and I had not remembered how often the Trinity is named in traditional liturgical worship. Yet I was grateful as well, for my discomfort caused me to think carefully. I was again reminded of how it is that we can call ourselves sons and daughters of God. It is *in Christ* that we can be bold and reasonable to name Father, Son, and Holy Spirit, and in this naming we actually share in their love, thus finding our own identity. "May they be one, as we are one," Jesus prayed the night before he died for us.

But many have forgotten this. They think we are God's "children" just because we are his creatures. They think that the Trinity is simply a complicated theological formula, the best that humans can do in contemplating an unknown God. They even say that the doctrine is outdated, because it was put in the creed in ancient Greek philosophical language.

They suggest that it distracts us from the center of the faith, that is, from the proclamation of the gospel. But in fact, the two things go together: we proclaim Jesus as Savior in public, and then we celebrate the Trinity within the household of the Church. When we speak and think about Father, Son, and Spirit, we are not just making correct statements about God: we are being formed, shaped, molded within the living tradition that enfolds those who are in Christ. After all, Christians at the beginning of their new life in Christ are "baptized into the Name of the Father, Son, and Holy Spirit." The naming of the Trinity is the focal point of our affection; that One upon whom we set our affection shapes our identity. In speaking of the Triune God, we are at the Holy of Holies, the center of all things.

So then, it is not just theologians who are called to dwell upon the Triune Name. The most profound Christian mystics (or as I prefer to name them, spiritual theologians) are to be seen, in their communion with God, absorbed wholly in contemplation upon the One who became incarnate, and so gaining more and more insight about the Godhead — Father, Son, and Spirit. This is true of the early theologians of the church, from the second to fifth century; it was true of Augustine, the Cistercians, Loyola, Marie of the Incarnation, and the Wesley brothers in the West; it was true of the Cappadocians, Symeon the New Theologian, St. Gregory Palamas, and John of Kronstadt in the East. All these Christians witness to the centrality of the incarnate Son, and to the mystery of the Trinity, the source of all love.

This study, then, is self-consciously marked by the intimate mystery of the Triune God — Father, Son, and Holy Spirit — and by the wonder of the Incarnation, through which God, in divine ecstasy, brings us to life and health. Standing against the presumption of much scholarship in this age, we do not aim to learn anything "new" about this God. In invoking the Trinity we stand at the abyss of the mystery of the ages, and at the edge of all things new. After all, it is the Ancient of Days who has acted already in an utterly "new" way in the person of Jesus, and who "makes all things new" by drawing us, through the reviving Spirit, into life. Rather, we hope to add to the recovery of a perspective that has too often been sealed in the reliquaries of the past — an appreciation for the Trinity as the shaping source of life. Renewed meditation upon those themes that have been central in the Church's life and thinking — the incarnate Son and the Triune God — will surely nourish the ecstasy and intimacy that is meant to characterize our communion, both with God and with each other. As a structural reminder of the One after whom all life is patterned, I offer three "triads" of love, light, and life, each one centering around a Person of the Trinity, but not in distinction from the others, and each one written "giving thanks to the Father, who has qualified us to share in the inheritance of the saints in light" (Colossians 1:12). It is my prayer that by concentrating mind, and heart, and will upon him, we will "see to it that no one makes a prey of [us] by philosophy and empty deceit, according to the human tradition . . . and not according to Christ" (Colossians 2:8).

> Come, Holy Ghost, our souls inspire, and lighten with celestial fire;
> Thou the anointing Spirit art, who dost thy sev'nfold gifts impart.
>
> Thy blessed unction from above is comfort, life, and fire of love;
> Enable with perpetual light the dullness of our blinded sight.
>
> Anoint and cheer our soiled face with the abundance of thy grace:
> Keep far our foes, give peace at home; where thou art Guide
> no ill can come.
>
> Teach us to know the Father, Son, and Thee, of Both, to be but One;
> That through the ages all along this may be our endless song,
> Praise to thy eternal merit, Father, Son and Holy Spirit.

> *Veni Creator Spiritus,* Latin attr. to
> Rabanus Maurus (776-856)
> Tr. in English verse by
> Bishop John Cosin (1594-1672)

LOVE

Love bade me welcome: yet my soul drew back,
    Guiltie of dust and sinne.
But quick-ey'd Love, observing me grow slack
    From my first entrance in,
Drew nearer to me, sweetly questioning,
    If I lack'd anything.

A guest, I answer'd, worthy to be here:
    Love said, You shall be he.
I, the unkinde, ungratefull? Ah my deare,
    I cannot look on thee.
Love took my hand, and smiling did reply,
    Who made the eyes but I?

Truth, Lord, but I have marr'd them: let my shame
    Go where it doth deserve.
And know you not, sayes Love, who bore the blame?
    My deare, then I will serve.
You must sit down, sayes Love, and taste my meat:
    So I did sit and eat.

GEORGE HERBERT, 17TH C.

A

The Holy Tryst and the Great Story:
The Incarnation, the Holy Spirit, and the Human Spirit

Two experts, seeking to introduce today's student to the writings of the mystics, or spiritual theologians, of the Christian community, explain their topic thus:

> Reading mystical writers — even if they are mediocre stylists, poorly educated, and separated from us by antiquated theologies and questionable methods of exegesis — may be an illuminating experience. It allows a rare glimpse of that mystery that surrounds our entire existence. For a Christian the translation of doctrine into experience . . . may also mean a homecoming into his or her faith, a feeling of "So that's what it was all about." . . . What counts as a mystical text? . . . The history of the term itself has proven too slippery to provide hard and fast answers. . . . "Mystical" applies to the hidden (Christian) meaning of the Old Testament, to the hidden presence of Christ in the Eucharist, and . . . to the universally Christian experience of God's presence in Scripture. All these meanings convey the idea of a reality concealed by surface appearances but . . . potentially manifest to all Christians. Indeed, I doubt whether before the late Middle Ages the word ever referred to a purely private, inner experience. (Dupré and Wiseman, *Light from Light: An Anthology of Christian Mysticism*, pp. 3-4)

What these scholars say about "mysticism," a word derived from the Greek, *mysterion*, applies very well to that other slippery term "spirituality," which is so popular today. (Indeed, where in the West we use the term "mystic," Eastern Christians often use the term "spiritual theologian.") Dupré and Wiseman warn us against too narrow a notion of mysticism, against the idea that we are speaking about the private spiritual experiences of an individual or an elite group. Instead, they firmly anchor writings of the spiritual theologians within the grand biblical narrative, referring to the Old Testament, the presence of Christ at the table, and the outpouring of the Holy Spirit so that all Christians may meet God in the Scriptures.

Christian spirituality should not, then, be understood in the narrow sense of a private esoteric experience, for it is about the human spirit and the Spirit of God. As well, for spirituality to be Christian, it must not float free from the great story of which we are all a part, the holy "meta-narrative" of God's dealings with the world, with humanity, with Israel, and with the Church, God's "New Israel." Whenever Christians set themselves to study the Holy Spirit and the human spirit, we are especially aided by our brothers and sisters from ages past. This is particularly so in our own rootless day, since many of us have short memories and are frequently blinkered by contemporary and skewed ideas about the nature of spirituality. We envisage subjective experiences. We think of some heroic effort of the human spirit to pierce the numinous, to glimpse or taste the ineffable. We contrast the spirit over against the body, the spiritual over against the material. Our mental furniture is crowded by the partitions placed there by the Enlightenment, especially that sharp distinction of nature and "super-nature."

Deep Knowledge in the Body of Christ

In all of this emphasis upon private individuality, concerted effort, and the supernatural, we miss the mark. For the fact that our spiritual ancestors *recorded* the sights that they glimpsed, the sounds their inner ears caught, suggests that they did not intend to hold these things to themselves. Their experiences were valuable because they took place within the context of the believing and thanksgiving ("Eucharistic") community, and because in them Christ, the head of the body, was lifted up. God's Spirit, that One who enlivens the whole family of Christ, has enlivened those spiritual theologians, mystics, hymnodists, and liturgists whom we so admire. And so they spoke; indeed they *speak*. Moreover, they interpreted what they had experienced within the context of the believing community — consequently, their *experiential theology* was not at odds with more cognitional or dogmatic thinking about God. To use the Eastern Orthodox adage, "a theologian is one who prays." As Dupré and Wiseman put it, "It remains generally true that mystical texts place a greater emphasis upon the communally or individually *experienced* presence of God than related systematic or pastoral ones do. This provides the reader with no pretext for discarding the theoretical husk in favor of some alleged core of pure experience" (p. 5).

So we see that Christian spirituality deals with experience, but not out of context, nor at the expense of theology. What is most fascinating is how the writings of our spiritual mothers and fathers kindle our hearts, and deepen our understanding. Not a few people have remarked upon how they awaken within the reader a warmth, an insight, or view of Christ that is more than rational. In this enlivening power, the spiritual writings follow after the pattern of the Scriptures themselves, for the Bible is meant not simply to teach information *about* Christ, but to be an icon, a window, a means to meet God and to be met.

In the texts from Scripture and in the spiritual writings of those who have followed in the biblical tradition, we are invited, as part of the Christian family, to taste and see, not simply to grasp ideas rationally. (Note that we are called to not *less* than a rational response, but to something that is *more* — richer, deeper, greater than a proposition or assertion of something). The Latin verb *sapere* ("to taste") rather than the verb *cognoscere* (to know intellectually) best describes our pursuit. Remember that the very term *homo sapiens* is defined by this verb *sapere*, which implies a wise, sensible, experienced, judicious, inspired mode of knowing. Moreover, though this book might be thought of as a dialogue between the author and the reader, it is my fervent hope that it is not simply a two-way discussion, or grist for solely intellectual study. Indeed, this written study has grown out of group reflection, Christian worship, the confession of the ecumenical creeds, and the communion of believers as well as out of scholarship. It is for that reason that I invite the reader, or a group of readers together, to enter this discussion as part of the larger ideal context within which Christians read the Scriptures and worship. We learn best together, as a community of saints, spread across time and space — rather than through a study that is conceived and executed in an isolated, disconnected, novel, or purely cerebral manner. As we meet through the instrument of written words, it is my prayer that we will come to see and celebrate the communion we have with God as something that is the birthright of all of us together, not of the specially placed saint or separated ascetic. "For we all, with unveiled faces, beholding/reflecting the glory of the Lord, are being transformed into the same image from one degree of glory to another; and this comes from the Lord, the Spirit" (2 Corinthians 3:18).

Meeting in the God-Man

Though St. Paul speaks of glory, and though we are concentrating upon *spirituality*, the world into which we are entering is not a world of the spiritual over against the material, of the sacred over against the profane. The centerpiece of our Christian story, the Incarnation of God, should warn us against this kind of divide: the Word became flesh. That ancient hymnic passage from Philippians 2:5-11 says it all:

> Let the same mind be in you, the one in Christ Jesus,
> Who, though he was in the form of God,
> Did not regard equality with God something to be seized,
> But emptied himself,
> Taking the form of a slave,
> Being born in human likeness,
> And being found in human form,
> He humbled himself and became obedient to the point of death —
> That is, the death of the cross!
>
> Therefore God also highly exalted him, and gave him the name
>   that is above every name,
> So that at the name of Jesus, every knee should bow,
> Heavenly, earthly, or under the earth,
> And every tongue should confess that Jesus Christ is Lord
> To the glory of God the Father.

In this passage, we see God's embrace of the whole world, flesh and all, death and all — an embrace that shows the character and the glory of God. Attention to God as Creator and Re-creator should also warn us against this divide between spirit and matter. The Spirit hovered on the

16

waters; the Spirit calls the faithful to "come," to hope for a new cosmos vivified by God's own Spirit.

The Points of Contact

All of life, not simply human life or what goes on in spirits over against bodies, is therefore touched by what we consider spirituality. God's point of entry for us may be deep within, as the Holy Spirit works in the center of our beings, speaking within our spirits. At the same time, when we are welcomed by God, we come to participate in the Body of Christ (that is, we have communion with *persons* in Christ), and so are not simply touched in a nonmaterial, non-corporeal manner. Moreover, we must remember that God's point of entry into the world was through the medium of the flesh: God became a baby, in a concrete place and a particular time.

With this in mind, we come to our working definition: *Christian spirituality is the study and experience of what happens when the Holy Spirit meets the human spirit.* This definition is not meant to exclude God's contact with the entire person, including the body. Indeed, Christian spirituality is profoundly *incarnational,* since that meeting-place between spirit and Spirit, that holy tryst, finds its example *par excellence* — indeed, its prototype and its cause — in Jesus, the God-Man. Our Christian story is the marvelous drama of a "holy tryst" — a holy meeting in which God, through his very own love, brings humanity (spirit, soul, body) to himself. As the Orthodox theologian John Zizioulas asserts, "The mystery of the Church . . . is deeply bound to the being of man, to the being of the world, and to the very being of God" (*Being as Communion,* p. 15). Let us not hope to find a spiritual life unconnected to that one tangible, wondrous place in which perfect God and perfect humanity are joined. In observing the tendencies of the contemporary search for spirituality, we must beware of that wrongheaded quest for "religious *experience without faith* . . . a religion of *pure experience*" (Dupré and Wiseman, p. 23). Such a quest recently has been proposed to the troubled Anglican faith community by Bishop Michael Ingham, who, in his *Mansions of the Spirit,* cautiously valorized an "esoteric" search for that mystical experiential point beyond doctrine where "all faiths meet" (pp. 119-23). But to do this is to place that One from whom are all things and in whom all things converge in a subordinate position; it is to miss the staggering import of the unique and revolutionary Incarnation of God the Son. It is to worship experience, and not that One from whom all experience flows.

God's Ecstasy and Intimacy in the Grand Story

In contrast to a view like Ingham's, we hear the witness of a multitude — thinkers, prayers, writers, liturgists — who do not despise the rational, who do not dismiss or relativize theology, but who have learned to bring the human mind (the *nous* in Greek) "down into the *heart*," into the center of their being. There they are met by God, that same God of Abraham, Isaac and Jacob, the God of Israel, the God who became flesh in Jesus, the God who poured out the divine Spirit upon the Church, the God who enlivens the Scriptures (written on *material* pages) for those who seek truth, love, and life. Intimacy becomes possible because God is love, sharing intimacy within the Persons of the Trinity, and because God delights also to move out to us — to "stand outside" the Godhead ecstatically. By *God's* great ecstasy, intimacy with him becomes reality. Thus, in concert with the first apostles, there are other mature Christian witnesses who have "seen" God's glory with what they call "noetic" (from *nous*) sight — opened eyes, not separated from but integrated with the heart and the eyes of the body. These pilgrims, in their writings, *confirm* the biblical narrative and the creeds by what they have experienced in prayer.

And what is this grand story that informs our life together? It can be comprehended, suggests Bishop N. T. Wright *(The New Testament and the People of God)*, if we think of a great play in five acts — Act I, God's creation of a good world; Act II, the fall or disruption of that good creation; Act III, God's call of Israel to be a light to the world and his ongoing dealings with Israel and Judah; Act IV, God's climactic coming in Jesus, that One who is at once the New Israel and the New Adam; and Act V, the sending of the Spirit by the Father and the Son into God's Church, as the promise of a completed new creation when Jesus returns. The pattern of this story shows us that we, who seek to live faithfully within the final Act, need to understand spirituality in terms of the story's climax: the life, death, resurrection, and ascension of Jesus. This climactic Act IV, where Jesus is central, is thus the turning point of the human story. In him we see what happens when the human spirit and the Spirit of God are perfectly united, and so we see what God purposes to do in us. The Christian family, since the time of Pentecost, has become a participant in the ongoing final act, and awaits its consummation, when the new creation, begun in the Holy Spirit, will be made complete after the judgment and return of Jesus the Christ.

Here, then, is the story in brief: Adam and Eve walked with God; fallen humanity, its spirit wounded, lost that ease of communion; redeemed humanity has been sent the enlivening Spirit, who is himself a promise of the unimaginable intimacy to come when "we shall be like him, for we will see him as he is." This is not an optimism born of confidence in the inner capacity of the human spirit, although we cannot ignore the wonders held within the "very good" (Genesis 1:31) human creation of God. Out of God's ecstasy comes divine-human intimacy.

The Divinity of Jesus, the Person of the Holy Spirit, and the Trinity in the New Testament

Before continuing we must do some troubleshooting, due to an unfortunate impact that some twentieth century New Testament scholarship has made upon (even Christian) readers of the Bible. There is a widespread opinion that these intertwined orthodox teachings concerning the divine and human natures of Jesus, the personhood of the Spirit, and the communion of the Trinity are concoctions of the third to fifth centuries, and not anticipated in the New Testament *per se* (perhaps with the exception of the Fourth Gospel's "high" Christology, in which the Son is identified with God).

In fact, we could read deeply in all four Gospels and find, within the structure of their narratives, a clearly implied teaching that Jesus is not simply an emissary from God, or an inspired teacher. In John, Jesus is from the outset introduced as the Son who was "in the beginning with God." In Mark, the term "the Son of God" probably has a double meaning, reflecting a common title for "Messiah" in the Jewish world, but moving beyond this toward a fuller declaration of divinity in the Roman centurion's confession at 15:39. In Luke, Jesus is heard to "rejoice in the Holy Spirit" with the exclusive statement "No one knows who the Son is except the Father, or who the Father is except the Son" (10:22). However, it is more profitable, for the purpose of clarifying theology, to consider New Testament passages that are intended as catechetical instruction; hence,

Paul's instructive letters offer more clear expositions of the role of Jesus and the Triune God. Moreover, if we find evidence of "high" Christology (that is, the belief that Jesus was divine) and of trinitarian teaching in Paul's letters, this is particularly impressive. After all, these letters are, according to the scholarly consensus about the chronology of the New Testament documents, the earliest strand of Christian writings. Thus, the theological "raw material" for the later creeds would be found in our earliest Christian documents, and a harmonious development between the first and fourth centuries of Christianity would be suggested.

A careful reading of these letters will disclose what must have been for some a shocking move by the apostle — the implicit (at some points explicit) identification of Jesus with God himself. We begin with Philippians 2:5-11, which may actually represent an earlier statement than Paul's letters, since many believe that this is his adaptation of a hymn or creedal statement already known by the community. This narrative is familiar, with its check-mark formation: Jesus, the richest of all, forfeits his "wealth" to plunge into the fallen world of humankind, and even into the degradation of a criminal's death, so as to be exalted above the heavens, and worshipped by all. On the surface, the passage seems only to indicate Jesus' pre-existence, and does not clearly establish his equality with God — though we might wonder why it is said that he does not "clutch" at this! However, the final three verses give us pause: "Therefore God has highly exalted him and bestowed on him the name that is above every name, that at the name of Jesus, every knee should bow, in heaven and on earth and under the earth, and every tongue confess that Jesus Christ is Lord, to the glory of God the Father" (Philippians 2:9-11).

What *is* the "name that is above every name"? Why, it is the Hebrew name for "the Lord," YHWH in the Hebrew (see Exodus 3:14-15 and the meditation upon this passage in the following section) or *Kyrios* in the Greek versions of the Old Testament. Some will object that Paul is not addressing a Jewish group, and that in the Greek context *Kyrios* did not necessarily imply divinity, but was simply a title of majesty and respect. Be this as it may, we cannot rest with this explanation of Paul's intent when he uses this title. For at the very point where Paul says that Jesus' name is *Kyrios*, he also unmistakably echoes the words of the book of Isaiah: "By myself I have sworn, from my mouth has gone forth in righteousness a word that shall not return: 'To me every knee shall bow, every tongue shall swear'" (Isaiah 45:23). Moreover, this verse is lodged within Isaiah's scathing denunciation of idol worship, in which God declares again his holy name, the LORD, in whom "all the offspring of Israel shall triumph and glory":

> Assemble yourselves and come, draw near together, you survivors of the nations! They have no knowledge *who carry about their wooden idols, and keep on praying to a god that cannot save.* Declare and present your case; let them take counsel together! Who told this long ago? Who declared it of old? *Was it not I, the LORD?* And there is no other god besides me, a righteous God and a Savior; there is none besides me. Turn to me and be saved, all the ends of the earth! For I am God, and there is no other. By myself I have sworn, from my mouth has gone forth in righteousness a word that shall not return: *'To me every knee shall bow, every tongue shall swear.' Only in the Lord*, it shall be said of me, *are righteousness and strength;* to him shall come and be ashamed, all who were incensed against him. In the LORD all the offspring of Israel shall triumph and glory. (Isaiah 45:20-25; my emphasis)

In the light of the prophet's strong monotheism, it is highly unlikely that Paul (or the hymn/creed he is quoting) would be suggesting anything other than Jesus' identification with the LORD, the one true God of all.

This can be clinched by turning to what might seem an unlikely spot for christological teaching, 1 Corinthians 8:1-6. Here Paul is giving practical instruction to the Corinthians regarding whether they may eat food that has been offered to idols. (This was a common practice in the ancient world, where much of the food for sale at the market had been previously "devoted" to a deity.) In the course of this contentious debate, Paul drops a theological bomb in the playground of any who might think that the monotheistic God is a mere "monad" — a divine Atom, or simple Unit. In a deft restatement of the beloved Jewish Shema, the Hebrew declaration of God's holiness and peculiarity, Paul sets us thinking about the relationship between Father and Son. "Hear, O Israel, the LORD our God, the LORD is one" (Deuteronomy 6:4) is now cast in this way:

> *"There is no God but one."* For although there may be so-called gods in heaven or on earth — as indeed there are many "gods" and many "lords" — yet for us there is *one God, the Father,* from whom are all things and for whom we exist, and *one Lord, Jesus Christ,* through whom are all things and through whom we exist. (1 Corinthians 8:4b-6; my emphasis)

21

We are hard pressed to characterize Paul's declaration except by the term "binitarianism." What is most striking is how he introduces this statement without any warning or defense, but simply as a belief that he shares with the Corinthians, so that he can get on with the business at hand — to discuss the problem of the existence of false gods and the propriety of eating food associated with them. Here, in the midst of a pragmatic point, we find a specifically Christian definition of monotheism, which Paul assumes that his believing readers share with him ("but not all possess this knowledge," 8:7). It is a formation of monotheism that includes Jesus, the Lord, along with God the Father.

These two passages, with their implicit and explicit identification of Jesus as Lord, suggest to us that the benediction of Romans 9:5, sometimes translated as referring generally to God, instead specifically identifies the Son as human and divine: "To them [Israel] belong the patriarchs, and of their race, according to the flesh, is the Christ, *who is God over all, blessed forever.*"

To this early "high" Christology, whereby Father and Son are both understood to be God, we must add the Person of the Holy Spirit. We begin with the obvious linking together of Father, Son, and Holy Spirit in triadic formulae studded throughout the New Testament:

> Go therefore and make disciples of all nations, baptizing them in the name of the Father and of the Son and of the Holy Spirit. (Matthew 28:19)

> And because you are sons, God has sent the Spirit of his Son into our hearts, crying, "Abba! Father!" (Galatians 4:6)

> But [Stephen], full of the Holy Spirit, gazed into heaven and saw the glory of God, and Jesus standing at the right hand of God. (Acts 7:55)

> Take heed to yourselves and to all the flock, in which the Holy Spirit has made you overseers, to care for the church of God which he obtained with the blood of his own Son. (Acts 20:28)

> Now there are varieties of gifts, but the same Spirit; and there are varieties of service, but the same Lord; and there are varieties of working, but it is the same God who inspires them all in every one. (1 Corinthians 12:4-6)

The grace of the Lord Jesus Christ, and the love of God and the communion of the Holy Spirit be with you all. (2 Corinthians 13:14)

There is . . . one Spirit, just as you were called to the one hope . . . , one Lord, one faith, one baptism, one God and Father of us all. (Ephesians 4:4-6)

But, some scholars have argued, it is not at all clear that "spirit" is to be understood as a person in the New Testament. After all, there is no distinction made between upper and lowercases in the Greek text, so perhaps we are translating "Spirit" in an anachronistic way, reading back the creedal formulae into the Bible. To this, we must respond that although the Holy Spirit is, in a sense, the "reserved" or "shy" Person of the Trinity, and One who has an intimate connection with humanity and creation, there are ample indications that the New Testament writers did not consider him to be a mere substance, or an emanating power from God. For example, in the Fourth Gospel, Jesus speaks about the Holy Spirit throughout by using the pronoun "he," which is grammatically surprising when it is connected, as it is here, with the Greek word for "spirit," which requires a neuter (rather than a masculine) article. Secondly, throughout the New Testament, the Spirit is pictured as having the attribute of will: the Spirit counsels (John 14:26), reminds (John 14:26), guides (John 16:24), speaks (John 16:13), convicts (John 16:8), searches (1 Corinthians 2:10), knows (1 Corinthians 2:11), teaches (1 Corinthians 2:13), dwells (1 Corinthians 3:16), gives life (2 Corinthians 3:6), cries out (Galatians 4:6), leads (Romans 8:14), bears witness (Romans 8:16), has desires (Galatians 5:17), helps (Romans 8:26), intercedes with deep sighs (Romans 8:26-27), strengthens (Ephesians 3:16), and can be grieved (Ephesians 4:30). All in all, however, the strongest action that we may attribute to the Holy Spirit is his supportive action in witnessing to, or revealing, the glory of the Son. We may conclude with St. Paul's explanation concerning the identity of the Divine Agent, the LORD, who imparted glory to Moses' unveiled face. The Old Testament narrative of the Sinai event tells us:

Whenever Moses went in before the LORD to speak with him, he took the veil off, until he came out; and when he came out, and told the people of Israel what he was commanded, the people of Israel saw the face of Moses, that the skin of Moses' face shone. (Exodus 34:34-35)

In his reference back to that event, Paul indicates that, though Moses and the people did not know it at the time, this Lord was none other than the Spirit: "When anyone turns to the Lord the veil is removed. *Now "the Lord" is the Spirit*, and where the Spirit of the Lord is, there is freedom . . . for this comes from the Lord who is the Spirit" (2 Corinthians 3:16-18).

So, then, though they do not contain a systematic working out of the Persons of the Trinity, the writers of the New Testament books adore the Persons of Father, Son, and Holy Spirit, glorying in the revelation that they are unified in action, each and together worthy of the name "God" or "Lord." It would take several centuries for this mystery to be expounded in more detail, as the Church responded to various mistakes in emphasis and understanding regarding the communion of the Three-in-One. Yet the theologians of the third to fifth centuries did not create the doctrine of the Trinity out of whole cloth. Their raw material was the witness of the apostolic community, as lived out in the Church, and presented *in nuce* in the New Testament writings. Though a great deal of modern scholarship makes the teachings about Christ's nature as the God-Man, the personhood of the Spirit, and the communion of the Trinity seem like academic affairs, they are far better thought of as rich jewels, provocative secrets that God has given to us, his beloved people. If we treasure these, and see our lives as informed by a God who is personal in a way that far exceeds our understanding, we place ourselves in a location where we may come to appreciate God's enlivening power in our lives. For it is as the Persons of the Trinity come to be with us, historically through the Incarnation of the Son, and continually through the ministrations of the Spirit, who lives within the Church, and yearns for each of us, that we discover our own spirituality.

The Holy Spirit and the Human Spirit

The study of the Holy Spirit in relation to the human spirit and the world is a vast topic that has occupied numerous theologians and biblical exegetes. We can only scratch the surface of the riches awaiting us as we come to know more about the Spirit, but some few general points may be helpful at this initial point of our discussion. We can begin by looking at a few words.

In the Hebrew Bible several words are used that are associated with the English word "spirit" and that come to be translated as either *pneuma* ("spirit") or *psyche* ("soul") when they are used in the Greek New Testament. These words include the following Hebrew nouns: *ruach*, which (like the Greek *pneuma*) can mean "wind" or "spirit" and is used of the physical phenomenon, the human spirit, and God's Spirit; *nepesh*, which is more generally associated with the Greek word *psyche* and which means "life" or "soul"; *neshamâ*, which means "breath" or "blowing" and is frequently understood as a synonym for *nepesh*. These three nouns, though somewhat distinct, have overlapping "semantic domains" (that is, they can be used synonymously in some cases), are associated with verbs that mean "to breathe," "to blow," or "to give life," and are found frequently in combination with each other or other words (for example, *nepesh haya:* "the breath/soul of life" given to the animals in Genesis 1:30).

Ruach is the word associated with God's Spirit, though it can be used for human beings, along with *nepesh*. (The life-force of animals is also spoken of in terms of *nepesh*, but *ruach* is never used to describe the animation of nonhuman creation.) God's own Spirit is the initiating Agent in the Hebrew Bible. First, the Spirit of God is introduced to the reader of the Bible in its opening verses — "the Spirit (Hebrew: *ruach*) of God moved upon the face of the waters" (Genesis 1:2). Though humankind shares with all animals the "breath of life" (1:30), we are created in a particular manner: in the first creation story (1:27) "after the image of God"; in the second story (2:7) through the intimate action of God, who "breathes" into human nostrils the "breath of life" so that Adam becomes a living "soul" (*nepesh*) and then carefully distinguishes Eve from Adam so that human beings would know communion with one another.

As we follow down through the divine saga about creation, Israel, Jesus, and the new community of the Church, we see the ministration of the Holy Spirit at all the key points: anointing prophets, priests, and kings (e.g. 2 Kings 2); granting repentance to the penitent (Psalm 51:10-11); promising a new covenant within a rejuvenated people of God (Ezekiel 36–37); hovering over the adolescent virgin Mary at the beginning of a "new creation" in Jesus (Luke 1:35); descending upon the young Messiah at the onset of his ministry (Luke 3:21-22; 4:18-21); revealing the downfall of Satan and the uplifting of the lowly through the conquest of the Son (Luke 10:21); imparting life to the disciples as Jesus "breathes" upon his own (John 20:22); recreating and filling the church at the Pentecost gathering (Acts 2:4). Because of the direction of this great story, Christians look forward with St.

Paul to the time when they will possess, like the risen Jesus, incorruptible bodies animated by the Spirit of God — "Spirit-animated" bodies in the place of "soul-animated" bodies that now must die (1 Corinthians 15:43-49). Though in our bodies we bear the image of Adam at the present time, we hope at the end to fully bear the image (body, soul, and spirit) of Christ himself — dust will be taken up into glory.

In heeding this story, in hearing it told in different tones by our older siblings, mystics, prayers, theologians, poets, and liturgists — who have lived well within Act V, in learning from them to turn our faces towards Jesus, we understand more and more what it means to live faithfully within a drama that is not yet complete:

- We affirm God's good creation, learning to love creature-hood in itself, and coming out of ourselves *ecstatically*, as we trace the finger of the Father in his creative work.
- We frankly admit the fallen condition of humanity, learning to be "unshockable" when faced with its problems and vices, and cry out with God's saints, "Lord have mercy on me, a sinner!"
- We look to the Incarnation of Jesus to make a real difference, for he holds us all in his heart — *intimacy* with him and with each other is made possible by his death, for he pleads for us, and fosters our warm response through his Spirit, and through the experiences of those who know him better than we do at present.
- We consider the being and action of the Triune God as the foundation, pattern and source of our own human fellowship, looking to that Holy One to inform and correct our skewed ideas of communion and love.
- We remember that we are in the midst of a God-directed story that has a past, and that is promised a future fulfillment, on the basis of what God has done already in Jesus. Our understanding of reality must be shaped by acknowledging the ambiguities of our present situation, and looking to God to help us bear the tensions that this "in-between" position creates.

Perhaps we pay lip service to these truths, but suspect in the back of our minds that this ability to go out of oneself so as to be in intimate communion with God is something for the rare ascetic, the unusual mystic. But St. Paul, who himself had mystical experiences unfamiliar to many

(2 Corinthians 12:1), tells us that this is not so. Though a visionary in his own right, he emphasized that it is the prerogative of all God's people to share intimacy with God. In speaking about the life of the Christian community, he contrasts it with the peculiar experience of that Old Covenant prophet, Ezekiel, who was "comforted" while in exile by a bizarre vision of God. Ezekiel beheld, coming to him in obscurity, "the appearance of the likeness of the glory of the Lord." Christians are given, together, a greater gift: God has "shone in our hearts" to give "the light of the knowledge of the glory of God in the face of Jesus" (2 Corinthians 4:6). Ezekiel's personal and reserved vision of awe has been replaced by God's startling invitation to all of us to approach him in Jesus. Together, we have been given the greatest vision of all, and are meant *together* to see this One more and more clearly, and so to join in God's generous communion. May the suspicion that this is only for the future, and only for a few, thus be banished from our mind as we become more intimately acquainted with those who have gone before. May we instead sense the lively work of the Holy Spirit in them as their words warm our hearts, inclining us to our Divine Lover and to each other. May we see through their eyes of hope the reason for our very life — to be in communion with God and with each other, to taste and see that the Lord is indeed good.

FURTHER MEDITATION

> If you are a theologian you truly pray. If you truly pray, you are a theologian. (St. Evagrius, *Chapters on Prayer*, 61)

> Trinity! Higher than any being, any divinity, any goodness! Guide of Christians Higher in the wisdom of heaven! Leads us up beyond unknowing and light, up to the farthest, highest peak of mystic scripture. (Pseudo-Dionysius, *The Mystical Theology*, I)

> Christ is the *way and the door*; Christ is the ladder and the vehicle, like the Mercy Seat placed above the ark of God and the *mystery hidden from eternity*. (St. Bonaventure, *The Soul's Journey into God*, 7.2)

> Do you not see how this light shines now in the hearts of the faithful and the perfect? (St. Gregory Palamas, *Triads*, 2.3.18)

God the blessed Trinity . . . joined and united us to himself, and through this union we are kept as pure and as noble as we were created. By the power of that same precious union we love our Creator and delight in him, praise him and thank him and endlessly rejoice in him. And this is the work which is constantly performed in every soul which will be saved, and this is the godly will. . . . (Julian of Norwich, *Showings*, chapter 58)

Lord, who hast form'd me out of mud,
And hast redeem'd me through thy bloud,
And sanctifi'd me to do good . . .
Enrich my heart, mouth, hands in me,
With faith, with hope, with charitie;
That I may runne, rise, rest with thee.

(George Herbert, *Trinitie Sunday*)

Love divine, all loves excelling,
Joy of Heaven, to earth come down,
Fix in us Thy humble dwelling,
All thy faithful mercies crown.
Jesus, thou art all compassion,
Pure unbounded love Thou art;
Visit us with Thy salvation,
Enter every trembling heart.

(Charles Wesley)

The New Testament offers itself . . . as a set of stories, and a single Story. . . . It offers itself as the true story, . . . the true history of the whole world. (N. T. Wright, *The New Testament and the People of God*, p. 471)

The mystery of the Church . . . is deeply bound to the being of man, to the being of the world and to the very being of God. (Zizioulas, *Being as Communion*, p. 15)

The cross is not something that God does unwillingly or only because he can't think of a better way. At the heart of Philippians 2, and at the heart of Paul's theology . . . is the news that the one true God consists through and through, of self-giving love. . . . For this God to become human, and to die for sinners, is not a category mistake. (N. T. Wright, *What Saint Paul Really Said*, p. 69)

The goal for the Christian is union with God in love. (Lossky, *Vision of God*, p. 116)

Truly our God is a God who hides Himself, yet He is also a God who acts — the God of History, intervening directly in concrete situations. (Timothy [Kallistos] Ware, *The Orthodox Church*, p. 209)

FURTHER READING

Downey, Michael. *Understanding Christian Spirituality*. New York: Paulist Press, 1997. On the uniqueness of Christian spirituality.

Dupré, Louis, and James A. Wiseman, O.S.B. *Light from Light: An Anthology of Christian Mysticism*. Mahwah, N.J.: Paulist Press, 1988. Helpful introductory essays and selections from spiritual theologians (the above quotations from Pseudo-Dionysius, St. Bonaventure, and Julian of Norwich are from this source).

Egan, Harvey D. *An Anthology of Christian Mysticism*. Second edition. Collegeville, Minn.: The Liturgical Press, 1996. Another helpful introduction, with extensive selections, to spiritual theologians (the above quotation from St. Evagrius Ponticus is from this source).

Humphrey, Edith M. "God's Treasure in Jars of Clay." Available online at http://www.edithhumphrey.net/god's_treasure_in_earthen_jars.htm. A response to pluralism, in particular to the writings of Bishop M. Ingham.

Ingham, Michael. *Mansions of the Spirit: The Gospel in a Multi-Faith World*. Toronto: Anglican Book Centre, 1997. In a cautious pluralism, the bishop attempts to "square the circle" by offering a perspective which he calls "grounded openness." Though irenic towards Christian "exclusivists," he is influenced in his analysis of the issue by the Theosophist Frithjof Schuon, who pictures mystical religions in a spectrum, all of which point to the unknown Reality.

Lossky, Vladimir. *The Vision of God*. Translated by Asheleigh Moorhouse.

Crestwood, N.Y.: St. Vladimir's Seminary Press, 1983. An Orthodox study of the "vision of God" from the time of the Scriptures through the fourteenth century.

Ware, Kallistos. *The Orthodox Church.* Second revised edition. London: Penguin, 1993.

—————. *The Orthodox Way.* Crestwood, N.Y.: St. Vladimir's Seminary Press, 1995. A compelling and accessible introduction to Orthodox spiritual theology.

Wright, N. T. *The New Testament and the People of God.* Minneapolis: Fortress Press, 1992. An involved tracing and explanation of Scripture's "grand narrative": not for the beginner.

—————. *What St. Paul Really Said.* Grand Rapids: Eerdmans, 1997. An accessible introduction to Paul's theology in relationship to the rest of the New Testament, for the layperson.

Zizioulas, John D. *Being as Communion: Studies in Personhood and the Church.* Crestwood, N.Y.: St. Vladimir's Seminary Press, 1993.

FURTHER REFLECTION AND DISCUSSION

1. How would you define "mystery" and "mystic"?
2. How do we maintain both the personal and the corporate understanding of communion with God?
3. How can Christians affirm the uniqueness of Christ and the specific nature of God's Holy Spirit without appearing arrogant in this pluralistic age?
4. What is the relationship between Scripture, tradition, reason, and experience in our understanding of the Christian life?

B

Separation from God and Approach

It's Not All about Us

In the last section, we established a working definition: *Christian spirituality is the study and experience of what happens when the Holy Spirit meets the human spirit.* This, then, directs us as Christians to begin our study of spirituality with the Incarnation itself, that is, with *God's approach* to us. To begin this way around is in conflict with the general perspective of many teachers on spirituality today, who assume that spirituality is fundamentally about *us*. This preoccupation lies behind, for example, the lament of Lauren Artress, Episcopal priest and Western proponent of the spiritual practice known as the "Labyrinth Walk": "we lost a sense of connection to ourselves and to the vast mystery of creation" *(Walking a Sacred Path)*. Certainly these connections are involved in the spiritual life. But to focus on them is to focus on ourselves first and foremost. What about the *primary* communion to which we are called, what about our connection to the Spirit of Truth, the One to whom our spirits are called to respond?

A truncated spirituality, intent mainly upon finding an inner connection to the self, does not truly represent the mind of Christ. As Christians, we proclaim the good news that God has himself visited us, dramatically and decisively, in the One who is God-with-us, Jesus the Lord. This One died our death, conquered it in the resurrection, and ascended to the Father in triumph and glory. As a result of these particular events, the Holy Spirit has also come to dwell intimately with God's people, working out the reconciliation that has already been accomplished in Christ. This is why sometimes, when reading Paul's words, we are not always sure whether Paul is using the word "spirit" (*pneuma*) in order to speak about the redeemed human spirit, or about the Holy Spirit. So, for example, in 1 Corinthians 2:10-13, there is a seeming ambiguity in the use of the word as it applies to the Christian. Are we meant, in verses 12 and 13, to think that we have received an enlivened human spirit from God, so that we should understand and interpret spiritual truths, or the Spirit of God himself, or both?

Such ambiguity does not mean that Paul considers the human creature's spirit to be identical, by virtue of his or her own nature, with God's Spirit; rather, it shows Paul's deepest desire: that we should have the mind of Christ, God's Spirit joining intimately with ours. Part of the mystery of the Incarnation is that God has assumed human nature, taking it up into himself so that it might be both healed and glorified: body and soul, we have been visited by our Creator, and we see the location of this mystery in Jesus himself. All those things that are "out of joint" — our spirit, will, heart, mind, passions and body which tend to war against each other, our interpersonal relationships, our relationship with other parts of creation — all these things find their healing because of the initiative of God.

Two Challenges

In considering spirituality in the light of our Christian story, two challenges emerge for us today — our needy creaturely status; and the particularity of God's Spirit over against other concepts of divinity, freedom, or power. These two challenges must be taken seriously without (on the one hand) inculcating in ourselves a "low view" of humanity, or (on the other) fostering a triumphalism that declares God's Spirit only to be active among those who call themselves Christians. Instead, we must affirm a sober and full assessment of the fallen human condition and human nature, alongside a joyful response to the particularity of God's clearest revelation — his glory in the face of Jesus.

The Old and New Testaments, we have seen, are studded with moments in which Deep calls to deep, the Divine Spirit reaching out to the human spirit, a holy tryst as the result of God's own initiative. They are, indeed, organized around the central tryst, the Incarnation of God the Son, in which God "comes down" in utter identification and "takes up" human nature. However, we must also go on to take account of the separation between humankind and God, and so consider some of the ways that God approaches us, or teaches us to approach him, given our present condition. To take serious account of Genesis 3 (the Fall) as well as God's initial declaration of the creation as "very good" (Genesis 1:31) is part and parcel of a sober and full assessment of the human condition. Michael Downey, describing spirituality as it can be observed, even across religious divides, says that there are two "constants" with spirituality: "(1) the awareness that there are levels of reality not immediately apparent and (2) the search for personal integration because of fragmentation or depersonalization" (*Understanding Christian Spirituality*, p. 23).

These two constants point to a universally recognized phenomenon of the separation between humankind and God: "the angels keep their ancient places; Turn but a stone and start a wing! 'Tis ye, 'tis your estrangéd faces, That miss the many-splendoured thing" (Francis Thompson, "The Kingdom of God"). The constants also point to the tragedy of disintegration, that is, our present lack of what St. Thomas Aquinas called the "original justice" of the human being, that human being who has forgotten that he or she has a "heart" in which to meet God. Christian spirituality, then, holds together two tendencies that seem at first blush to be self-contradictory — God's creation is "very good" because humans are created in the image of God, so that when one looks within the human spirit, one can find God; but humankind at the same time is tragically separated from God, and distorted within, so that communion and integration seem well-nigh impossible. Authentic Christian spirituality can thus say, with St. Isaac the Syrian:

> Be at peace with your own soul; then heaven and earth will be at peace with you. Enter eagerly into the treasure house that is within you, and so you will see the things that are in heaven. . . . The ladder that leads to the kingdom is hidden within your soul. . . . Dive into yourself and in your soul you will discover the stairs by which to ascend. (*Ascetical Homilies*, 2)

Authentic spirituality also cries out, aware of the bankruptcy of the human soul, "Lord Jesus Christ, have mercy on me, a sinner."

Paradise Lost: A Grace?

Let us go to the Scriptures to consider this puzzling part of the picture — our separation from God and God's approach to us, including the means of approach that he has offered to us. In reading Genesis, the renowned theologian Karl Barth surely exaggerates when he expostulates about humankind, "There never was a golden age. There is no point in looking back to one. The first man was immediately the first sinner" (*Church Dogmatics* IV, 1, p. 507). It is, however, the case that the narrative of God's good creation is pursued closely by the story of the Fall. Genesis 3 tells a story of unraveling relationships and creation "undone," or at least spoiled — *fear* separating humanity from their evening communion with God, *curse* separating the serpent among the animals, *enmity* pitting the woman and her offspring against the serpent and its offspring, *domination* complicating the relationship of husband and wife, *pain* surrounding the conception, birth, and nurture of children, and *toil* bedeviling the cultivation of the earth. Craft, deception, hatred, awareness of vulnerability, and displacement: these are the signs of the great rupture.

Yet the disturbances themselves are not devoid of grace. Despite the questions we may raise, it is clear that the first limitation placed on Adam and Eve was somehow for their good. That is, though we may not know exactly how or why, the sanction against eating from the Tree of the Knowledge of Good and Evil was a protection for them, and a symbol of their positive obedience to God's will. God continues his interventions even after the disobedience, calling out to the hiding couple (Genesis 3:9), interpreting their acts to them by means of question and judgment (3:14-19), clothing their nakedness by means of skins taken from living animals (3:21), and driving them out from the garden which shields the now-forbidden Tree of Life. The actions all contain a dark element, but they also afford humanity the dignity of realism. God has taken Adam and Eve's plight seriously, and he puts poignant signs of their present condition in every life context. What seems at first glance a mere "punishment" is actually a limiting grace: for humankind to "live forever" in their current condition would be true hell. What seems at first glance mere "penance" is the means by which we are reminded of our frailty and need for God. Some of the ancient fathers of the Church suggested that the moment of disobedience brought about a loss of "glory" which had surrounded the first couple, so that now they knew their nakedness. Until the Tree of Life again may be offered to humanity, the vulnerability and awkwardness are a constant reminder, like the pain reflex, of our dependence. The divine answer to the arrogant self-reliance of humanity (the desire to be "as God") is to allow the limitations of creatureliness to be felt in full strength. The process of dying, to which humanity now is subjected, is no mere consequence, but a strong intimation of the source of our life — not in ourselves, but in our Creator and Re-creator.

Covenant and Crisis

We see the protecting hand of God continually outstretched throughout the saga that follows. God "comes to Abram in a vision," calling himself Abram's shield, and promising him offspring (Genesis 15): the ratifying covenant is enacted entirely by the Almighty, as Abram falls into a visionary trance. God's chosen, Abram, is not himself required to "pass through the pieces" of the carcass slaughtered for the covenant, but witnesses God's initiating power in the darkness, in the divinely provided figures of a smoking firepot and a flaming torch. The covenant is entirely God's doing, but embraces Abram, his future family, and eventually, all the families of the earth who will be blessed through Israel (12:3). The sleeping Abram, the darkness, the slaughtered animals are on the one hand; the signs of light and warmth, and the oracle of God are on the other. Here is an ambivalent situation — separation and an impaired communion that require a covenant, over against the ease of Adam and Eve who walked with God in the garden. Abram sleeps, even while God reaches into our world through his connection with the patriarch.

More striking ambiguity is to be found in the dramatic vignette several chapters later. Here Abram, now Abraham, is tested to the extreme point, and learns, through crisis, the character of the One whom he worships. Genesis 22, known in the Jewish community as the Binding of Isaac, the *Aqedah,* is a difficult chapter for Christians to read as well. Yet we must not short-circuit the process, but abandon ourselves to the drama and power of the story. Do we think only the contemporary reader is horrified to hear God's command at the outset: "Take your son, Isaac"? Must not Abraham and Isaac, recipients of God's promise, also have been shocked to suspect that the God they worshipped might be like the bloodthirsty gods worshipped around them? Imagine the anxiety of Abraham, caught between a revelation of God and a command to commit an unthinkable act. Readers of the entire book of Genesis will feel the same dissonance. Is this not the same God of Abraham who has just heard the pitiable cries of Isaac's half-brother Ishmael, and rescued him? Abraham was in conflict and so are we, as we hear the story: and we are supposed to be! For the story is about separation and approach to God, about learning who God is, and who we are. It is not some moralistic tale from long ago encouraging us to slavishly obey the precepts of religion. It is a story about mystery, devotion, provision, and promise. It is about seeing the life-giving hand of God amidst testing and confusion, the context in which the entire human family finds itself since the Fall. It is about faith brought to birth, and faith rewarded.

Abraham does not understand everything, but he understands that he must be wholly, not selectively, devoted to God. Abraham adores his son, but he knows that his love of God must be greater — yet how can these two loves be opposed? Abraham does not know how, but he knows God will honor the promises he has already made about Isaac — he "will provide," as he said to Isaac.

And the sacrifice is finally not required — for God is *not* vengeful or bloodthirsty. His desire for our devotion, and for our obedience is keen: his desire to bless and to make and keep promises is even greater. And there is one further thought for us to have, as Christians — the sacrifice that God did not require of Abraham, he made himself. It is through God's own gift, the death and resurrection of Jesus, the offspring of Abraham, that all the world is blessed. For the first Hebrew hearers, the mysterious story of Abraham ended with an evocative, exciting promise: for us, in the Christian community, it is fulfilled and explained by the coming of the main character of the great drama, Jesus. The willingness of Isaac to do his earthly father's behest is a small shadow of the utter obedience of the Son who came for us. The willingness of Abraham to lose his own son is likewise a picture of the Father, who for the love of the world gave his Son. This strange subplot of the story of Abraham and Isaac is illumined by the main story of the One who dies on our behalf.

On Names and Naming

The strangeness of the human condition is evoked most strongly in the story where Jacob receives his family name, Israel (Genesis 32:22-32). Jacob has been directed by God to return home to the land of his birth with his large family after his sojourn with Laban, concerned about the enmity between himself and Esau that he has created through his own deception. He sends his family across the Jabbok ford, and stays himself at the stream, where he finds himself confronted by a stranger who wrestles with him and will not reveal to Jacob his name. Jacob continues to wrestle with the visitor until daybreak, and asks a blessing: he receives the name "Israel" — literally "he strives with God" — and the hair-raising realization that his opponent is in fact the Almighty himself. That very One who has directed Jacob across the Jabbok has now been hindering him for the entire night. God visits Jacob and blesses him, but that very visitation is a "mixed" blessing. The patriarch emerges with a new name, and a wound. God's approach has given him a glimpse of the great mystery: separation and approach are intermingled. The struggle has taken place in the dead of night, as Jacob is completely alone. Yet morning dawns, and as it does, the patriarch's new name is given as a commencement blessing to his family, that is, to the people of Israel. The dark night of isolation is tied up with God's plans for Israel, and indeed, for the whole world. But Jacob will sport a limp, and Israel will abstain from meat derived from the thigh muscle as a reminder that concourse with God may issue in much wrestling of the spirit. The "dance" of the wrestling match, with its engagement and retreat, is a picture of our strange condition. We will never master the Wrestler, but his aim is to name us, even when this also deals us a wound.

At the Mountain

God's dealings with Moses and the people in Exodus disclose the same dynamic. The initial call of Moses in Exodus 2:23–3:22 begins with Moses in a solitary place of separation, requires that he remove his sandals because of the separateness (holiness) of the revelation, and is all about a distant, but concerned God, employing his chosen intermediary to respond to the Hebrew people. God approaches, but with reserve; Moses encounters God, but with reserve. Here the Almighty does disclose his name, YHWH, but that name itself is a great mystery, translatable in several ways, and revelatory of God's activity, though not his essence — "I am who I am"; "I will be who I will be"; "I cause to be what I cause to be."

After the long saga of redemption, the escape from Egypt, the crossing of the sea, the trudge through the wilderness, Moses comes with his people to their goal, the foot of the mountain, whence they have been called to "worship YHWH" (Exodus 3:18; 19:17), the holy God of all creation, who was forging a special relationship with the Hebrews for the sake of the whole world. We have seen already that the Divine Name is not divulged freely, so that Jacob was not given this name, though the Almighty named him. It is to Moses and the Hebrews that the divine name is finally revealed, though this revelation itself is shrouded in mystery. It may be helpful to remember that the name of God himself, YHWH, as printed in the Hebrew Bible, underscores the mystery of a God who is wholly other, yet concerned and connected with his people. In the later Hebrew texts, which added vowel "pointings" (small marks) to the consonant-only sentences (originally all that the scribes used to tell the ancient stories of the Torah) we find a peculiarity. The strange name YHWH, a mystery connected with the verb "to be" (I am who I am? I will be who I will be? I cause to be what I cause to be?), now is further complicated. The scribes have taken the consonants YHWH and added to them the vowel pointings of the noun "Adonai" ("Lord"). In reading the Scriptures aloud, ancient rabbis never vocalized this word, with its strange combination of consonants and vowels, nor do they to this day. Instead, the vowel pointings are there as a reminder to the reader *not* to pronounce the holy name YHWH, and instead to substitute the honorific title "Adonai," Lord. In our English Bibles, wherever we see the name LORD capitalized, this is a way of signaling that strange anomaly, the YHWH consonants marked by the Adonai vowels. So the capitalized LORD should speak to us about God's great mystery, his being by which we have life, and his complete holiness, so that we should revere even his name. After all, humanity has leave to name the animals, but not to name God!

It is this ineffable but loving LORD who speaks many words to the people through Moses, and then calls upon Moses and the elders to climb the mount, and worship him "at a distance" (Exodus 24). Moses begins by enacting a blood covenant upon all the people at the foot of the mountain, a sign of God's connection with them; this liturgy is followed by a mystical meal in which the seventy and Moses eat and drink, beholding a dazzling theophany of God, while God restrains his power, not "laying a hand" on them despite their irregular proximity; finally, Moses himself goes to the apex, where for forty days and nights he beholds and even enters "the appearance of the glory of the LORD" (34:17). There he receives the stone tablets, and special instructions about the tabernacle, to be built by "heart offerings of the Israelites" (25:1), "so that I may dwell among them" (25:8). What follows seems to us of Gentile birth to be chapters of abstruse regulation about worship procedures but are actually passages that disclose the wonder and the mystery of the Sinai epiphany. The purpose of Moses' experience on the mountain was not simply to receive the Law, wonderful though that was; for, says God, he speaks to Moses about the tabernacle, about the Sabbath, and about the Decalogue, so that "they shall know that I am the LORD their God, who brought them out of the land of Egypt that I might dwell among them" (29:46).

All that happens at Sinai is a poignant picture of separation from God, human sinfulness, and God's approach. The slope of the mountain, the three stages of reception (the people at the foot, the elders further up, and Moses at the top), the role of Moses as mediator, the contrasts of darkness and light, the extraordinary theophany and awesome signs — all speak of a God who is both revealed and concealed. God spoke, and yet, as Hebrews puts it, those "words made the hearers beg that not another word be spoken to them" (12:19). Humanity, left to itself, cannot "endure the order that is given (12:20)"; still, God approaches.

Natural and Ascetic Connections

This paradox — that humanity was made for communion with God, but that this communion is no longer natural to them — finds its subtle expression in the many stories of Israel. Throughout the books of Samuel and Kings, the reader witnesses two contrasting models by which God reaches human beings: the first might be called the "national" model and is represented by God's concourse with kings and priests; the second may be understood as the "ascetic" model, and is represented by the prophets. The many images associated with Moses, who was both prophet and priest, on the mountain, are now bifurcated, split. So in 1 Kings 8:22-46, Solomon sums up the first stream in his Temple prayer of dedication. The king speaks in a holy place, a place that he has just seen filled so full with God's glory cloud that the priests could no longer officiate. He dedicates the Temple by recalling God's covenant with David, highlighting the states of sin and innocence, conceding that human beings are prone to sin, but focusing upon confession, associating affliction and natural disaster with alienation from God, calling to remembrance God's action in history, particularly the Exodus from Egypt. Here, it would seem, is the "ordinary" mode of God's concourse with humanity, in which God's grace is mediated, and God's Temple is seen as the point of juncture between two separated parties: "Hear the plea of your servant and of your people Israel when they pray towards this place; O hear in heaven your dwelling place" (8:30).

The second stream contrasts and complements the first, and may be seen in the experience of Elijah (1 Kings 19:1-18). Elijah meets with the LORD not in the Temple or in the holy city, not in a politico-religious place, but first in the desert, and then, through God's strength, on Horeb, where Moses first heard God speak. The prophet flees to the wilds during a time of desolation, with Queen Jezebel's price on his head, whereas Solomon had prayed at a high moment of triumph, with the newly built glory-filled Temple before him. There are no great prayers, just the gasp, "It is enough, O LORD, take away my life, for I am no better than my fathers" (19:4). Elijah can initiate no great conversation with the Almighty; all his words have been spent before Jezebel's priests. Yet God communes with him, first through a ministering angel who feeds him, then through a forty-day journey, and finally in the cave, where he hears the questioning voice of the Almighty, "What are you doing here, Elijah?" There follows an extraordinary series of Exodus-like phenomena — wind, earthquake, fire — but the narrator tells us that God is not in these. Then the still, small voice speaks, and by Elijah's humble and awestruck response, we gather that *this* is the location of the LORD. The same question comes a second, then a third time. Elijah answers, pouring out his heart to God, and God neither confirms his prophet's despair nor argues with him. Instead, the LORD gives his prophet a commission, reassuring him that he is indeed not alone in his fidelity to the LORD.

Both in the "ordinary" place of civil, kingly, and priestly worship, and in the "extraordinary" place of seclusion and prophetic lament, God meets his people. Both streams, though aware of God's presence in different modes, acknowledge the ambivalence of the human condition: humanity is separated from God through sin; yet God approaches. The first stream admits the separation, and provides a "solution" that God condescends to dignify: "The LORD has said that he would dwell in thick darkness; I have built you an exalted house, a place for you to dwell in forever"

(1 Kings 8:12). The second admits that even in this fallen world God's presence can be discerned in God-sent phenomena, but he is not *in* them nor can he be contained: the LORD passes by, comes and speaks as he wills. God's Spirit was to be discerned in the glory that filled the Temple; God's Spirit was to be heeded in the voice of sheer silence.

Lament and the Dark Night

The Old Testament witness, then, knows well about our separation from God, but also gives hope that God acts to breach that gap. Nor do the Hebrew writers shy away from the experience of utter desolation, what the mystics would come to call the "dark night of the soul." Both the Psalms and the book of Lamentations inscribe within our canon this sense of desolation as a regular part of human experience for those who are in covenant-relationship with the LORD: "My God, my God, why have you forsaken me? Why are you so far from helping me, from the words of my groaning? O my God, I cry by day, but you do not answer; and by night, but find no rest" (Psalm 22:1-2); "I am one who has seen affliction under the rod of God's wrath; he has driven and brought me into darkness without any light; against me alone he turns his hand, again and again, all day long" (Lamentations 3:1-3). Liturgical practice has further dignified such moments, admitting the "lament" genre within the worshipping life of first the Jewish, then the Christian communities.

It is unfortunately the case that some contemporary expressions of Christianity have forgotten, or are embarrassed by, this moment of dark reflection, and instead espouse an unrealistic and warped view of spiritual victory. In many Christian communities who do not follow the disciplines of liturgical rhythm, one is hard-pressed to find any moments of "lament": the relentlessly upbeat, both in song and in prayer, is the norm. In such congregations, a sense of alienation or unworthiness may assault Christians who are in a period of great turmoil or spiritual dryness: there is no authentic voice offered to them, and so a sense of unreality may well set in. Corporately, lack of attention to the down-then-up rhythm of the biblical story is equally dangerous. Just as an earlier generation missed the fullness of the gospel by concentration upon judgment and duty, so today's typical (Western) "seeker-friendly" worship services frequently pull the congregants into a place of false security and canned joy.

41

When we direct our attention towards the rhythm of the biblical story, however, we see that God makes use of the "lows" as well as the "highs" in history, and that separation is an essential moment in the process that God directs towards reconciliation and communion. This begins, of course, with the "severe mercy" of death and limitation imposed upon humanity by a loving God in Genesis 3; it continues with the scattering of arrogant people in Genesis 11; then the imprisonment of Joseph; the wandering in the desert; the chaotic time of Judges, by which the Hebrews were called to repentance; the division of North and South; the judgment of the North; the Exile; the chastisement of the returned Judeans by the Seleucids; the Roman rule. All this culminates, of course, in the humiliation and self-offering of Jesus, who on the cross places the lament of Psalm 22 in the starkest light possible. Jesus' sense of utter abandonment, and the objective bearing of our sin as he "became sin" for us, issues in his triumphant declaration: "It is finished; God has done it" (Psalm 22:31//John 19:30).

To speak of this dark moment, and indeed to analyze the other "troughs" in the corporate and personal experiences of the Church, requires care. We have spoken both of a sense of abandonment and of the objective separation from God that results from sin. It is important not to play off the subjective and objective here. A popular Christian poem entitled "Footprints in the Sand," deals with the paradox of human separation from the Lord of life. The source of this poem is a matter of some controversy, since it has been published in three different versions by three different authors, and has, in its various forms, been reproduced on posters, cards, and other devotional paraphernalia. It seems that we owe its earliest appearance, in 1936, to a fourteen-year-old girl, Mary Stevenson:

Footprints in the Sand
One night I dreamed I was walking along the beach with the Lord.
Many scenes from my life flashed across the sky.
In each scene I noticed footprints in the sand.
Sometimes there were two sets of footprints,
other times there was one only.
This bothered me because I noticed that during the low periods
    of my life,
when I was suffering from anguish,
sorrow or defeat,
I could see only one set of footprints,

so I said to the Lord,
"You promised me Lord,
that if I followed you,
you would walk with me always.
But I have noticed that during the most trying periods of my life
there has only been one set of footprints in the sand.
Why, when I needed you most, have you not been there for me?"
The Lord replied,
"The years when you have seen only one set of footprints,
my child, is when I carried you."

Stevenson's poem, though sentimentalized and commercialized in our culture, emerged from the profound and honest experience of a desolate young Christian. This adolescent reminds us of our particular and irrevocable relationship with God. Hers is a poetic re-enactment of Paul's great consolation in Romans 8:38-39: "For I am convinced that nothing . . . in all creation will be able to separate us from the love of God in Christ Jesus our Lord." In one sense, Jesus was the final and greatest Lamenter, crying out for his own, "My God . . . why have you forsaken me!" There is nothing that we can add to that Great Alienation, by which our communion with God has been forged. This young girl has perceived the mystery of our seeming abandonment: God has carried us, and continues to do so. Our abandonment is, in this sense, only apparent.

Yet those who are closest to the Lord witness that our sense of separation is not always easy to bear: indeed, one wonders whether we only sense the separation, or whether it is indeed a condition, though passing, of our temporal existence. Because God enters into our time, and because our human time has been, or will be, taken up into God's eternity, separation is not the final word; but it is an accurate description of our state, at least seen from the human side of our relationship with God. Could it be that Paul uses the *future* tense in Romans 8:39 advisedly? Nothing "*will be* able" to separate us from that One who is Love and Light and Life. Our entire lives are riddled by moments — poignant moments — of separation. Elsewhere, Paul reflects upon the ambiguity of our current situation, placed between the ascension and the final return of Jesus:

But we have this treasure in earthen vessels, to show that the transcendent power belongs to God and not to us. We are afflicted in every way, but not crushed; perplexed, but not driven to despair; persecuted, but not forsaken; struck down, but not destroyed; always carrying in the body the death of Jesus, so that the life of Jesus may also be manifested in our bodies. For while we live we are always being given up to death for Jesus' sake, so that the life of Jesus may be manifested in our mortal flesh. . . . So we do not lose heart. Though our outer nature is wasting away, our inner nature is being renewed every day. For this slight momentary affliction is preparing for us an eternal weight of glory beyond all comparison, because we look not to the things that are seen but to the things that are unseen; for the things that are seen are transient, but the things that are unseen are eternal. (2 Corinthians 4:7-18)

Notice that in describing his plight as an ambassador who represents Jesus, Paul speaks both of "persecution" and of the natural corruption of the "mortal flesh." Both these sorrows are entailed for a Christian who lives, as we all do, in the present age, and both are part of the present affliction that will issue in glory. To the surprise of many who rightly stress the once-for-all nature of Jesus' suffering, we must acknowledge that there is a very strong theme across the New Testament books regarding the Church's "communion" of suffering and "participation" in the suffering of Christ (e.g. Romans 8:17; 2 Corinthians 1:5, Philippians 3:10; Hebrews 10:32; 1 Peter 5:9, Revelation 1:9). It is both true to say that Jesus suffered "for" us, in terms of substitution, and to say that he suffered "for" us as our representative or pioneer (and so we participate in his suffering). Only the God-Man, Jesus, could be, as C. S. Lewis puts it, the "Perfect Penitent," the Sufferer *par excellence* who brought about atonement. Because of his death we need not die eternally. But, one of the mysteries of intimacy with him is that we are brought into his communion of suffering, and that God *uses* our suffering for his good purposes. Paul explained that, as an apostle, part of his charge was to "fill up what was incomplete" in Christ's suffering, as he suffered for the edification of the first-century Church. Likewise, he explains in Romans 8:18-27 how the Spirit is at work within the whole Church, so that we may groan, as in childbirth, participating with our inchoate prayers in the birth of the new creation, which is ultimately God's own work. It is *God* who invites us into such intimacy with him that we may share in the suffering of the Son, in the lament of the One who is the Great Lover of humankind.

Layers of Separation

Here, then, is a point of dissonance, of conflict, with the current worldviews espoused by many outside the Church. For the Christian, suffering and death are not pointless; nor are they natural, in the strict sense of the word. Instead, Christians are called to see the ambiguity of our status as those afflicted but not destroyed. Several "layers" of separation from happiness, from life, and from God, need to be sorted out. There is first of all that separation that comes as a normal consequence of our own, personal sins. "In him there is no darkness," as John writes, and what is dark in us dare not come into the light. Next, there is that separation that comes to us as the inevitable result of the Fall, in which we participate both unwillingly (for we are dying, corruptible and prone to sin) and willingly (when we deliberately walk in darkness). There is a shadow cast over our world, a shadow that even affects the children of light, for their bodies are in the process of dying; sometimes their bodies, wills, minds, spirits, are not "in sync," and they are subject to the invariable distortions, attacks, and dangers that accompany this age. Finally, there is that alienation, that separation, that suffering that comes to those who are in communion with Christ, especially to the mature, as they are embraced by God's will to save the world.

This third type of separation, paradoxically, brings us to God's own heart. It is a separation-in-communion. We plumb, with ever-so-shallow a plumb line, into the depth of that One who cried over the death of Lazarus, over the unrepentant city of Jerusalem, and over the whole of his wayward and hurting creation. We join with him, for a moment, in Gethsemane, if not Golgotha. Separation, then, is in the first sense "normal," though not God's will for the individual Christian; it is in the second sense "inevitable" though not God's first plan for his image-bearing creatures; it is in the third sense "spiritual" because it occurs when the sisters and brothers of Jesus start to take on their God-given roles as priests and rulers, mediating God's love (through Christ) to others.

Suffering and Transformation

It seems, too, that as we glimpse this third layer of suffering, a new transformation or miracle takes place: here we must only preview the hope en-

45

visaged in our third triad, where we will more fully explore the wonder of the new creation. These things are intertwined, however — separation and suffering with healing and transformation, for "what is not assumed is not healed" (St. Gregory of Nazianzus, called "the Theologian"). Within the mystic "exchange" established by God, those who participate by the Spirit in Christ's afflictions are given the grace to be transfigured, by a transformation of mind and heart, those wounds that they have received from the first and second levels of separation. That is, the mature Christian receives the separation that comes from his or her own particular sins as a means of God's love to one's self and to others — he or she knows that God chastises his beloved, and that unresolved sin will "hinder prayers" (1 Peter 3:7). Thus, the one who, in praying, seeks intimacy with God, keenly perceives the emptiness caused by sin, and so is driven back to God's will. The witness of a Charles Colson, who paid in prison for his offenses, is instructive here — individual human witness is here turned to the glory of God. Again, the Christian who knows well about Jesus' submission to the Father is prepared to see creaturely suffering as "use-able" (though not directly inflicted) by God for the transformation of the world. It is in this way that Paul understood his "thorn in the flesh," that undefined scourge that drove him to depend upon God and made him ever aware of the Source of his strength. In this way, the first two levels of suffering can be brought into the service of the One who also calls us to suffer wrong "for his name's sake." Let us make no mistake about it: the long night of the soul, the alienation from God, is not useless. Our sense of abandonment, our momentary separation, is part of our calling to participate in Christ's suffering, and is part of the whole picture. In fact, the visionary John can speak about the Enemy of God being conquered by "the blood of the Lamb" *and* by "the word of their [the faithfuls'] martyrdom" (Revelation 12:11).

At risk of alienating some of my readers, but for the sake of realism, I want to cite a poignant example of how this might work today. The Christian community should be humbled, and has been clearly blessed, by the posthumous witness of a young man, called "Gary" by his academic friend Richard Hays. Gary lived as an uneasy member of the gay subculture for over twenty years. At first hopeful concerning the (then) new pro-gay interpretations of Scripture, he was not entirely satisfied with their depiction of that subculture, nor with the permission they were granting for a lifestyle that he experienced as separating him from

God's purposes. Gary contracted HIV, and as it became likely that he had not much longer to live, he spent a bittersweet week with his old friend Hays, laughing, praying, and studying the Scriptures together. During this eleventh-hour retreat, Gary came to clarity about many questions he had, repented, and was given peace by Christ. He was not "reoriented" during this time of spiritual healing, but he covenanted to remain chaste. Finally, he died of AIDS.

Gary's sober and vibrant witness speaks with ongoing life to his brothers and sisters today, across the gulf separating life and death — for we are one body. Gary understood that his own sins had played a role in his physical predicament, for he had, in sin, embraced a lifestyle that was laden with risks. Here was the first level at work. Gary also witnessed that he had received wounds from the body of Christ, both from skittish "orthodox" who could not empathize, and facile "progressives" who insisted that homoerotic behavior was God's will. Here was the second level at work: he was harmed even by those who should have been agents of healing in this fallen world. After his repentance, he did not sense within himself a "reorientation" to heterosexual desire, but in a dark night of the soul came to understand that "brokenness" can be used by God for the strengthening of the Church: we are all "awaiting the redemption of our body." Here, again, is the second level of separation at play, an alienation from wholeness that is tied up with the context of our fallen world. Yet God could use this, even this, to his glory. Finally, it is clear that Gary wanted to complete a project with his theologian friend Richard Hays, in order to enrich the present hurting Church. He died prematurely, having only conducted, but not yet publicized, his study on what the Bible says about homoeroticism and on what his living a homoerotic lifestyle had done to him. That work was completed by Hays alone, who withheld his friend's name. However, everything that Hays tells us suggests that Gary would have been prepared to suffer for his witness to the truth. Given today's cultural climate, such attacks inevitably would have come to him from agents in the churches as well as in the world at large. No doubt Hays believed that Gary had suffered enough, and was prepared to take upon himself the probable heat, knowing that the article would anger some, but hoping that it would also encourage others in both clarity and compassion. But Gary's simple witness tells it all: "Are homosexuals [then] to be excluded from the community of faith? Certainly not. But anyone who joins such a community should know that it is a place of transformation, of discipline, of learning, and not merely a place to be comforted or indulged" ("Awaiting," p. 380).

I am grateful for the courage of my unknown friend, who allowed Jesus to take his "compulsion and affliction" and use it for transformation: he is a beacon in great darkness. His efforts, along with those of his friend Hays, in entering into this raging and Church-splitting controversy, are for us a powerful symbol of God's power made perfect in weakness, embodying our present situation "in between the times." God's Spirit is at work among us, yet full glory remains a future hope. Gary's fidelity reverses the symbol of disintegration (between man and woman, mind and will) described by Paul in Romans 1. He speaks in the same vein as the women at the tomb, who witnessed to the disciples and so (in the words of an Orthodox Vespers hymn) "cast away the ancestral curse" of strife between Adam and Eve. Together, Gary with Hays witness redemptively about Christ's grace, love, and fidelity. In the darkness, the light shines. In Christ, there is neither "gay" nor "straight."

Separation and Sanctity

From Moses, to Jesus, to the present day, we see that separation, though painful, is creative, and indeed, is entailed in God's approach to us. This has been the startling discovery of many who have been called "mystics" or "spiritual theologians" — those athletes in the spiritual world who have trained their bodies, minds, and will, to come to a place where intimacy with God comes more easily. In the anonymously written ancient tale *Joseph and Aseneth* (written perhaps in the late first to early second century A.D.) we read a fictional account of the remarkable pilgrimage of the patriarch Joseph's Gentile wife, Aseneth, from darkness to light. Her transition involves a long period of separation, including prayers of desolation, and a snapshot of the abandonment that the convert of the ancient world would anticipate as a result of conversion: "Be mindful, Lord, of my humiliation and have mercy upon me. Look at my orphanage and have compassion on the afflicted" (*Joseph and Aseneth* 13:1); "And now I am an orphan and desolate and I have no other help save in you, Lord, and no other refuge except your mercy, Lord, because you are the father of the orphans, and a protector of the persecuted, and a helper of the afflicted" (12:13). To be an "orphan" and "desolate" is taken up into God's plan, and

Aseneth herself receives a new name — the "metropolis" or "mother-city" of refuge for those who flee to God.

Gregory of Nyssa, who lived when the Church was being perse-cuted in the fourth century, knew this well. He traced a paradigm for the spiritual voyager on the basis of Moses' Sinai revelation of God in light, cloud, and darkness. There is, at the critical moment in this jour-ney, a point at which the soul's "Spouse" [Christ or God] "approaches but does not reveal Himself" *(Commentary on the Song of Songs)*. Because of both the imperfection and the creaturely nature of the human being, the pursuit of God goes on forever, as does God's self-revelation. Hav-ing received "the arrow of love," the Beloved attains eventually to a "sat-isfied dissatisfaction" of the God whose love is, in the end, ceaseless. As we complete our ruminations about "separation," St. Gregory reminds us of a separation from God that is more basic even than the Fall. To our three levels of complicating alienation we must add the fundamen-tal distinction or break between God and humankind, between Creator and creature. That "division" is no tragedy, but part and parcel of our identity and God's grandeur. It must be accounted for in the mystery of God, who reveals himself to us as we can bear it: revelation invariably involves concealment, since God is God and we are not. The commu-nion that he forges with us remains a tantalizing "mystery" that leads us to know more and more of him, but never in completion — and at this, we wonder! As Kallistos Ware puts it, where knowledge of God is con-cerned, "The eyes are closed — but they are also opened" *(The Orthodox Way*, p. 15).

FURTHER MEDITATION

How shall I describe, Master, the vision of Your countenance? How shall I speak of the unspeakable contemplation of Your beauty? How can the sound of any word contain Him whom the world cannot hold? How can anyone express Your love for mankind?

. . . Thus as far as I am human, I know that I see nothing of the di-vine realities, and I am totally cut off from the invisible. But by divine adoption I see that I have become god and I have become a participator of intangible things . . . but also as even now You have allowed me to look upon you, Saviour, so after death grant me to see you! . . .

49

If you lay bare all my disorders and actions, O King immortal, do not show them to all. . . .

But may your immaculate light, the light of Your countenance, hide my works and the nudity of my soul, and clothe me with joyfulness so that with confidence without shame I may be placed at the right hand with the sheep and with them I may glorify You forever. (St. Symeon the New Theologian, *Hymns of Divine Love*, Hymn 25)

When the purgative contemplation oppresses a man, he feels very vividly indeed the shadow of death, the sighs of death, and the sorrows of hell — all of which reflect the feeling of God's absence, of being chastised and rejected by Him, and of being unworthy of Him as well as the object of His anger. . . . God humbles the soul greatly in order to exalt it greatly afterwards. (St. John of the Cross, *The Dark Night of the Soul*, 6)

Prayer is the substance of eternal life. It gives back to man, in so far as he is willing to live to capacity — that is to say, to give love and suffer pain — the beatitude without which he is incomplete; for it sets going, deepens and at last perfects that mutual indwelling of two orders which redeems us from unreality, and in which the creative process reaches its goal. (Evelyn Underhill, *An Anthology of the Love of God*, p. 127)

The Greek noun *mysterion* is linked with the verb *myein*, meaning, "to close the eyes or the mouth." The candidate for initiation into certain of the pagan mystery religions was first blindfolded and led through a maze of passages; then suddenly his eyes were uncovered and he saw, displayed all around him, the secret emblems of the cult. So, in the Christian context, we do not mean by a "mystery" merely that which is baffling and mysterious, an enigma or insoluble problem. A mystery is, on the contrary, something that is *revealed* for our understanding, but which we never understand *exhaustively* because it leads into the depth or the darkness of God. The eyes are closed — but they are also opened. (Kallistos Ware, *The Orthodox Way*, p. 15)

FURTHER READING

Hays, Richard. "Awaiting the Redemption of Our Bodies." In *Homosexuality in the Church: Both Sides of the Debate,* edited by J. S. Siker. Louisville: Ky.: Westminster/John Knox, 1994.

St. Gregory of Nyssa. *Commentary on the Song of Songs.* In *From Glory to Glory: Texts from Gregory of Nyssa's Mystical Writings,* translated by Herbert Musurillo. Crestwood, N.Y.: St. Vladimir's Seminary Press, 1979.

St. Isaac the Syrian. *Ascetical Homilies of St. Isaac the Syrian.* Brookline, Mass.: Holy Transfiguration Monastery, 1985.

St. John of the Cross. *The Dark Night of the Soul.* In *The Collected Works of St. John of the Cross,* translated by K. Cavanaugh. Washington, D.C.: Institute of Carmelite Studies, 1976.

St. Symeon the New Theologian. *Hymns of Divine Love by Symeon the New Theologian.* Translated by. G. A. Maloney. Denville, N.J.: Dimension, 1976.

Stevenson, Mary. "Footprints in the Sand." http://footprints-inthe-sand.com/. Cited above by permission. For a discussion of the debate surrounding this poem's authorship, see the article by Debra Fieguth, "Whose Footprints?" *Christian Week* 14, Issue 9, August 2000.

The Cloud of Unknowing. Edited by James Walsh. New York: Paulist, 1981. An anonymous classic on the problem of separation and approach.

Underhill, Evelyn. *An Anthology of the Love of God.* Edited by Barkway and Menzies. London: Mowbray and Co., 1953. An introduction to the work of a well-known contemporary spiritual theologian in the Anglican tradition.

Ware, Kallistos. *The Orthodox Way.* Crestwood, N.Y.: St. Vladimir's Seminary Press, 1995.

FURTHER REFLECTION AND DISCUSSION

1. In what way can the focus upon ourselves ("subjectivity") prevent us from understanding what it means for Christians to be spiritual?
2. How can we understand God's use of separation and suffering without abandoning trust in a good and just God, and yielding to a fatalistic or monstrous picture of an unknowable deity "beyond" good and evil?

3. Is it helpful to understand the "dark night of the soul" as not simply an individual experience, but as an event common to God's people, insofar as we are united to the sufferings of Christ?

4. Is the notion of *felix culpa* (the "fortunate fall"), found in many medieval hymns, a valid way of expressing God's use of separation and alienation, or is it theologically suspect?

5. In what sense does the natural separation of Creator from creation help us to understand the importance of personal boundaries, alongside fellowship and communion?

C

Word and Wisdom, Knowledge and Faith

Word, Wisdom, Knowledge, and Faith: Ecstatic Gifts

God's loving remedy to our situation of separation typically has been understood in terms of word and wisdom, knowledge and faith — word, wisdom, and knowledge coming to us from God, with faith evoked as our human response to these gifts. A moment's commonsense reflection leads us to see how ecstasy and intimacy are bound up with word and wisdom, knowledge and faith. The giving of a word, with an intention to communicate, involves an act of ecstasy, or standing outside of oneself; we can see this when we consider how those afflicted with serious autism are cut off from others, even sometimes to the point of being unable to speak. Wisdom involves an intimate knowledge of someone or something, and so also a delight in "the other." Knowledge requires the ecstatic act of careful concentration upon the other, and faith is directed outward, as well (unless, like *The Sound of Music's* Maria, we celebrate *fideism*, an absurd "I have confidence in confidence *a-lone!*").

Word, Wisdom, Knowledge, and the Ego

Of course, there are philosophers and popular thinkers who will tell us that a word is simply an expression of one's self; that wisdom is decided by contract or by conventions agreed to by several individuals; that knowledge is an indication of the ego, not of the other; and that faith in oneself is the only kind of confidence that makes sense. However, this kind of division of the self from the rest of the cosmos is counter-intuitive, and has led to the solipsistic, self-absorbed thinking that characterizes twenty-first-century culture. There may well be a philosophical problem in understanding how we know the other. But Descartes' *cogito ergo sum* ("I think, therefore I am") and Kant's division of knowledge from reality do not detract from how most people characterize their thinking — we aim to understand someone or something *else* when we think. Though we may not actually "grasp" the other, this is our desire in trying to understand. Self-consciousness, or making one's self the object of thought, is a second order action that may, in fact, be doomed from the start: "O to see ourselves as others see us!"

Real knowledge and communication have a different aim. Their purpose is not to navel-gaze but to move out to the other. We witness this the first time an infant smiles at her mother, delights in a toy, encounters a dog. Some psychologists think that a first revelation for such an infant is that the mother is "other" than him; others, however, suspect that the first early surprise is that his hand is in fact attached to him, and not independent of him. Maybe that is why he chuckles so hilariously at the appendage: how can he see himself? All this is, of course, speculative, because we cannot get inside a three-month-old's head. We cannot be sure whether the human being is first startled to discover that *others* are separate from himself, or first astonished to learn that he can be self-reflective, and even study *himself* as an object.

Whichever is the case, it is clear that human beings know themselves both to be with others and separate from them, and that communication is early, urgent, and natural. The word becomes a primary means of communion, and wisdom is born of our collective life, not of individual brilliance. Despite our emphasis upon individuality since the time of the Enlightenment philosophers, it would seem that the community, rather than the individual, is primary. Our Christian experience on this matter is borne out by the significant role assigned to word and wisdom, which (or *who*) are intimately connected to the Lord in the Scriptures. Let's look at this pair before moving on to consider the gifts of knowledge and faith that are given to direct our paths.

The Shadowy Figures of Wisdom and Word in Jewish Writings

In the Hebrew Bible and rabbinic Jewish traditions, word and wisdom become increasingly important. Genesis 1 speaks briefly about God's "spirit" hovering over the waters of chaos, and about the word by which he created ("God *spoke,* and it was so"). These details about word and spirit are picked up poetically in Psalm 33:6 — "By the *word* of the Lord the heavens were made, and all their host by the *breath ("ruach"* = spirit) of his mouth." When we move beyond the exilic period, into what is called the "intertestamental" period, word and wisdom take on ecstatic roles, moving out to humanity and the creation, even as they are ever more exuberantly described by the authors of books written during this period. Indeed, in some writings they assume a curious identity, at once united to and distinct from God, that goes beyond the poetic device of personification. Some specialists trace a progression from mere figure of speech to an uncanny "hypostatization" — that is, they see "Wisdom" and "Word" in the process of becoming persons in these later writings. An actual chronological crescendo into "personhood" may not be possible to prove, given the vicissitudes of history. What we can say is that, when we study the texts of the Old Testament, the Apocrypha (Old Testament books accepted by Roman Catholic and Orthodox), the noncanonized works called the Pseudepigrapha, the rabbinic writings, and the writings of the New Testament, these two motifs of wisdom and word seem to grow in theological significance.

At the first stage we encounter, in Proverbs 8:1–9:6, "Lady Wisdom," a poetic figure who is contrasted with "Folly" (who is no "lady"!). Wisdom takes her stand in the paths, besides the gates, and at the entrance to the public square, crying out for the foolish and simple to "pay attention":

> Hear, for I will speak noble things, and from my lips will come what is right; for my mouth will utter truth; wickedness is an abomination to my lips. All the words of my mouth are righteous; there is nothing twisted or crooked in them . . . for wisdom is better than jewels, and all that you may desire cannot compare with her.

Her appeal is laden with metaphor and imagery, as she likens the acquisition of wisdom to the finding of riches and honor, to the eating of fruit and the discovery of gold. As might be expected, she is connected both with rulers and with the LORD himself. We may be a little surprised to hear about her primordial past and her help as a skilled worker beside the Creator, but, on the whole, the language may be understood in poetic terms:

> The LORD created me at the beginning of his work, the first of his acts of old. Ages ago I was set up, at the first, before the beginning of the earth. When there were no depths I was brought forth, when there were no springs abounding with water. Before the mountains had been shaped, before the hills, I was brought forth; before he had made the earth with its fields, or the first of the dust of the world. When he established the heavens, I was there, when he drew a circle on the face of the deep, when he made firm the skies above, when he established the fountains of the deep, when he assigned to the sea its limit, so that the waters might not transgress his command, when he marked out the foundations of the earth, then I was beside him, like a master workman; and I was daily his delight, rejoicing before him always, rejoicing in his inhabited world and delighting in the sons of men.

Indeed, the reader is forcibly reminded of the metaphoric language as the proverb moves from Wisdom's own speech, to the fanciful description of her home and her table in chapter 9. The invitation to dine closes with the didactic purpose of the entire extended parable: "Leave simpleness, and live, and walk in the way of insight." For a few brief moments, then, during the course of Wisdom's speech, the reader may have lost his or her literary bearings, drawn by evocative language into Wisdom's world. When we forget that this is a parable, we may well be tempted to construct theological propositions regarding the identity of this figure, and her relationship to God. The end of the passage, however, cues us to return to the confines of the parable's function.

In a later book, the apocryphal Wisdom of Solomon, the tendency of the figure Wisdom to take on a life of her own is even more pronounced. Perhaps written toward the end of the first century B.C., the book goes beyond parable to provide a theological exposition and psalm of praise concerning Wisdom that invites the reader to move into territory uncharted in Proverbs:

> Wisdom is radiant and unfading . . . the spirit of Wisdom came to me. . . . Wisdom, the fashioner of all, taught me. For in her there is a

spirit that is intelligent, holy, unique, manifold, subtle, mobile, clear, unpolluted, distinct, invulnerable, loving the good . . . all-powerful, overseeing all and penetrating through all spirits. . . . For she is a breath of the power of God, and a pure emanation of the glory of the Almighty. . . . For she is a reflection of eternal light, and an image of [God's] goodness. Though she is but one, she can do all things, and while remaining in herself she renews all things. . . . She reaches mightily from one end of the earth to another. . . . She glorifies her noble birth by living with God, and the Lord of all loves her. . . . Who has learned thy counsel, unless thou hast given Wisdom and sent thy holy Spirit from on high? And thus the pasts of those on earth were set right, and men . . . were saved by Wisdom. . . . For thy immortal spirit is in all things. (Wisdom of Solomon 6:12–12:1)

This section includes as well a historical review of Israel's history, in which Wisdom is depicted as the protector of Adam, as the salvation of the world from the flood, and as the rescuing guide of Abraham, Lot, Jacob, Joseph, Moses, and the people of Israel as a whole. Throughout, she is linked with God's "spirit" and "holy Spirit," so that we are encouraged to understand her role as intimately connected with the will of the Almighty. At the same time, she is pictured as communing directly with the righteous and the wise, inspiring them. For the imaginative reader it is as if she is a person: we are enjoined to "praise," "love," and "honor" this one who lives, with God, in honor in the heavenlies, but who also dwells as teacher among humankind. She is at once the darling of God and the spouse of godly humanity. Indeed, we are hard-pressed to distinguish her boundaries — is she a being in herself, an aspect of God, or a gift given to righteous and receptive humanity? Interestingly, in a sense we are directed away from questing after her identity: her major action is to give voice to the prophet and the worshipper (11:1; 10:20) rather than to call attention to herself. The reader of Wisdom of Solomon, however, can hardly escape the sense that in hearing about Wisdom, we have encountered a figure much more striking, indeed, more concrete, than a mere figure of speech.

Perhaps it is simply that the length of this passage leads us to dwell upon Wisdom as having a personhood of her own. Indeed, in this same book we discover a briefer, but similarly picturesque depiction of God's *logos*, which can be more easily read as symbolic. The "Word" comes to the aid of the Hebrews at the time of the Passover:

For while gentle silence enveloped all things, and night in its swift course was now half gone, thy all-powerful word leaped from heaven, from the royal throne, into the midst of the land that was doomed, a stern warrior carrying the sharp sword of thy authentic command, and stood and filled all things with death, and touched heaven while standing on the earth. (Wisdom 18:14-15)

Where Wisdom was pictured by the ample use of nouns and metaphors, as well as in her active capacity, the Word is described simply in terms of action verbs; this naturally leads the reader to think of the personal aspect of Wisdom, but to read the Word passage as symbolic. We remain uncertain: in the book of Wisdom, are both Wisdom and Word intended metaphorically, or is there a hint of something more with one or both? It is hard to be sure. We do know that some rabbis and philosophers (notably Philo) tended to speak about the Word in quasi-personal terms, as a figure with semi-divine status; this makes it more likely that Wisdom of Solomon's depiction of both Wisdom and Word strays beyond poetry into the realm of theological mystery.

But as though to leash speculation and call the wayward back to the foundation of Jewish piety and practice, two other apocryphal books, Sirach and Baruch, tie the figure of Wisdom firmly to the possession of the Torah, the first five books of the Old Testament:

I [Wisdom] came forth from the mouth of the Most High. . . . Alone I have made the circuit of the vault of heaven and have walked in the depth of the abyss. In the waves of the sea, in the whole earth, and in every people and nation I have gotten a possession. Among all these I sought a resting place. . . . Then the Creator of all things gave me a commandment and the one who created me assigned a place for my tent. . . . He said, "Make your dwelling in Jacob. . . ." . . . *All this is the book of the covenant of the Most High God, the law which Moses commanded us.* . . . (Sirach 24:3-23; my emphasis)

Who has gone up into heaven and taken her [Wisdom], and brought her down? . . . [God] found the whole way to knowledge, and gave her . . . to Israel whom he loved. Afterwards she appeared upon earth and lived among men. *She is the book of the commandments of God, and the law that endures forever.* (Baruch 3:29–4:1; my emphasis)

These two writers seem to be well aware of the picture of mysterious Wisdom, the one who dwells with both God and humanity, and who guards the secrets of the cosmos. Despite the mystery associated with her name, they want to make it clear that she is important specifically because of her connection with the Torah of Moses: to obey the Torah, they insist, is to come to know Wisdom; it is because Israel has been given the Torah that this nation can say Wisdom dwells within her walls. Any "esoteric" wisdom claimed by visionaries who report that they have "ascended the heights" or "plumbed the deeps" is always trumped by that Wisdom who is, in herself, "the Torah that endures forever."

Notice the concentration upon Torah! Even before, but especially after the fall of the Temple in A.D. 70, the center of rabbinic religion came to be Torah: Torah was considered God's complete wisdom and word, coming from the heavens to Israel, and the source of her glory. To obey the "words" of Torah is the source of wisdom. In the rabbinic teaching, from the first century A.D. on, the identification of the two, wisdom and word, is complete. The images come together — Torah, Word and Wisdom — existing even before the creation of the world, related to God in an intimate way, eternal, and giving graces to humankind. The Jewish tradition, though nervous of too much mystery, comes by the end of the first century to adapt the visionary stories about Wisdom, and to co-opt the Greek philosophers' words regarding a "hypostatic" Word, so that these stories and speculations are made to apply to the Torah. Here, they declared with optimism, we may find true wisdom and God's own word.

The rabbis, then, understood Torah, which subsumed God's Wisdom and Word, to be what identified Judaism — and even today, Torah remains the core of Judaism. Buried amidst this use of wisdom and word as cheerful boundary markers for Judaism, however, we encounter one pessimistic story. In the corpus of apocalyptic visions known as 1 *Enoch*, there is a suggestion that no one, not even Israel, is a fit home for Wisdom:

> Wisdom could not find a place in which she could dwell;
> But a place was found (for her) in the heavens.
> Then Wisdom went out to dwell with the children of the people,
> But she found no dwelling place,
> And she settled permanently among the angels.
> Then Iniquity went out of her rooms,

And found whom she did not expect.
And she dwelt with them,
Like rain in a desert,
Like dew on a thirsty land.

(1 Enoch 42:1-3)

Of course, 1 Enoch was neither accepted as a sacred book by the forma-
tive rabbis of the late first century, nor was it later canonized among the
Christian community (though it is quoted in the letter of Jude, and was
certainly read by some Jews and early Christians as authoritative). However, this esoteric book with its strange story about Wisdom serves as a
reminder that true Wisdom is the prerogative of God *alone*; nothing, not
even the possession of Torah, ensures that God's people can *contain* wisdom. This passage in fact offers a strong riposte to what might be con-
strued as one scribe's smug confidence when he treats the topic.
"Baruch," a pseudonymous writer whose book likely dates in its present
form from 150-50 B.C., exults:

> She [Wisdom] is the book of the commandments of God, and the law
> that endures for ever. All who hold her fast will live, and those who for-
> sake her will die.
> Turn, O Jacob, and take her; walk toward the shining of her light.
> *Do not give your glory to another, or your advantages to an alien people.*
> *Happy are we, O Israel, for we know what is pleasing to God.*
>
> (Baruch 4:1-4; my emphasis)

1 Enoch less optimistically sends Wisdom back home, for there is no human place fit for her to dwell — not even Israel.

Out of the Shadows

Indeed, in the Christian sequel to the story, we are told that the wisdom,
the word of God, *is* given to those once considered "an alien people."
Though humanity can offer no fit dwelling, a stunning reversal takes
place, orchestrated and enacted by the (re-)creating God who by wisdom
and word can bring to life the dead, and who will call into being a people
that was no people. So in the New Testament, both God's wisdom and

word are revealed as the same person come among us. The *Logos* (Word) is most prominent, appearing both in gospel and in vision. In the Gospel of John's first chapter, we hear of the One created alongside God in the beginning, and who was what God was: the language is rather philosophical, reminding us of Philo, but it reaches into our world. The Word has become flesh: will we respond to the plaintive cry that this One "came to his own but his own did not receive him"? Here, even as Jesus is called the Word, there are echoes of Wisdom, who in the ancient mythology was also rejected! What had been a mythic story concerning humankind's repudiation of wisdom now is enacted in human history. This declaration of God among us is described in cosmic proportions in the Revelation of Jesus to John. At the climax of its drama, when the forces of evil are finally vanquished, and just before the New Jerusalem appears, we greet a warrior figure who reminds us of the leaping Word from heaven, about whom we read in the Wisdom of Solomon:

> I saw heaven opened, and behold, a white horse! He who sat upon it is called Faithful and True, and in righteousness he judges and makes war. His eyes are like a flame of fire, and on his head are many diadems; and he has a name inscribed which no one knows but himself. He is clad in a robe dipped in blood, and the name by which he is called is The Word of God. And the armies of heaven, arrayed in fine linen, white and pure, followed him on white horses. From his mouth issues a sharp sword with which to smite the nations, and he will rule them with a rod of iron; he will tread the wine press of the fury of the wrath of God the Almighty. On his robe and on his thigh he has a name inscribed, King of kings and Lord of lords. (Revelation 19:11-16)

In the New Testament, then, there is no more ambiguity about the personal quality of the Word. The curtains are pulled back, and that shadowy figure encountered in the earlier writings emerges in full light and full force. The Word is clearly a person — indeed, the Word is *the* Person by which all others are measured. The event of the Incarnation means that God has done an utterly new thing; yet it may be that the earlier literature provided hints, muted and obscured figures of mysterious Wisdom and Word, in order to prepare God's people. Jesus, in his incarnate role as a human being, is figured most naturally as the Word in the New Testament, and by this title we most readily recognize him. Some have said that the figure of Wisdom in the ancient Jewish writings actually prefigures the Holy Spirit, whose *work* is sometimes also pictured by Christian writers as having a feminine cast, as in Romans 8:18-27, where the Holy Spirit acts as midwife to the cosmos. (On the whole knotty problem of masculine and feminine names and imagery, and the human roles of male and female, see section II C.)

Meditation upon the ancient texts about Wisdom discloses, indeed, many connections with the Holy Spirit — Wisdom is associated with God's spirit, dwells both on high and with humanity, and guides and protects. However, the figure of Wisdom also paves the way for believers to understand Jesus himself. For example, St. Paul speaks of our Lord as the One *"who became for us the Wisdom of God"* (1 Corinthians 1:30). Moreover, Jesus himself utters words in the Gospels that echo Wisdom's compelling invitations in the Apocrypha: "Come to me, you who labor and are heavy-laden. . . . Take my yoke upon you . . ." (Matthew 11:28-29; cf. Sirach 24:19, 51:23). Jesus was, after all, the first Person from the bosom of the Father to come and dwell intimately with humankind. He is, in historical terms, the first *Paraclete* ("one called alongside") from God — the encourager, the teacher, the strengthener of his people. It is through his work that the way is cleared for the Spirit to come in fullness, leading the people of God to all wisdom and truth.

Paradigm for Personhood

If we have been taught as Christians that the older figures of God's Word and Wisdom are fulfilled in the Person of the incarnate Son, Jesus, what does this tell us about the character of personhood? Careful thought concerning how this Person is in the world and amongst the Godhead makes for bracing theology — it is also supremely practical! John's Gospel begins with this telling description:

> In the beginning was the Word and the Word was *toward* God, and the Word was God. He was in the beginning *toward* God, and without him not anything was made that was made.

In English this literal translation of the Greek is awkward, so that our versions have tended to use the preposition "with" to describe the relationship of Word and God. In fact John's wording says, precisely, that "the Word was toward God" (**pros** *ton theon*). Here is a fascinating challenge to our "default" or automatic thinking about personhood. Ever since the Enlightenment, people have assumed that to be a person is to be an *individual*, one who is defined by separateness from others, by the categories of "I" and "not-I." Here we return to the primal experience of our infant, who smiles at her mother even before the discovery of her own hand — we are, in the first place, persons because we are *toward* others, not *over and against* them.

This essential characteristic of communion does not mean that there is no integrity in personhood. Indeed, the pattern of the Trinity, with each Person in intimate relation — one Being, yet *distinct* Persons — may be informative for us. We might be tempted to assume that the Spirit of God, whose role is to glorify Father and Son, sounds *sub*-personal, too adaptable to the other, and must as a "force" rather than a "person" indwell both deity and the created order. The Scriptures tell us otherwise, insisting that the Spirit is indeed a person who can be grieved, who can counsel, whose glory is to remain in intimacy with us, to encourage human redeemed persons and the Body of Christ as a whole. We may be confused as to how the human Jesus can indeed truly be a human person, "intruded" upon as he is by God's will and being — one of the heresies of the past is that the Son was comprised of a human body and a divine Spirit, a half-and-half mix! Or, we may suspect that the Son is less a divine person than the Father, for the Son is subject to his Father, and does the Father's will. But personhood is neither defined by autonomy nor by autocracy — the Son's unique personhood is shown in a willing humility, a giving of his life not only in love to the Father, but out of love for those who are not even worthy! "Herein is love, not that we loved God, but that he loved us." We might paraphrase, saying, "Herein is personhood, not to will autonomously, but to be and to act for the sake of others."

This is, of course, a mystery. Persons are made for other persons, but we cannot give what is not authentically ours to give. A full-blown person is not merely a "foil" for others (that is, a contrasting means by which another is identified), but has an integrity of his or her own. It is, indeed, out of strength, out of a robust *being* and a decisive *doing* that a person can love and give. As Michele M. Schumacher puts it, in her book *Women in Christ: Towards a New Feminism*, "the one . . . who experiences herself as eternally loved and forgiven, and thus as authentically free . . . is really capable of giving herself to God and to other human persons; for one cannot truly give what is not in one's possession" (p. xii). Of course, there is a sense in which God is the only "self-possessed" One; and even here, Persons of the Godhead are towards each other, living a mutual life. Most probably those who are redeemed (and probably also human beings in their glorified state) can only echo God's integrity, through love and grace, for we are *creatures*, albeit creatures called to bear the divine image. The divine paradigm of true Being and free Doing eludes us, for we cannot know this side of eternity, in our fallen condition — indeed, we may never know, because of our created nature — how it is that God, the truly authentic One, can give so utterly of himself. Perhaps it is not in our nature to be true "integrities" or to be complete "sacrificers." This remains to be seen. But at the very least, we learn from the personhood of the Son and the Holy Spirit, who fulfill the shadowy figures of Word and Wisdom, that to be a person is not to be independent in the absolute sense. (We must tread more lightly in our discussion of the Father, whose nature is known through the Son and the Spirit. The creeds tell us that it is from the Father that the other eternal and divine Persons *eternally* proceed: he is the source, the fountain, but has also himself been *always* in relation to those Others. So it would seem that even the Father is not to be understood as "independent": can we say that the Persons possess each other, and it is in this sense that they are "self-possessed"? Thought fails us.)

What we can say is that, given our knowledge of the Trinity, personhood is tied up intimately with community, and with complementarity of Persons: the Trinity, a communion of irreducible Persons in complementarity and love, is our bedrock in understanding what it is to be alive. This leads us back to our understanding of Christian spirituality: authentic spirituality is the characteristic of a person in Christ who has enough wisdom and insight regarding self and others, and enough love and strength through the Spirit, that he or she can dare to be "ek-static" and so to enter into true intimacy with "the other," an intimacy that will include both word and silence.

Mystery and Communication Meet Here

Besides telling us about what it means to be a person, word and wisdom also help us to understand how it is that we *know* and how it is that we truly *speak* with each other. The ancient philosophers used the term *logos* in connection with reason, proposition, and communication. That sense of reasonable utterance is not left behind when John tells us that the *Logos* became flesh. Indeed, in the One who is the Word, who has himself visited us in God's great living Story, we have a coming together of mysterious personhood with "proposition" or "communication." One of the most dubious assumptions of our age is that proposition and mystery, and proposition and narrative, are at odds. Mystics and theologians, poets and philosophers have been at war for long ages, and the war is at its height in our postmodern environment. Yet in the Christian story, we meet both One who *is* the Truth, and who *speaks* the truth. We must resist the current postmodern romance with narrative and mystery, at the expense of proposition. Postmodern Christian theologians and laypeople alike now are happy to "tell the story of Jesus and his love" and to speak wistfully about "spiritual experience" — but they have become nervous about making statements of doctrine, or claims about the nature of God and God's world. This is to lose any sense that God can tell us things that are true. It is to suggest that revelation is always like an impressionistic painting, or an evocative poem, and that the significance of revelation lies in the mind or imagination of the recipient. The fact is that the Bible itself contains various genres, not simply poetry and vision, wonderful though these are! God uses different modes to speak with us, including the voice of assertion or precept.

Many of us belong to confused ecclesial communities whose theological "thinkers" have, for the past generation, played off mystery and doctrine, experience and tradition. In the midst of this woolly-headedness, we have created an environment of so-called "inclusivity" that has brought about a colossal collision not only of stories, but also of precepts and of practice. In the American atmosphere of polarization, this collision has meant for emotive explosion and sometimes uncharitable defamation of character; in my own Canadian context, "politeness" seems to reign, and fear of the fireworks, so that much doubletalk and ostrich behavior abounds. On both sides of the border, the iceberg has been hit, and the churches are being divided, but few understand the depth and size of the barrier upon which they have foundered. The critical debates over same-sex eroticism and the particularity of Jesus as Savior continue to polarize and confuse: these are very important issues, because of what they entail. But it is hard to get at the *reasons* for the current state of affairs, because of two factors. First, we do not recognize that many have mistaken the biblical narrative for one of their own making, replacing the gospel of Jesus (which includes repentance and transformation) with a "gospel" of so-called inclusivity. Second, rigor in careful propositional thought, and a sense of history have both been forfeited, even by many of the educated, in our culture. Many are trying to think of many impossible things before breakfast — we have banished reason to the basement, and put experience in her place in the parlor and the master bedroom!

All this may sound political and beside the point in a discussion of Christian spirituality. But it is not, for we are called by our Lord Jesus to come into soundness of "body, soul, and spirit" through the ministrations of the Holy Spirit in the Church. Our mind matters, as John Stott once insisted. One of the greatest needs for the Church as a whole, and for each of us, is to see the call for an integrated life, where mind, body, and spirit are joined in the center of our beings, the heart. This happens, I believe, in only one place: in the presence of the Lord himself, who heals everything and us all.

What we need is to return again to our first love, to worship. We need, in the presence of God's worshiping people, past and present, and in the presence of the adoring angels and archangels, even when we are physically alone, to hear yet again God's very own story, to know that he is with us, and to fall down before the standing slaughtered Lamb. St. Gregory of Palamas, who lived during the thirteenth century, speaks of those who, in the presence of God, find that "the morning star rises" in their hearts (Triads 2.3.18); this brilliant Light is far "superior to the light of . . . knowledge . . . that comes from Hellenic [i.e. philosophical] studies." Scripture, he tells us, is the lamp that shines in our dark places; but in seeking the Lord's face, in worship, in quiet adoration, we prepare a space where the Sun itself can shine. So we behold, perhaps only for brief glimpses at first, the "Star of the Morning."

Sustained, and then finally unceasing worship of this One who is Word and Wisdom bring us to increasing love, and to growing knowledge. We come more clearly to understand the propositions, the words, the path, by which he directs us. In the worship, in the remembrance, in the reasoning, comes an authentic living and an increasing faith, because this takes place before the very face of God, and in the light of the Sun of Righteousness. Mary Magdalene, in coming to the garden at the climax of Jesus' own story, heard her name called. She was given a message, a message that included both a story and a proposition, to give to the apostles. The story was that the Son was "going back" to the Father. The proposition was that as a result of all these events, Jesus' own obedient life, death, glorious resurrection, and impending ascent, this God was now "my Father and your Father, my God and your God." It was from entering into the story of Jesus, from being intimately named by the Namer of all the living, from being told the conclusion of the story, and from being entrusted with a true proposition, that Mary's identity was sealed, and her own ecstatic mission was born. So, "casting aside the ancestral curse," she "elatedly told the apostles, 'Death is overthrown! Christ our God is risen, granting the world great mercy!'" (Troparion, tone 4, Orthodox Divine Liturgy). This woman, from her place at the margins of society, was brought into the center of God's life, God's actions, God's truth, and God's very own mission, by which he claims his own.

Knowledge and Faith: Knowing the Lord

We move on, then, to a discussion of knowledge and faith, two very prominent concepts in the New Testament, and especially in the epistles of Paul. Human faith comes from "hearing" or knowledge of what God has done (Romans 10:17), and so we must begin with knowledge. In speaking about how it is that Christians "know," the apostle takes his point of departure from the promises of the Old Testament prophets. There we hear, unequivocally, that "knowledge" is the prerogative of God alone (Isaiah 40:12-18), and that knowledge of God's will coincides with an intimate knowledge of the Lord himself:

> Behold, the days are coming, says the LORD, when I will make a new covenant with the house of Israel and the house of Judah, not like the covenant which I made with their fathers when I took them by the hand to bring them out of the land of Egypt, my covenant which they broke, though I was their husband, says the LORD. But this is the covenant which I will make with the house of Israel after those days, says the LORD: I will put my law within them, and I will write it upon their hearts; and I will be their God, and they shall be my people. And no longer shall each man teach his neighbor and each his brother, saying, "Know the LORD," for they shall all know me, from the least of them to

the greatest, says the LORD; for I will forgive their iniquity, and I will re-member their sin no more. (Jeremiah 31:31-34)

The prophet anticipates a new era: having the Lord's law written in the heart will mean that God and his people are intimately joined, so inti-mately joined that "mediation" is not necessary, for all God's people will know the Lord, and all will be forgiven. This is to be an action of God himself, who is the author of all knowledge. So Jeremiah passes on the promise that God's people will know *about* God's will in an internal way, and so they will also *know God*. It may help for us to remember that in the Hebrew Bible, "to know" did not mean simply to receive an idea, but also was applied to the special knowledge that a husband and wife share re-garding each other: "And Adam knew his wife Eve." This kind of commu-nion between God and his people is suggested throughout the tormented verses of the prophet Hosea, in which our "love-crazed" God seeks Israel as Hosea seeks his wayward wife. The Lord's pledge, recorded by Jere-miah, that we should intimately *know* the Lord was fulfilled, says St. Paul, when God acted in Christ and in the Holy Spirit:

> You are a letter from Christ . . . written not with ink but with the Spirit of the living God, not on tablets of stone but on tablets of human hearts. Such is the confidence that we have through Christ toward God. . . . Since we have such a hope, we are very bold, not like Moses, who put a veil over his face so that the Israelites might not see the end of the fading splendor. But their minds were hardened; for to this day, when they read the old covenant, that same veil remains unlifted, be-cause only through Christ is it taken away. Yes, to this day whenever Moses is read a veil lies over their minds, but when a man turns to the Lord the veil is removed. Now the Lord is the Spirit, and where the Spirit of the Lord is, there is freedom. And we all, with unveiled face, beholding the glory of the Lord, are being changed into his likeness from one degree of glory to another; for this comes from the Lord who is the Spirit. (2 Corinthians 3:3-18)

Paul is applying to the entire Christian community the free status that Je-sus bequeathed to his apostles when he said, "No longer do I call you ser-vants, for the servant does not know what his master is doing; but I have called you friends, for all that I have heard from the Father I have made known to you" (John 15:15). Again, following his vision of the fall of Satan, Jesus rejoiced in the new era:

> I thank thee, Father, Lord of heaven and earth, that thou hast hidden these things from the wise and understanding and revealed them to babes; yea, Father, for such was thy gracious will. All things have been delivered to me by my Father; and *no one knows who the Son is except the Father, or who the Father is except the Son and any one to whom the Son chooses to reveal him.* (Luke 10:21-22; my emphasis)

God, then, has revealed to infants, and indeed emboldened Christ's own community, so that together we can have true knowledge of who he is, and what he is doing — this veil lifted, we may actually anticipate in the present our complete transformation of the future. Knowledge of God brings about change of the sort that can be likened to Jesus' own transfiguration on the mountain. This is why, throughout the correspondence with the Corinthians, St. Paul is at pains to describe the quality and depth of Christian knowledge, seeking to go beyond spiritual milk to feed them with solid food. Ten times in the first letter he uses the little phrase, "Do you not know?" In the second letter, he is more positive, encouraging the church to hold on to what it does know, even while challenging them with regards to spiritual pride and the wrong evaluation of esoteric knowledge. The knowledge that God has given to them comes from the "foolishness" of the cross — "For you *know* the grace of our Lord Jesus Christ, that though he was rich, yet for your sake he became poor, so that by his poverty you might become rich" (2 Corinthians 8:9). Moreover, although some Christians have grown in this knowledge more than others, and some of the body has the gift of the Spirit to speak words of knowledge in particular circumstances, the knowledge of God himself is not a specialized gift, as it was under the old covenant. Rather, knowledge of God is the shared and *common property* of all who are in Christ: "For it is the God who said, 'Let light shine out of darkness,' who has shone in *our* hearts to give the light of the knowledge of the glory of God in the face of Christ" (4:5).

This is an astounding statement, considering the fact that St. Paul himself claimed to have had "unutterable" spiritual visions and revelations, times of special ecstasy and unspeakable intimacy with the Lord. These he speaks about, though with irony and reserve, in 2 Corinthians 12, a passage that can only be considered an "anti-apocalypse." That is, for the reader "in the know" about apocalyptic visions and how they were recorded in Paul's day, this passage presents a teasing "form" of an apocalypse, without any recorded revelation of secret things. The apostle sets us up in order to frustrate our desire for "dope" concerning that other world. So, in 2 Corinthians 12:1-12, St. Paul makes reference to the levels of heaven, to visions and "words" from the Lord, to things experienced in an altered state, and even to an interpreting spiritual "messenger" — though, in this case, the visionary Paul has received a messenger from *Satan*. All these details are introduced because the apostle has been challenged in his ministry by so-called "super-apostles" who are claiming to be superior to Paul because of their esoteric knowledge. So the Corinthians' true apostle admits that he, too, has had his "mountaintop" experiences: but he is embarrassed to have to mention them in order to get the attention of his people, and complains that they have driven him to "play the fool." After all, it is their common bond in Christ, and what they know *together* that Christ has done and is doing in their midst, that should commend them to each other. However, if they demand to know, St. Paul also has seen with spiritual eyes, and heard with the spiritually-open ear.

Nevertheless, all this is beside the point to him. He will not stake his reputation on these things, nor will he base doctrine upon secret revelations vouchsafed to him. For there is "one thing needful" — to follow the Lord's pattern of humility, and to hear the word, "My grace is made perfect in weakness!" Paul's physical reminder of his revelatory exploits is not a glowing face like that of Moses, nor stigmata like the saints, but an unidentified "thorn in the flesh" that reminds him of his dependence upon Christ. If other Christians can learn anything from his personal experiences concerning that other world, let them learn from this mark of humility. For whatever our experience, it is only significant if it points to the common knowledge that the body of Christ has been given, the open heart that together we share, because we are in Christ. The ultimate revelation, or apocalypse, is Jesus Christ himself, and what God has done in his Son. Thus, as Christ's own, we are *privileged* to hear; as Jesus declared to his disciples, "many . . . desired to see what you see, and did not see it, and to hear what you hear, and did not hear it" (Luke 10:24). *Together* we are privy to "the mystery . . . hidden for ages and generations but now made manifest to his saints — Christ in you, the hope of glory" (Colossians 1:26b, 27b). That mystery will not play second fiddle to any boastfulness regarding idiosyncratic esoteric spirituality!

St. Paul, then, is wholly convinced of the act of God in Jesus that radicalizes every human prerogative to spirituality and by which we are brought together into the communion of the Godhead; he has, and we should have, no use for those who claim special privilege and status on the basis of their own spiritual exploits. As he emphasizes throughout his correspondence, knowledge of God and of God's ways belongs to the Christian community as a whole:

You were enriched in him in every *word* and in all *knowledge*. (1 Corinthians 1:5; my emphasis)

Now we have received not the spirit of the world, but the Spirit which is from God, that we might understand the gifts bestowed on us by God. (1 Corinthians 2:12)

"For who has known the mind of the Lord so as to instruct him?" But we have the mind of Christ. (1 Corinthians 2:16)

Back at the dawn of our world, Adam and Eve were seduced by the tempter to think that their heart's desire was to "be as God." So they ate of the Tree of the Knowledge of Good and Evil, and forfeited, through the process of dying, the godlike potential that was given to them by the Creator. Jesus, the One who resisted temptation as our new Adam, and who became himself fruit upon a cursed tree, won again our birthright, and reopened Paradise. Indeed, his victory went beyond "Paradise regained" so as to regain our *real* heart's desire, to be *with* God, and so to be "like God" by grace, in Christ Jesus himself. For, indeed, the tempter told only a half-truth: we have come to know evil (at least in part) but have ceased to understand the good. Jesus, our true representative, is the One who has thoroughly understood evil, not from the inside, but by receiving the worst that it can do to humanity, in his own person on the cross (and, says the creed, by his descent to Hades).

Because Jesus assumed *this*, our curse and punishment, we may be healed in the arena of knowledge, so that we begin to understand with all the saints, and eventually beyond even the ken of the archangels (what wonder!), "the good" — God himself! From the side of that incarnate One came blood and water, recreating and washing his new Eve, the Church: "at once, there came out [from his side] blood and water. He who saw it has borne witness — his testimony is true and he knows that he tells the truth — so that you also may believe" (John 19:34). So Paul says in 2 Corinthians 11:2 that it is his desire "to present you [i.e., the Church] as a pure bride to her one husband." All this has been accomplished and prepared in Christ, yet the result is not automatic. Danger still lurks, and so we are enjoined, "Since we have these promises, beloved, let us cleanse ourselves from every defilement of body and spirit, and make holiness perfect in the fear of the Lord" (2 Corinthians 7:1).

Some of this may not "wash well" with those of us this side of the Reformation, who rightly emphasize the grace of Christ, his gift of redemption to us. Yet we must remember that Christianity is not Gnosticism: we are *not* a movement that believes in salvation through *knowledge*. No, our salvation is a result of the faithfulness of God himself, and it is a salvation that calls us to participate fully in Christ. There remains the "impossible possibility" (to use Barth's phrase) that even having "known" about God's grace, even having "tasted" of Christ's goodness, some might turn away and refuse God's desire to sanctify, to draw us deeper into the only goodness that there is. And there is no standing still in this life: we are either moving more into God's will or away from it (though, as with all life, the progress is not always immediately apparent, and there are fluctuations). Without getting into the tortured theological debate about election and free will, we may recognize that the Scriptures issue injunctions to holiness, and warnings about apostasy and carelessness, *for a reason*. Our life in Christ is a gift, and our continued growth is a gift, but it does not happen automatically. Just as God placed Adam and Eve in a caretaking position in the pristine world of Eden, so now the redeemed humanity, in Christ, is called to respond to God's work in us, so that time and space are redeemed for the sake of holiness. This begins with, but does not end with, our own lives and our own relationships.

We tread carefully here to avoid the impression that this relies upon us, for all of it comes from the initiative of God. Yet we are called, in a certain sense, to "co-operate." (Perhaps we could coin the word "sub-operate.") Just as the God of the Hebrews said to his own people, "You shall be holy, for I am holy" (and assumed that this required a response), so the rhythm of the Pauline letters says, "God is like this and God has done this in Christ," "*therefore* present your bodies as a living sacrifice, *holy* . . ." (Romans 12:1). Jesus said to his listeners, "*Be* therefore *perfect* (*teleioi*, that is, complete, with integrity, fulfilled) just as your heavenly Father is *perfect*" (Matthew 5:48). Again, it is not Christianity, but the Gnostic movement, that assumed its converts, the "spirit-ones" to be *already* perfect. The Incarnation, and God's reclaiming of the cosmos and of humanity, does not mean that we can claim an inner, inalienable "holiness." This is something held for us in trust as we are in Christ; we are at the beginning of an ongoing life of transformation in which we are marvelously, and graciously, called to participate. "I no longer call you servants, but friends," Jesus says to his disciples in John 15:15.

Let us make no mistake about it. The advent of God the Son changed the whole of the fallen created order, so that, in a sense, the distinction between the holy and profane has been abolished. This means that nothing is to be, by its inner nature, whether material, emotional, psychic, or spiritual, left outside of God's rule — but things are not *automatically* rendered holy just because they have some claim to existence, nor are people rendered holy because of their knowledge alone. Things and people need to be "set aside" for God, a work that begins when we are incorporated into *Christ*, "the Holy One of God" (Luke 1:35, Acts 4:27), and that continues as we stay in Christ. Yet this is a work that does not exclude our own will, and our own heart-desires.

Thus Paul enjoins his people, "Now as you excel in everything — in faith, in utterance, in knowledge, in all earnestness, and in your love for us — see that you excel in this gracious work also" (2 Corinthians 8:7). In the end, knowledge about God and knowledge of God means desiring to become like him, in Christ. And he will answer our prayer, for he is faithful to do what he has promised.

From Faith to Faith

This brings us, then, to the whole wondrous matter of *pistis* — a double-duty word in the Greek that means both "faithfulness" and "faith." It should be clear by now that faith is not the opposite of "knowledge," nor of "reason." Rather, the faith or trust that we have in Christ is itself a gift of God that does not bypass our minds, but is deeper than what we can think. And that faith is based upon the faithfulness of Christ Jesus himself, who as God incarnate showed forth God's faithfulness and, as obedient Son, had faith, trusted in the Father, to accomplish the mystery of the ages. As a mind-opening experience, open your English version of St.

Paul's epistles, and every time you come to the phrase "faith *in* Jesus" or "faith *in* Jesus Christ," try substituting "the faith" or "the faithfulness *of* Jesus Christ," a translation that is equally valid. See what difference this makes to your understanding of the gospel, how it becomes apparent that this is God's work from first to last, not something to "earn" — even by means of our own faith! In the gospel, the good-news drama, God is shown to be faithful and true — that is, righteous. In the life, death, resurrection, and ascension of our Lord, we see the character of our loving and just, merciful and truthful God, who deals with human sin and rescues us from the tragedy of death, by his own costly actions. This story of Jesus, this gospel, reveals the mystery of goodness, the One who is at once righteous and true and just and loving: "For in [the gospel] the righteousness of God is revealed by [Christ's] faith(fulness) for [our] faith" (Romans 1:17; my translation).

In the light of what God has done in Christ, there is no need for us to go far afield to find ultimate reality. We need neither to ascend to the realms of heaven nor trek down to the abyss (Romans 10:5-7), nor need we search feverishly for methods, spiritual techniques, and unseen power. For this One who is the very active Word of God is near us: indeed he has visited us, has plunged into the matter of this world, rescued us from the darkest regions, and now dwells intimately with us through the Spirit. It is due to *his* questing, *his* agony, and *his* victory that "everyone who calls upon the name of the Lord shall be saved" (Romans 10:13). Faith, then, does not mean believing "in spite of the evidence." Faith is not a human accomplishment or work. Human trust, or faith, simply responds to the faithful work of the God who creates out of nothing, and gives life to the dead. Our confidence in God responds to this story of all stories, and so can stand the test, during trial, and during times of suffering when the end cannot yet be seen; yet that faith is not "blind" nor "mindless," but has a God-given grounding in history, in God's actions for Israel and the world, as well as in a Person, in the character of the creating and resurrecting Lord of all.

"For Christ is the *fulfillment* of the Torah, to bring about righteousness for everyone who has faith" (Romans 10:4; my translation). Nor is that the end of this eternal drama: "for those to whom he gave righteousness, he also glorified" in Christ Jesus (Romans 8:30). Word and Wisdom, knowledge and faith thus come from the Father of lights, in the Son, and grow intimately within us through the ministrations of the

Holy Spirit, so that we, God's people, can be what we are intended to be — bearers of the very image of God, whose Love far exceeds anything we can think or imagine.

FURTHER MEDITATION

This is eternal life, that they may know you, the only true God, and Jesus Christ, whom you have sent. (John 17:3)

Let us not, then, turn aside incredulous before the superabundance of these blessings; but let us have faith in Him who has participated in our nature and granted in return the glory of His own nature, and let us seek to acquire this glory and seek it. . . . For the Lord has promised to manifest Himself to the one who keeps [his commandments], a manifestation He calls His own indwelling and that of the Father, saying, "If anyone loves Me, he will keep my word, and My Father will love him, and We will come to him and will make our abode with him" (John 14:23) and "I will manifest Myself to him" (John 14:21). (St. Gregory of Palamas, *Triads* 2.3.16)

But thanks be to God, who in Christ always leads us in triumph, and through us spreads the fragrance of the knowledge of him everywhere. (2 Corinthians 2:14)

Suppose that . . . he himself alone were to speak, and we were to hear his Word, not through any tongue of flesh or voice of an angel or sound of thunder or involved allegory, but that we might hear him whom in all these things we love, might hear him in himself without them, just as a moment ago we two [Augustine and his mother], as it were, rose beyond ourselves and in a flash of thought touched the Eternal Wisdom abiding over all. If this were to continue, and other quite different visions disappear, leaving only this one to ravish and absorb and enclose its beholder in inward joys so that life might forever be such as that one moment of understanding for which we had been sighing, would this not surely be: "Enter into the joy of your Lord"? (Augustine, *Confessions*, Book 9.10)

Thou whose almighty Word
Chaos and darkness heard,
And took their flight,
Hear us, we humbly pray,
And, where the gospel-day
Sheds not its glorious ray,
Let there be light!

Thou who didst come to bring
On thy redeeming wing
Healing and sight,
Health to the sick in mind,
Sight to the inly blind,
O now, to all mankind,
Let there be light!

Spirit of truth and love,
Life-giving, holy dove,
Speed forth thy flight;
Move on the waters' face,
Bearing the lamp of grace
And in earth's darkest place
Let there be light!

Holy and Blesséd Three,
Glorious Trinity,
Wisdom, Love, Might,
Boundless as ocean tide
Rolling in fullest pride,
Through the world, far and wide,
Let there be light!

J. Marriott, 1813

FURTHER READING

I Enoch. Translated by E. Isaac. In The Old Testament Pseudepigrapha I, edited by James H. Charlesworth, pp. 5-89. Garden City, N.Y.: Doubleday,

1983. Taste this non-canonical apocalypse for a disorienting of ancient "wisdom," and as a contrast to the revelations disclosed in the Christian Scriptures.

Schumacher, Michele M., ed. *Women in Christ: Towards a New Feminism.* Grand Rapids: Eerdmans, 2003. A collection of helpful essays from a Roman Catholic perspective on personhood and women in the Christian tradition.

Hays, Richard B. *The Faith of Jesus Christ: The Narrative Substructure of Galatians 3:1–4:11.* Revised edition. Grand Rapids: Eerdmans, 2002. Hays's masterful discussion of the phrase "the faith of Jesus Christ" versus "faith in Jesus Christ" in the letter to the Galatians. Not for beginners.

Walsh, Brian J., and J. Richard Middleton. *The Transforming Vision: Shaping a Christian World-View.* InterVarsity Press, 1984. The authors put forth the biblical story to help us negotiate this generation's difficulty with knowledge and the concept of truth.

FURTHER REFLECTION AND DISCUSSION

1. What is the relationship between worship, faith, and mission in the Church?
2. How do we avoid, in our discussion of the Son as the Word, and the likening of the Holy Spirit to Wisdom, the heresy of "modalism" — that God "appears" in different forms, and is not eternally one Being in three Persons?
3. If the understanding of Jesus as God's revelation is common to all Christians, and the greatest "apocalypse," what do we make of Christians who have had special experiences, or who obviously have special wisdom, insight, or gifts?
4. What are the benefits and dangers of seeing the Persons of the Trinity as a pattern for human personhood?

LIGHT II

Christ, whose glory fills the skies,
Christ, the true, the only Light,
Sun of Righteousness, arise,
Triumph o'er the shades of night;
Day-spring from on high, be near;
Day-star, in my heart appear.

Dark and cheerless is the morn
Unaccompanied by thee;
Joyless is the day's return,
Till thy mercy's beams I see;
Till they inward Light impart,
Glad my eyes, and warm my heart

Visit then this soul of mine,
Pierce the gloom of sin and grief;
Fill me, Radiancy Divine,
Scatter all my unbelief;
More and more thyself display,
Shining to the perfect day.

CHARLES WESLEY, 1740

The above quotation from 2 Peter provides for us a scriptural commentary on the great revelatory event of the transfiguration of Jesus, that shining epiphany of God the Son on Mount Tabor, recorded in all three of the Synoptic Gospels (Mark 9:2-13, Matthew 17:1-13, and Luke 9:28-36). This story, which in each Gospel foreshadows the humility of the cross, speaks powerfully of the divine love and light that has entered our world. The epistle writer tells us that for the apostles, this sight of the transformed Jesus "confirmed" or "made sure" the "prophetic message" of the Old Testament; it is to the apostles' testimony concerning this Jesus, recorded now in the New Testament Scriptures, that we are to pay attention, because their apostolic witness is indeed "a lamp shining in a dark place." It is by way of Jesus, the Sun of Righteousness, that we together with the prophets and the apostles come to understand the Holy God, from whom streams all light.

Perhaps those of us who are creedal, or "orthodox" (in the sense of maintaining "upright doctrine"), have been tempted to treat such matters in terms of sheer doctrine, the jealous hoarding of a dragon sitting upon its treasure. Have we adopted statements about the Son and the Trinity as "shibboleths" (see Judges 12:6) to guard our identity, rather than as realities by which we become who we are meant to be? May it not be so! Trinitarian life, made known to us through the Incarnation, has to do with the very One whom we worship: "orthodoxy" means not simply "upright *doctrine*" but also "upright *worship*." It is as we worship, through the open door provided by Jesus, that we find our own true identity: coming to know God intimately means coming to find our own nature, for we are *made* for worship. St. Augustine, great father of the Western Church, is often quoted in this regard: "You have made us for yourself: our hearts are restless, until they find their rest in you" (*Confessions* 1.1.1). To gaze upon Jesus the Son, to contemplate his life, and to listen to his teaching, means that we come to understand the triune nature of God; to set our affections upon that One means that we will come to understand ourselves as well. For in speaking of the Triune God, we are at the Holy of Holies; to understand the center helps all that circles around find its true place.

Thus it is that our glimpse of the Son (and so of the Triune God) *transforms* us in a way that affects the whole of us, and not simply our minds! To some this has not seemed to be so. More and more frequently one hears of even faithful Christians who consider the proclamation that Jesus is both God and Man, and the Church's teaching concerning Trinity to be theological "constructs" simply designed to keep us from heresy. To many Christians today, the doctrines appear abstruse and difficult, coded in ancient Greek and philosophical language, and even a distraction from the "gospel." Those who say this have usually either reduced the gospel to a simple scheme by which the individual can be assured of acceptance by God, or diluted it into a bromide hardly distinguishable from, "What the world needs now is love, sweet love." But the good news is both richer and more focused than either of these alternatives. The good news concerns the one true God, who is faithful, loving, righteous, and merciful, and it is the ultimate expression of God's character in the gift of *himself* to fallen humanity — an action initiated by the Father in his Son and through his Holy Spirit. As those who have been entrusted with this good news, we begin by announcing to the world that Jesus (sinless, crucified, risen, and ascended!) is the Majestic Lord and Savior over the two dread enemies of humanity: sin and death. Once we see that this gospel has been accepted, it is our great joy to introduce to our new friends the astonishing plan of God — the plan by which he means to reveal his nature, to enfold us in his own love, and to make us, together, *like* him. God's mending is to be followed by God's making. It is not simply a matter of Paradise regained (as Milton would have it), not simply a U-shaped story that we tell, but a matter of something beyond our imaginations, a checkmark-shaped story in which "the sky's *not* the limit."

In the light of *this* gospel, we come to see that orthodox christological teaching (i.e., Jesus is both God and Human, not half-and-half, nor one at the expense of the other) and trinitarian teaching (i.e., Father, Son, and Spirit are one yet three) are not simply matters of parroted catechism. Part of our being remade and transformed is that we come to have the mind of Christ; we are to be formed, shaped, molded within the living tradition that enfolds those who are in Christ. Many of the mystics, or spiritual theologians, both male and female, learned or not, wrote about an experience that is christologically focused and therefore triune-shaped. The celebrated scholar of spiritual theology, Louis Dupré, puts it this way: "I believe it is not exaggerated to claim that most of the writings of the Greek fathers between the third and fifth century centred around the Trinity. Not only was it the main subject of theological speculation, but it was also the source of spiritual inspiration" (Dupré and Wiseman, *Light from Light*, p. 12).

In Christ, our spirits respond to the Holy Spirit, who is united with the Father and Son forever. This response means that we are not simply *informed* about a key Christian doctrine, but that we are *formed* and *re-formed* by the Triune God who loves us. Our spirituality, if it is truly Christian, must be trinitarian-shaped. Hidden in the Old Testament prophetic words, then revealed in gospel event, in the theological reflections of the epistles, and in the prayers of Jesus, we come face-to-face with the Triune One, and so in our own lives find our spirituality informed by this Mystery. We come to have a family likeness with the One who has called all families into being.

Let us begin by training our gaze upon the fulfillment event of the transfiguration, allowing it to suggest to us those Old Testament moments where the Person of the Son and the mystery of the Trinity were intimated all along, for those with eyes to see. Then, we will move on to consider the deep teaching given by Jesus to his disciples in John 14–17, teaching that he delivered with the promise that the "Holy Spirit" would lead them (and us) into all truth. Finally, we'll look at the place that we ourselves are being given within God's glory and communion, as adopted children of God. Consideration of this great grace, that is, the potential for our illumination by God's very own light, will provide the backdrop for the second two topics of this triad — the witness of our holy siblings from the past, who have shone with God's own light, and the ongoing reflection of God's trinitarian communion that we behold in redeemed human relationships.

The Transfiguration of Our Lord

The transfiguration, found in Mark 9:2-13, Matthew 17:1-13, and Luke 9:28-36, is a key moment both in Jesus' own ministry and in the apprenticeship of his disciples. Meditation upon this scene, both in word and through icon, has been a powerful source of spiritual growth for Christians throughout the ages.

Let's begin our reading, according to the conventions of contemporary scholarship, with Mark's Gospel. As always with Mark, the *placement* of the event is key to its understanding. The overall structure of Mark's Gospel can be visualized as two "mountains" of revelation. The first mountain comprises roughly chapters one through eight, where the question "Who is this Jesus?" is given the answer "He is the Messiah," an-

This icon of the transfiguration includes, in detail, the journey up and down the Mount. A mid-16th-century icon by George the Cretan, it is found at the Dionysiou Monastery in Mount Athos.

Image compliments of St. Isaac of Syria Skete, www.skete.com

This 1403 icon of the transfiguration is written by Theophanes the Greek, one of the instructors of Rublev. It shows Jesus blessing Peter, James, and John, who have fallen down "in fear."

Image compliments of St. Isaac of Syria Skete, www.skete.com

ticipated throughout by the suggestiveness of the drama, and declared unequivocally at the climax by the mouth of Peter himself (8:29). The second mountain comprises chapters nine through sixteen, where the question "What kind of Messiah is he?" is initially answered by Jesus' own reproof of Peter, where the Lord teaches that he is "a Messiah who must suffer and so enter into glory" (8:31). This exchange is then dramatically played out in the ensuing way to the cross. The transfiguration event comes just after this double "hinge" or "valley" between these two great structures (8:27-38), when Peter has been both commended for his insight into Jesus' Messiahship, and challenged to accept (and emulate) Jesus' true nature, as one who suffers and so is glorified. In Jesus, the "kingdom" or "rule" of God has already "come" with power (9:1), although things are not yet completely restored; the disciples are about to have the veil pulled back so they can see the significance of this One to whom they must listen. As Cyril of Alexandria explained, when the three saw the glory of Jesus and Moses and Elijah, the kingdom of God had come *even at that point* for them (*Commentary on Luke*, Homily 51).

Mark's Gospel sounds several notes that are particularly evocative. First, Mark encircles the whole episode with the repeated word "alone" (Greek *monon*). Jesus initially takes the three disciples up with himself *alone*; at the conclusion of the vision, they see Jesus *alone*. This is a concentrated time with Jesus, a revelatory event that will shape their entire discipleship from this point on. Here they are, with a teacher who appears in glory that can hardly be described, so that even his garments glisten. Though they call him "Rabbi" (9:5), soon they will learn that he has taken on a more glorious double role. He is being presented to them as fulfilling the picture of both the Suffering Servant of God, who is connected with faithful Israel in Isaiah 42:1-4; 49:1-6; 50:4-11; 52:13–53:12, and the visionary Son of Man, whom the Father glorifies, as a representative of God's saints (Daniel 7:13-14, 26-27). Indeed, glory comes only through the route of suffering, and it is by this unlikely route that their Rabbi will win victory for them; this is what Jesus goes on to teach his disciples as they return down the mountain (9:9-13), though his teaching will not be fully understood until the end of the Gospel. It is interesting that in Mark the episode of glory is sketched very briefly; almost as much time is given to Jesus' lesson after they leave the moment of luminescence, with the Father's word reminding them (and us!), "Listen to him."

Matthew's version (17:1-8, followed by 9-13) follows the same contours as that of Mark, though he has told the story in a striking way, recalling great revelatory events of the past, specifically, the encounters of Moses and the prophets with the Almighty. His narrative is twice pierced by the expostulation, "Behold!"; in the scene that ensues, we are told that the apostles have seen "a vision." Indeed, the entire episode has the "rhythm" of an apocalyptic vision, as can be readily seen when we compare it with another visionary episode, such as that in Daniel 10:4-11. That is, the apostles see a wondrous sight, One whose face "shines like the sun," the major luminary of the sky — this glowing One is greater than the mere angel observed by Daniel, whose face was "like lightning" (Daniel 10:6); and yet, unlike the prophetic visions that Isaiah, Moses, and Elijah have of the Almighty God, this face can be seen! After beholding this wonder, the three hear a divine *bath qôl* (literally, "the daughter of a voice," the term used by rabbis for the echo of God's own word on earth). At this, they fall on their faces in awe, like many a visionary, and are touched and raised up, for God has something for them to do. Finally, on the way down the mountain, Jesus assumes the role of the interpreting heavenly being, a messenger frequently encountered in visionary literature. During their descent together, he explains the meaning of what has been revealed, so that the Gospel can comment: "then the disciples understood . . ." (17:13). It is, however, Jesus' whole life-direction — up to the cross, and beyond, to the resurrection and ascension — that provides the complete interpretation of their vision.

Luke's account, found in 9:28-36, underscores both the significance of this staggering event within the flow of salvation history, and its power to embrace us personally. Here is a scene of true glory: *doxa* ("glory") is the term used by Luke, reminding us of the appearance of God's glory (*kabod*) which led the Hebrew people by day and by night through the wilderness. The *Shekinah,* that remarkable and ineffable Presence of God, was seen by the Israelites in the cloud of glory, both as a protection and as a guide, during their sojourn in the wilderness. It had the effect of irradiating the face of their leader, Moses, after he had been in intimate contact with the LORD, both on Mount Sinai and in the "Tabernacle of Meeting." Jewish people throughout the centuries have commemorated this time of intimacy with God in the wilderness by erecting tabernacles during the feast of "Booths" — a reminder of their dependence upon the LORD in a harsh environment, and his closeness to them as he forged them to be his own people.

After about 1000 years, in their time of Babylonian exile, perhaps the

Jewish people had assumed that God had abandoned them, taking away his glory, which had been first in the portable Tabernacle, and then had resided in the Temple since Solomon's day. But in the vision of Ezekiel, the glory comes to the prophet, *not* confined to one place, not even to holy Jerusalem, but moving (as it were) on a celestial and fiery chariot-throne. Ezekiel's vision demonstrated that God was still with them. So it was that, after Ezekiel's era, rabbis of a mystical bent went in small conventicles, led by master seers, to contemplate the Ezekiel visions. Their hope was to themselves glimpse the glory throne, the heavenly court-room, and the attending Angel of God, who could give them esoteric insight into the meaning of the Torah, the sacred Law. Any of my readers who are of an adventurous bent may search out some of the later Enoch literature (e.g. *3 Enoch*) in order to learn what some of these mystical rabbis (called "Merkavah," that is, "Divine Chariot" mystics) might have discovered in their time of prayer and ascetic separation from the world!

In Luke 9:28-36, we watch another rabbi taking his inner group of disciples to a holy place to pray. They call him "Master," but through this event he will be revealed as *greater* than any mystical rabbi, indeed, greater than both the law-giver and the prophets. The very first verse of the narrative suggests that we are to expect something new — this event occurs on about the *eighth* day, which St. Ambrose reminds us was the day of Jesus' resurrection and symbol of the New Creation (*Exposition of the Gospel of Luke 7:6-7*); The other Gospels had detailed the "sixth" day, perhaps to recall God's creating power — says St. Ambrose — but probably to recall the prescriptions for celebration of the Feast of Booths (see Leviticus 23:39). Their master enters into significant communion with Moses and Elijah, both of whom had, in their lifetimes, powerful revelations of God's power, and poignant moments of intimacy. Moses, we remember, spoke with God "mouth to mouth"; Elijah was visited by God's still, small voice in a time of despair. These two great servants of God talk with Jesus about his death to come, in terms that clearly recall God's delivering power in past times — Jesus is being strengthened in order to accomplish his "departure" (literally, his *"Exodus,"* 9:31), his redemption of the people, in Jerusalem. The disciples, though they do not understand all this, are themselves embraced by the glory of the scene. Though they are afraid, the cloud of glory, the numinous presence of God, envelops them, too, and they are left with the sound of the Father's voice ringing in their ears: "This is my beloved Son, my chosen, listen to him!"

Let us collect the images and themes here: intimate prayer with God; communion with saints throughout the ages; the careful recollection of God's law and revelation in the past; the reminder of God's redemption of Israel, pointing forward to the cross; the personal gathering up of the disciples into the glory of God, weak though they were; the centerpiece of the whole drama, Jesus, alone left before them, with God the Father's own word directing us to focus upon him, the chosen One. Jesus has been transformed before them while in prayer and in the company of major players in the divine drama. He is in center-stage. The Father's voice speaks, leaving no ambiguity about who is in authority, making impossible a confusion of the human and divine.

At the same time, the glory on Jesus' face transforms his disciples. They, like Moses and Elijah, are illumined by the Divine Presence of the Holy Spirit! As Ambrose puts it, "It was a luminous cloud that does not soak us with rainwater or the downpour of storm, but from dew that sprinkles the minds of men with faith sent by the voice of almighty God" (*Exposition of the Gospel of Luke*, 7:19-20). Nor is the "faith" into which the three are initiated a matter of bare creed, for they are to become key leaders to mirror and pass on the mystery of God to other believers. There is no need to set up tents or booths of dwelling, for the disciples themselves are to become tabernacles — holy, portable shrines — of the Divine Presence, through what Jesus is about to accomplish. The communion of Father, Son, and Holy Spirit has stooped down to heaven, as evident in the declaration, the transfigured face, and the glory cloud. In this heavenly visitation, God has gathered up to himself those who are "with Jesus"; at the same time, the divine voice strengthens their identity (apostle, prophet, law-giver) as human before a mighty God.

Though they had a particular role to play in the formation of the early Church, these three apostles are also, as it were, stand-ins for the ongoing apostolic community, representing those of us who are, throughout the ages, and across the lands, in Christ. In this transfiguration of their Lord they have learned two great things, not simply with their minds, but in their hearts and in their bodies — first, God's love is transforming, and he delights to make us "partakers of the divine nature" (2 Peter 1:4b); second, God's authority is unquestionable, for he is God and we are his creatures. As the second Petrine epistle comments upon this event, "His divine power . . . has *called us* into his own glory" (1:1); "No prophecy ever came by *human* impulse" (1:21; my emphasis). Here is the grand paradox: God is God and will not give his glory to another; God, through Christ the Son, imparts his glory to his adopted and beloved human sons and daughters!

The Glory of Christ, and the Embracing Communion of the Trinity

It is in the shining face of Jesus, and in the glory seen most profoundly on the cross, that we catch a vision of the likeness of God. Some have assumed that God's people knew all about the divine Father in the era of the Old Covenant, but that when Jesus emerged upon the scene, and then at Pentecost, we came to understand about the Second and Third Persons of the Godhead as well. This is simply untrue. As Jesus himself remarked, "No one knows the Father except the Son and those to whom the Son reveals him" (Matthew 11:27; Luke 10:22). So, then, prior to the Incarnation, there was no knowledge of the Father. God remained named the mysterious YHWH, the "one who will be who he will be." He was known by his functions — by the "economy" of his dealings with humankind as Creator, as caller of Israel, as inspirer of the prophets, as anointer of kings, and so on. Indeed, many of the Church Fathers taught that the Old Testament LORD who "spoke" words to the Hebrews was indeed God the Son rather than God the Father, though not understood as such by the people. At any rate, it is the Son who reveals the Father to us: until we know that there is a Son, we cannot know that there is a Father. Similarly, it is the work of the Son that paves the way for the revelation and giving of the Holy Spirit. Yet, we may also see how it is that the Spirit, who overshadowed Mary, and who filled her with the prophetic word about her Son (even while he was in the womb), also prepared the way for the revelation of the Son. Again, we are told in John's Gospel that the Father delights to "glorify" the Son. These three, then — Father, Son, and Spirit — engage in an ineffable mutuality and order that is revealed to us (as far as we can understand it) through Jesus. We come to understand more and more about this trinitarian life through the living experience of his Church.

Jesus himself teaches us about this mystery in his most intimate instruction of the disciples, found in John 14–17. There, the One who is first described as the "light" that has come into the world, illuminates his friends, as they huddle together on that last dark night. He is, paradoxically, about to "enter into his glory," enthroned upon the cross. As he prepares them for the ordeal, we are privileged to "listen in" while he describes the unique communion that he shares with the Father and the Spirit. Each plays a role with regard to the other, but all share intimately and exchange characteristics, communing as One yet as Three in a way unimaginable to us. Jesus pictures for us a mode of being that joins equality and order together. The Father is in the Son, and the Son in the Father; the Son glorifies the Father, and the Father will glorify the Son; the Son comes from the Father and the Son goes to the Father; the Son does as the Father commands, to demonstrate his love for the Father. Jesus also speaks about the Spirit, that One *who* proceeds from the Father and *whom* the Father will send in the Son's name. In concert with the Father, the Spirit will glorify the Son; in concert with the Son, he will "not speak on his own" but will witness to the divine will. Through his coming, those things that belong to the Father, and therefore to the Son, will be given to the disciples (16:14-15).

It is out of this order and mutuality, out of what the ancient theologians called the inner "interpenetration" and "inter-permeation" of the Father, Son, and Spirit, that our life and glory as children of God spring. Some have described this divine movement and mutual indwelling in terms of a "dance," and so we might fancifully picture the mystery portrayed by St. John of Damascus, in his *Exposition of the Faith,* Chapter Fourteen:

> For they are inseparable and cannot part from one another, but keep to their separate courses within one another, without coalescing or mingling, but cleaving to each other. For the Son is in the Father and the Spirit: and the Spirit in the Father and the Son: and the Father in the Son and the Spirit, but there is no coalescence or commingling or confusion. And there is one and the same motion.

Yet the word that St. John and others use to describe this mystic phenomenon is *not* the Greek word for "dance" (*perichŏresis,* with a short "o"), despite the numerous assertions concerning the etymology of the word. That choreographical word *is* used in the ancient texts of the encircling movement of the cherubim in Ezekiel 1, whose wheels revolve around as they move in concert. But for our Triune God, another word is used (*perichōresis* with a long "o"): this is a word that implies a far deeper spiritual intercommunion than a mere inter-weaving dance! We are here on the border of mystery, or, as the unfriendly Edward Gibbon once remarked, at "the deepest and darkest corner of the whole theological abyss." For Jesus' words, along with the Greek Fathers' term, imply a complete "movement around and into," plus an utter "abiding within" — an indescribable ecstasy and intimacy. The later Latin Fathers, indeed, had to use *two* different words to describe the metaphor in completeness, *circumincessio*, which means "to proceed around and through" and *circuminsessio*, which means "to settle around and within." To think further upon the divine concourse is to evoke a spiritual blush, indeed, to tread on blasphemy; our search for a dim analogy in human experience will lead us far beyond the reserve of the dance.

God's being, then, goes beyond our imagination. The Son and Spirit "go out" from the Father eternally, even as each Person goes out to and indwells the Others, in abandon and intimacy. Only in the Godhead do we see the answer to the dichotomy that we tend to make, both intellectually and in our lives, between "mutuality" and "order." From the Father the Son is begotten, and from the Father the Spirit proceeds, through the Son — there is a certain order, yet it is eternal. The Father would not be the Father and Source without the Son and Spirit; nor would the Son be the Son without the Father and the Spirit; nor would the Spirit be the Spirit without the other two; they are *towards* each other. Thus, order and mutuality come together in harmony, not one at the expense of the other. Here is God's own answer to our faltering and power-hungry relationships. We need God's own pattern in this era which is experiencing both a crisis of authority and a disregard for the dignity of each person.

Holy is as holy does. And so, God displays his inner life as he deals with us! The ecstasy and intimacy that God hides within the mystery of the Trinity spill over into his dealings with creation, and especially with humanity. God is ecstatic — he stands outside of himself, going out to us in the Son, even to the extreme point of humility and death. He is also intimate, dwelling among us in the Spirit, in a manner that is nearer than our own breath. In the Incarnation God has assumed human nature, taking it up into himself so that it may be both healed and glorified: body and soul, we have been visited by our Creator, and we see the location of this mystery in Jesus himself. Our bond to the Father as his children springs, then, from the mysterious bond between divine Father and Son. St. Paul, in Romans 5, calls us "sons of God," not to exclude women, but because he here is adapting the Jewish label for Messiah, "Son of God," to suggest our new calling — to be "little anointed ones," "small 'c' christs." Our character as children of God comes about because of the work of the Spirit, who shares glory with the Father and the Son. 'In' Christ, and not destined to be orphans, we are adopted by God as true children.

Our Transfiguration (2 Corinthians 2:14–4:18)

This glimpse at the indescribable life of the Godhead, the interplay between Father, Son, and Spirit, teaches us that hierarchy and mutuality are not in conflict, but find their perfect harmony and expression in God. Their communion and fellowship, though perfect in itself, overflows into our world, as St. Paul was well aware. Though the untimely born apostle has no outward reference to the event of the transfiguration in Jesus' life, it seems clear that he had grasped the same implications from it that we find in the Petrine letters and in Jesus' Last Supper discourse. It is to 2 Corinthians, the epistle of "glory" that we must turn, in order to see a fuller working-out of the transfiguration and the energy of the Trinity in the life of the Church. Paul's great passage concerning a transfiguration for those who are in Christ elucidates that wonderful exchange, that startling promise first suggested here in the New Testament (5:21), and then embraced by those closest to God, both in Eastern and Western Christianity: "God became human, that we might become god (in him)." Great is the hope of glory to which we are called!

Paul has a great deal to say about the glory of the new covenant, and how God imparts Christ's glory to us, in 2 Corinthians 3–4. Here Paul declares that, in the Son, God has done something brand new. No longer are God's people led by a leader (like Moses), who must wear a veil over his face to hide God's glory; no longer do God's people have a veil over their hearts. Remember that in Exodus, Moses received revelation from the LORD with a bare and open face, then gave the message to the people; but then he went about his daily activity with his face covered. There are no such veils now! Jesus' obedient life, death, and resurrection have brought in a new era of "open hearts" and "open faces" (2:17; 3:2; 4:2; 5:16; 6:11-13; 7:2). Again, there is no longer a distinction between the sacred time of revelation and ordinary activity. God's revelation no longer requires a special mediator like Moses, or a specially separated place such as a mountain or tabernacle: rather, the unveiling is shared by everyone who has the gift of the Holy Spirit. All God's people and all their moments are holy. It is the open heart and face that Paul sets forward as our custom, our attitude, as the new people of God.

In this passage, Paul reminds us of the Exodus story, so that we can compare and contrast it with the new event in Jesus. The whole Bible, the story of Israel included, is God's great act of salvation for us: but the Jesus event has fulfilled the earlier story of the Exodus: in glory, the Jesus event "outshines" everything that has gone before. "Much more has the permanent come in glory!" (3:11). But all the events of the old covenant were leading up to this point: so Paul speaks about the unfading glory of the new covenant, without looking down upon the old covenant that is also a part of God's story.

All this may seem very high and exalted, part of "theological" discourse. But remember that Paul, in 2 Corinthians, was dealing with Christians in a time of difficulty, disunity, and stress. He is not distracting them with an unreal fantasy world, but is telling them a strong story of hope. This story of hope contrasts with the tragic drama of the Exodus account, where God's people were ungrateful and stubborn, spending forty years in the wilderness despite all the evidences of God's love and power. Paul is telling them a story about what it means to be the *faithful* community. That story about the faithful family is itself founded upon that greatest story of all time — the story about the Christ who ministered, suffered, died, rose again, ascended, and sent the Spirit. Paul pleads to the Corinthians that they not be like those in the Exodus story, in which leaders were disappointed and disrespected, in which people first stood in awe of revelation and then ignored it, where the laws remained on stone tablets and were not taken into their heart. That is not how it should be with Christians. Instead, we are "in Christ," we have the "light . . . shining in our hearts," we have seen God's glory "in the face of Jesus" (2 Corinthians 4:6).

As we follow Paul's argument, a curious progression takes place. Because the Corinthians have been seduced by false leaders, Paul has had to commence his letter with an attempt to regain their affections, reminding them that he is their teacher and "father in Christ," though ever at their service. He has had to argue for his role as leader. Yet, as he tells the story about the new covenant, he moves from his own position as leader to talk about the community as a whole. He seems at first to be establishing his own status as one "sent from God . . . standing in his presence"; but he ends by picturing the community *together* as engaged in the same ministry of reflection (3:18), "extended . . . more and more" (4:15) and brought "into God's presence" (4:14). Here is godly leadership — one that gains respect, and then leads the whole community into the common life and work that God has given.

Paul could have told them grand stories about his own mystical spiritual experiences. We know that he had them (2 Corinthians 12). But Paul is embarrassed to do this, even when he touches on these wonders. He is far more concerned with the Christian *community's* common understanding of Jesus, and its corporate transformation. In the Old Testament, Moses alone, with some of the elders, had a high moment of revelation and mystery: today, God's glory is shared among all the members of the Church. In the Old Testament, the prophet Ezekiel had an individual, special vision of "the appearance *of* the likeness *of* the glory *of* God" (1:28), which he described in very respectful terms. He would not say that he saw God, for no one can see God and live. There is a sense of distance with Ezekiel. But things are different now, says Paul. So Paul echoes and changes Ezekiel's words: "God . . . give(s) *us* the light *of* the knowledge *of* the glory *of* God" (4:6). We have an unhindered and *shared* vision. This vision of Jesus enables us to come near to God: the *light* of the *knowledge* of the *glory* of God are not distancing, but *approaching* terms. It is a new creation, a new state of affairs! Light has come out of darkness, and we, along with Christ, are to being made fit to bear the divine image: *"For God, who said, 'Let light shine out of darkness,'* made his light shine in our hearts, to give us the light of the knowledge of the glory of God *in the face of Christ"* (my emphasis). Something has happened so that God has been brought near in the face of Christ; that same glory that was on Mount Tabor, says Paul, is vibrantly present to the whole community through the Holy Spirit: "And we all, who with unveiled faces, behold and reflect the glory of the Lord as though in a mirror, are being changed from one degree of glory to another: for this comes from the Lord, who is the Spirit" (2 Corinthians 3:17).

Paul highlights the *common* sharing in this vision and our *common* transformation by using ordinary objects to describe this glory that has come to us in Christ. In 2 Corinthians, he uses the common things of his culture: public smells (2:14-16), a procession of victor and slaves (2:14; 4:5), written letters (3:1-3), veiled and unveiled faces (3:12-18), selling and giving (2:27; 4:1-2), treasures hidden in clay jars (4:7), health and disease (4:16). Such images and activities are used to reveal the gospel story about God's people and their life in Christ. Yet all these common images are seen as, in some way, joined to the unseen world. From the beginning to the end of his argument in this part of 2 Corinthians, Paul urges his hearers to see themselves as those who dwell in the presence of God (2:17), as those who are loved by the One who is greater than the Adversary, the so-called "god of this world" (4:4). We are to see ourselves as those who are blessed by God's creative activity (4:6), and also by Jesus' re-creating death and resurrection. Indeed, we are going to follow in the very pattern of Jesus himself, because "we know that the One who raised the Lord Jesus will raise us also, and bring us into his presence" (4:14). Everywhere, Paul tells us, we can see space, time, and our identity in such a way that they are reclaimed and filled up by God's very presence. Mundane symbols such as clay jars and mirrors, as well as sacred images such as fragrance and veils, are all taken up into a dramatic vision of the life of the people of God.

We already have remarked upon how another Christian teacher, St. Matthew, once described the role of the "scribe trained for the household of God" as one with the ability to take out of the treasury old and new things. Surely Paul is a scribe like that! With passion and persuasion, he reminds us of that grand story, the story of God's action in Christ. Paul's own struggles with his Corinthian "children" are taken up into a bigger narrative, and speak also to us, as the veil is lifted from our eyes. The Hebrew Scriptures and prophecies find their fulfillment in Jesus; our own stories and cultural expressions are also refined in Christ: because of the Incarnation, and the work of the Holy Spirit, all things that are good, and noble, and lovely, take their place in God's new story. There are to be no aliens or strangers, no good customs or beautiful traditions that God cannot transform. All God's children, with all their riches, come into their native home. Think of the final vision of the New Jerusalem, when the nations will be healed (Revelation 22:2), where nothing "unclean" or "accursed" will be found, and when a multitude will come into God's presence with "the glory and honor of the nations" (21:26).

Do things seem grim, drab, and troublesome? So were they for Paul and the Corinthians. Yet we can, with Paul, put our struggles in perspective. We can recall the truth God has taught us, we can place our afflictions alongside the greater agony of Jesus, and we can remember the complete vision of God's glory that is promised to us. Our own story itself takes on importance, when seen in the light of the great story; our own lives take on color, reflect glory, as we gaze upon that One, the Lord Jesus, who is far more splendid. "And we all, with unveiled faces, behold and reflect as in a mirror together the glory of the Lord." So we are changed.

In Paul's discussion, some of the same principles emerge that we discerned in the story of Jesus' transfiguration. Clearly, there is One who is the LORD, before whom we bow in awe. Paul also recognizes that the Father, Son, and Spirit work together to bring us with Christ into God's own presence. We must not "rely on ourselves but on God who raises the dead" and have been given the Spirit as the "guarantee" that God will in fact fulfill all this work (5:5) so that we are together with him. So we come to see that the fulfillment of God's work in Jesus has two purposes: — he intends to *restore* broken humanity, so that we again show forth the image of God; he intends also to *glorify* us, so that we are "changed into his likeness from one degree of glory to another." It is within the believing community, the corporate body of Christ, that this work takes place: so we turn to consider "the flame of love" that shines forth from our brothers and sisters of past ages who are still alive to God.

FURTHER MEDITATION

He was bright as the lightning on the mountain and became more luminous than the sun, initiating us into the mystery of the future. (St. Gregory of Nazianzus, *Oration* 3.19, *On the Son*)

"When he spoke, there came a cloud and overshadowed them." That is the overshadowing of the divine Spirit, who is not dark with the emotions of humankind but unveils secrets. This is also revealed in another place when an angel says, "And the power of the Most High shall overshadow you." The effect of this is shown when the voice of God is heard, saying, "This is my beloved Son; hear him." Elijah is not the Son and Moses is not the Son. This is the Son whom only you see, because they had withdrawn when he began to be described as Lord.... It was a luminous cloud ... that sprinkles the minds of men with faith sent by the voice of almighty God. (St. Ambrose, *Exposition of the Gospel of Luke* 7:19-20)

Thou hast shown us on Mount Tabor the live coal of the Godhead that consumes sins while it enlightens souls, and Thou hast caught up in ecstasy Moses and Elijah and the chief disciples.

On Mount Tabor

Thou wast transfigured on the Mount, O Christ God, revealing Thy glory to Thy disciples as far they could bear it.

Having ascended this mountain with Thy disciples, O Savior, and having been transformed, Thou didst make the dark nature of Adam shine again, by transforming it into the glory and splendor of Thy Godhead.

For in His mercy the Saviour of our souls has transfigured disfigured man and made him shine with light on Mount Tabor.

He makes bright the weakness of man and bestows enlightenment upon our souls.
(All the above are Orthodox hymns for the Feast of Transfiguration)

Christ, your glory fills the heavens,
Your love the world must know.
Morning Star, you triumph over darkness,
You are Jesus the Lord.

You are the Son of Righteousness dawning
That shall cause our hearts to sing.
Shine upon our faithless shadows
Bringing healing in your wings.

The light of your face is all we desire
Now walk by our side,
And turn our hearts to burn with fire.

You are the final word to be given,
You're the hope that sets us free.
Let the earth be filled with your glory
As the waters fill the sea.

Steve James © 1999 Jubilate Hymns Ltd.
All rights reserved. Used by permission.
Admin. by Hope Publishing Co.,
Carol Stream, IL 60188

O Joyous Light of the holy glory
Of the immortal, heavenly, holy blessed Father,
O Jesus Christ.
We that come to the setting of the sun,
When we behold the evening light,
Praise Father, Son and Holy Spirit, God.
Meet it is for You at all times to be praised
With gladsome voices, O Son of God, Giver of life;
Therefore the world glorifies You.

Vespers Hymn

FURTHER READING

Chrysostom, St. John. *Commentary on St. John the Apostle and Evangelist, Homilies 48-88. The Fathers of the Church, A New Translation.* Translated by Sr. Thomas Aquinas Goggin. Washington: Catholic University of America Press, 1960. See especially St. John's comments on John 14–17.

Humphrey, Edith. "Called to Be One: Worshiping the Triune God Together." In *The Trinity: An Essential for Faith in Our Time,* edited by Andrew Stirling, pp. 189-206. Nappanee, Ind.: Evangel Publishing House, 2002.

Just, Arthur A., Jr., ed. *Ancient Christian Commentary on Scripture: New Testament 3: Luke.* Downers Grove, Ill.: InterVarsity Press, 2003. See pages 158-61 for the ancient theologians whose commentaries are cited above concerning the transfiguration passage.

Lossky, Vladimir. *The Vision of God.* Translated by A. Moorhouse. Crestwood, N. Y.: St. Vladimir's Seminary Press, 1983. Many insights here from throughout the ages on the vision of Mount Tabor.

Von Speyer, Adrienne. *The Farewell Discourses; Meditations on John 13–17.* Translated by. E. A. Nelson. San Francisco: Ignatius Press, 1987. Astute comments and deep probing of the mystery of subordination alongside mutuality, in terms of the relation of Father and Son.

FURTHER DISCUSSION

1. How do we reconcile this promise of transformation with the current drabness, sinfulness, and suffering of human life?
2. What are some ways that Christian worship incorporates or can begin to take account of the mysterious as well as the creedal shape of our faith?
3. If the veil is now lifted, is there still a place for mystery in the Christian era? What are we to think of those who make present claims to vision or prophetic words?
4. Can we identify modern day spiritual movements or activities in the churches that tend to remove Jesus from "the center"?
5. How do we maintain both a reverence for God as unique and an appreciation of our calling to "participate in the divine nature"?

B

The Flame of Love —
The Witness of Our Older Siblings in the Faith

I believe . . . in the holy catholic church, in the communion of saints. . . .

This is one of those parts of the Apostles' Creed that has received varying amounts of attention and wildly divergent interpretations across the spectrum of Christian communities, as has its parallel in the Nicene Creed, "we believe in one holy, catholic, and apostolic Church." Indeed, many Protestants are uncomfortable with the very words, which seem redolent of Roman Catholicism — so much so that churches sometimes substitute "universal" for "catholic" and "the faithful" for "saints." These choices may be well-meant, but the difficulty with this "negative" manner of preserving the ecumenical creeds is that frequently members of Protestant communities know only what they do *not* believe concerning this article of faith (we are not Roman Catholics! we do not believe in a hierarchy or special group of saints!), but remain mystified concerning what they *ought* to believe. Negative statements go some distance in the creation of identity, but they are insufficient in the long run. That is, a group may survive for a while by acknowledging its reaction against something, but it must eventually come to understand what it is *for* and not simply what it is *against*.

The fact that so many contemporary Christians (including some Roman Catholics!) can declare, "I believe in Jesus and the Trinity, but not in the Church" means that the force of these creedal statements has been lost for them. Not a few of today's Christians would, for example, be offended by Cyprian's words: "You cannot have God for your Father if you have not the Church for your mother." To many, the bishop's words smack of "ecclesi-olatry" — worship of the Church — although until quite recently they would have been accepted even in Protestant circles inspired by Calvin and Luther. The default position for understanding Christian identity has all too often been that of a solitary believer before the face of God, rather than one who has been embraced by the body of Christ, and joined to the living organism of the Church. As the late Reformed professor of Old Testament Elizabeth Achtemeier put it (in her endorsement of the *Ancient Christian Commentary on Scripture* series), "Modern church members often do not realize that they are participants in the vast company of the communion of saints that reaches far back into the past and that will continue into the future, until the kingdom comes." On the other hand, it is true that knee-jerk hostility to the doctrine of the Church is less severe than it was twenty years ago. Fewer Protestants are ignorant of catholicity, and some are reclaiming this word to describe their own understanding of Christ's body.

Along with a newfound comfort with the word "catholic," several Protestant groups are also turning to their older siblings in the faith — to tradition — for nurture and even for worship patterns. Prophetically conscious of our generation's rootlessness, many are deliberately recovering a vision of the Church as more than a *local* or *present* phenomenon — they are looking to the body of Christ stretching across time and space. In the academic sphere, we have witnessed a change among Western Protestant theologians, who now refuse to continue the pole vault from the fifth century to the Reformation (yes, Virginia, there was a Church in the Middle Ages!), who are no longer dismissing their Roman Catholic colleagues as insignificant, and who are also heeding the witness of Eastern Orthodoxy. A potent symbol of this is the new InterVarsity series edited by Thomas Oden, entitled the *Ancient Christian Commentary on Scripture:* each volume provides access to selected commentaries by many ancient Christians, grouped section-by-section and organized around a particular book of the Bible. Such a tool is invaluable in helping the contemporary student to discover what the Spirit says *to the churches,* and not simply (in an individualistic sense) what the Spirit is saying to her or to him. This turn in Bible study has been accompanied by a return to ancient forms of liturgy in many onetime "non-liturgical" groups, which are rediscovering the benefits of confession, recitation of the creed, and so on, through the ministrations of

Robert Webber and others. In the light of the turmoil of our age, and the worry, across ecclesial bodies, that revisionism is distorting the gospel, creedal Protestants are discovering, in devout Catholics and authentic Orthodox, unexpected family likeness, and serious dialogue partners.

Yet recovery from amnesia is frequently a long process. The Reformation (and Counter-Reformation) was surely significant in reminding God's people that God's love is accessible immediately (that is, "without mediation") through the Person of Jesus and the ministrations of the Holy Spirit; as a reaction, it also had an unfortunate added effect. That is, many of God's people found themselves imaginatively distanced from the faithful who had gone before, and who together with us make up the Church, God's holy ones. "Mediation" became a dirty word, instead of a sign of the mutual love between members of the Church, created by the Holy Spirit, and embodied most fully in Jesus, our brother. How can it be that we care so very little for our other brothers and sisters of the past, when they are not dead, but alive to God? We need again to hear Jesus' words to the Pharisees — "And as for the resurrection of the dead, have you not read what was said to you by God, 'I am the God of Abraham, and the God of Isaac, and the God of Jacob'? He is not God of the dead, but of the living" (Matthew 22:31-32). Whom God has declared alive should not be considered dead to us! Nor do these live ones refuse to speak, for many have left luminous words to light our way, teaching how the incarnate and ascended Son and the indwelling Spirit transform the spirits and bodies of those who are in Christ. In this chapter we will dip into the writings of one anonymous believer, three renowned teachers of the Church, three early Eastern spiritual theologians, several Western mystics, and some contemporary God-seers of various traditions. May our meditation upon this brief selection work for us as a catalyst to chase away our amnesia, and free us from what C. S. Lewis dubs "chronological snobbery" — that mindset which assumes that nothing older than a few generations is of value to us.

Light in the Everyday: Joseph and Aseneth

We begin with a work whose author's name has been lost, but which provides us, in its anonymity, with a window into the faithfulness of a past age. This popular piece, beloved by early Christians, and probably by Jewish readers before them, has immortalized the obscure name of Aseneth (Genesis 41:45, 50 and 46:20), the Egyptian wife of the patriarch Joseph. Indeed, their story became so well known in the Christian family that they are named as a model couple in eastern liturgies for marriage, along with Abraham and Sarah, Jacob and Rachel. Though *Joseph and Aseneth* is a romance, intended for entertainment, and not for the purpose of setting down history, we find in it the deep devotion and yearning for spiritual illumination that was typical of an age that did not compartmentalize its art into "secular" and "sacred." At the beginning of the story, Aseneth, a proud noblewoman and follower of pagan Egyptian religion, is arrested in her smug existence by the appearance of one who belongs to the living God:

> What shall I now do, wretch that I am? . . .
> Now, behold, the sun from heaven has come to us on its chariot
> And entered our house today,
> And shines in it like a light upon the earth.
> But I, foolish and daring, have despised him
> And spoken wicked words about him,
> And did not know that Joseph is a son of God . . .
> And where shall I flee and hide,
> Because every hiding place he sees
> And nothing hidden escapes him,
> Because of the great light that is inside him?

Aseneth is brought to repentance, calling out to the God of Israel who "created all and gave life . . . who brought the invisible things out into the light." After a time of penitence, she is visited and blessed by a messenger of light, fed miraculously from God's own storehouse, and given a new name. As she returns to her daily life, she discovers herself wonderfully transformed:

> And Aseneth . . . saw her face in the water. And it was like the sun and her eyes were like a rising morning star, and her cheeks were like fields of the most high . . . and her head was like a vine in the paradise of God . . . and her breasts were like the mountains of the most high God.

Close on the heels of this transformation, she is received intimately by Joseph, who kisses her so that she receives the spirit of life, wisdom, and truth. From this point on, she becomes a symbol of refuge for Gentile God-seekers, a merciful matron and a witness of God's transformation for any who seek the Lord of truth. Though the date of this story's composition is obscure (probably somewhere between 200 B.C. and A.D. 200), and its author is long lost, the fanciful writing served to inspire generations of believers, and to remind them of how the ordinary life is brought into the light of God, and therefore transformed.

This romantic story of a Gentile priest's daughter "converted" to the God of Joseph, and inwardly transformed by that light, was read by Christians in terms of the search of the Son of God for all who are his own. What Aseneth says poetically of Joseph is theologically astute when applied to the Christ — indeed, "nothing escapes *him*, because of the great light that is within him." Though Aseneth is an obscure name in the Hebrew Bible, she becomes, through the creative love of unknown members of God's family (probably first Jewish, then transmitted by early Christians), a symbol of God's transforming and welcoming love. Her prominence in the Orthodox wedding ceremony down through the ages and the continued use of her name in Christian cultures as far removed as Ireland and Armenia, serve as a reminder that God delights in the ordinary, whom he can, by his presence, make extraordinary.

Aseneth's story is a popular filling out of the principle we discover in Matthew's genealogy of our Lord: in that list of noteworthies, we find three unusual women figures (Tamar, Ruth, and "the wife of Uriah"), all of whom had "spotty" histories. From the onset of the gospel, we learn that "what is not assumed by God is not healed" — God takes up our everyday lives, and makes of these something beautiful. The light shines, not simply exposing the darkness, but illuminating what was once dark: "Those who were not my people I will call 'my people,' and her who was not beloved I will call 'my beloved'" (Romans 9:25). All this has been done so that we may become, together with Christ, a dwelling place of God in the Spirit.

The Negative Way: St. Gregory of Nyssa

Let us take, as a contrast to this "popular" light, one of the four great Fathers of Cappadocia. St. Gregory (335–c. 395) was bishop of Nyssa during the period when the Emperor Diocletian was persecuting the Church.

Along with his more formally trained brother, St. Basil, and the other St. Gregory ("The Theologian" of Nazianzus), Gregory of Nyssa played a major role in the Council of Constantinople and was instrumental in helping the Church to sort out the doctrines of the Trinity, Jesus the God-Man, and the Church. Besides laboring over a significant book of systematic theology, known as the *Catechetical Oration*, he was also a champion of the monastic movement, and himself followed a poignant path in his quest for God's presence — a path that is known as the "negative way" (or *via negativa*, to use the Latin). For him, life was not to be compartmentalized: the creedal and corporate life of the Church is united with that personal and intense adoration into which we are called by the Holy Spirit. Throughout his writings St. Gregory emphasizes the themes of light and darkness, separation from God, glory through Christ, intimacy and ecstasy, silence and the Word. By these images, he suggests the deep (though often brief) ecstasy into which the Christian is called by the One who first "wounds" the human soul and then woos it with love. St. Gregory is best known for two pictures of this communion: the ascent of Moses to Mount Sinai, and the beloved's approach to the bride. Though we prepare ourselves for God, as did Moses, it is God who, through the Son and the Spirit, comes to us, as to a bride. Let's learn from St. Gregory as we contemplate three passages, first from his *Sixth Sermon on the Beatitudes*, next from his *Life of Moses*, and finally from his *Commentary on the Song of Songs*.

Gregory is concerned in his sermon on the Beatitudes to explain how it is that Jesus can promise the clean of heart that they shall see God, when throughout the Scriptures, we are told that no one can see God and survive.

> For he says, "Blessed are the clean of heart, for they shall see God." . . . How is it then that the voice of the Lord, which promises that God may be seen if we are pure, should not contradict those who, according to St. Paul, evidently speak the truth if they contend that the contemplation of God is beyond our power?

His concern here is not simply that the Scriptures should not contradict themselves, but that we, as creatures, even redeemed creatures, should never lose our sense of the ineffability, majesty, and "otherness" of the One who differs from everything created. The wonder of the Incarnation, and of our communion with God, is sure to be lost, along with our ability to worship in Spirit and in truth, if we become presumptuous, thinking that we can "grasp" God himself by any human means — including reason or contemplation. Nevertheless, Jesus has given a solemn promise to his people, and so St. Gregory continues, explaining how it is that we can come to first "see who God is" through various media, and then finally, come to know God *himself.*

> . . . Since such is he whose nature is above every nature, the Invisible and the Incomprehensible is seen . . . in another manner. Many are the modes of such perception. For it is possible to see him . . . by way of inference through the wisdom that appears in the universe. . . . When we look at the order of creation, we form in our mind an image not of the essence, but of the wisdom of him who has made all things wisely. And if we consider . . . that he came to create man not from necessity, but from the free decision of his Goodness, we say that we have contemplated God by this way, that we have apprehended his Goodness — though again not his Essence, but his Goodness. . . . Hence it is clear . . . that the Lord speaks the truth when he promises that God will be seen by those who have a pure heart. . . . For he . . . becomes visible in his energies. . . .

Here we meet for the first time the important distinction between God's *energies* (God as seen in the outward marks that he makes upon our sensible world) and his hidden *essence*, which is known to him alone. This distinction will become helpful to spiritual theologians who come in the centuries after St. Gregory, as they strive to explain how it is that they have beheld God in intimacy, and have been gathered into God's fellowship, without *becoming* God, or piercing the elusive mystery of his utter holiness. After describing how it is that God can be seen by his general workings in creation, St. Gregory goes on to hint at a more intimate manner of "beholding" God, made accessible through the wonder of the Incarnation, by which the image of humanity is restored:

> . . . The Lord does not say it is blessed to know something about God, but to have God present within oneself. . . . I think that the Word expresses some such counsel as this: There is in you, human beings, a desire to contemplate the true good. But when you hear that the Divine

Majesty is exalted above the heavens . . . do not despair of ever beholding what you desire. . . . For he who made you . . . imprinted on [you] the likeness of the glories of his own Nature, as if molding the form of a carving into a wax. . . . Hence, if a man who is pure of heart sees himself, he sees in himself what he desires, and thus he becomes blessed, because when he looks at his own purity, he sees the archetype in the image. . . . Though men who see the sun in a mirror do not gaze at the sky itself, yet they see the sun in the reflection of the mirror no less than those who look at its very orb.

In his sermon, the bishop does not go very far in explaining the way that *this* route to *seeing* God opens up before us. This is explained more fully in his spiritual explorations patterned upon the *Life of Moses*, which are adventurous, and in the realm of pious opinion (*"theologoumena"*), as he signals throughout by his modest use of phrases such as "I think," "in my view," and "it seems to me." St. Gregory uses the ascent of Moses up Mount Sinai to describe the Christian journey of maturation. First there is an experience of light, by which one puts aside dark ideas of God, wrong doctrine about God — this, it would seem, is the stage at which he envisages his congregants during the sermon that we have just sampled. But as one matures, there is a second stage: the entry into God's cloud, where one discovers that nothing in the whole creation that can vie with the Glory of God, and in which one discovers that the created world itself is given its glory through the Word, who became incarnate. Finally, there is the hard way of darkness, in which the seeker sees God by *not* seeing and knows God by *not* knowing. These last two stages are described in the *Life of Moses* as follows:

When, therefore, Moses grew in knowledge, he declared that he had seen God in the darkness, that is, that he had then come to know that what is divine is beyond all knowledge and comprehension. . . . True being is true life. This being is inaccessible to knowledge. Thus, what Moses yearned for is satisfied by the very things which leave his desire unsatisfied. . . . This truly is the vision of God: never to be satisfied in the desire to see him. But one must always, by looking at what he can see, rekindle his desire to see him more. Thus, no limit would interrupt growth in the ascent to God, since no limit to the Good can be found, nor is the increasing desire for the Good brought to an end because it is satisfied.

Knowledge gives way to the deeper knowledge of love, which can never be satisfied, but grows more and more — we can never exhaust our understanding of the One whose essence is beyond anything we can think or imagine. Indeed, Gregory moves away from talk of "understanding" to talk of an intense, even erotic love, which draws us deeper and deeper into the mystery of God. This ecstasy is most tellingly described in his *Commentary on the Song of Songs*, that book of the Bible that many Christian commentators have read as speaking of the unparalleled intercourse between Christ and the Church, God and the soul:

> The soul . . . looks for him but cannot find him. . . . But the veil of grief is removed when she learns that the true satisfaction of her desire consists of constantly going on with her quest and never ceasing in her ascent, seeing that every fulfillment of her desire continually generates a further desire. . . . Thus the veil of her despair is torn away and the bride realizes that she will always discover more and more of the incomprehensible and unhoped for beauty of her Spouse throughout all eternity. . . . For she has received within her God's special dart, she has been mortally wounded by the arrow of love. And *God is love*. [She] is wounded by a spiritual and fiery dart of *eros*, for *agape* that is strained to intensity is called *eros*. And no one should be ashamed of this whenever the arrow comes from God and not from the flesh. . . . The bride then rightly recognizes the difference between herself and her Lord. As Light, he is the object of beauty for our eyes; he is a sweet odor for our sense of smell; and Life for those who partake of him. *He that eateth him*, as the Gospel says, *shall live*. . . . Our human nature, nourished by virtue becomes a flower — but it does not offer nourishment to the Husbandman, but simply adorns itself. For he has no need of our goods. . . .

Found with her heavenly Lover, the soul is both at rest, that is, at peace in her rightful place *with* him, while at the same time fully aware of the distinction between herself and that great One. Unity and distinction are twin truths for the one who has thus *seen* God and yearns to see more and more, in joy unending.

Personal Confession and Enduring Liturgy:
St. Augustine and St. John Chrysostom

Gregory of Nyssa provides us with reading that we readily recognize as mystical, though we have seen that he did not neglect practical and doctrinal discussion during his ministry. For some, the bishop's intimate discussion of the soul's journey may seem too esoteric to be understood, although it tantalizes us to expect more and more from God's hand. We may feel on more familiar ground with the two celebrated theologians who followed Gregory, and who tower over the Church: in the West, St. Augustine of Hippo (354-430), and in the East, St. John Chrysostom of Antioch (347-407). These two, as rough contemporaries, provided the Church with distinct but complementary ways of coming to terms with life in the Spirit. St. Augustine, author of many types of writings, is perhaps best known for his personal work, *The Confessions*, which has so marked the Western Church, both in its Roman Catholic and Protestant expressions. St. John "*Chryso-stom*" was a celebrated preacher, as his nickname "Golden-mouthed" proclaims, but it is as one who passed on beautiful words for corporate worship that he is remembered, week in and week out, especially in the Eastern Churches. Through these servants of God we will consider two aspects of our tryst with God — that born of personal intellectual meditation, and that which comes through corporate worship.

There is probably no ancient theologian about whom we have such a complete account of his personal quest for truth as Augustine of Hippo. Augustine's parents postponed baptizing him, as did many parents of that day. (There was, from the second century even to Augustine's time, a deep-seated fear among many Christians of committing sin after baptism, as this seems to have been connected with the unpardonable sin. Such scrupulosity may seem odd to us, but no doubt they would find many of the presumptions of twenty-first-century Christians odd, as well. It would seem that the human race, even those who are coming to know God, find it difficult to account for both the mercy and the holiness of God, and tend to err on one side or the other.) As a youth, Augustine "sowed his wild oats" both physically and philosophically: he retained a long-term mistress, sired a son, and flirted with the most prominent ideologies of his day, including Manichaeism (a Gnostic religion which denigrated the material world) and neo-Platonism (which also drove a wedge between the spiritual and the material). The turning point of his life came on Easter in the year 387, when he was baptized by the great St. Ambrose, and then embarked on a voyage with friends and his saintly mother, St. Monica, who had prayed for him for decades.

At the port town of Ostia, Augustine and his mother entered into a conversation regarding spiritual things that was so deep it verged on a mystical experience, so that it has been described as an "intellectual ascent," made possible by the "flame of love." This glimpse of the light answered, at least in part, to Augustine's keen longing for Beauty: "Late have I loved you, O beauty, so ancient and so new. . . . You were with me, and I was not with you (*Confessions* 10.27). In speaking with God, he describes his garden "vision" with Monica as beginning with their meditation concerning the resurrected life, and as proceeding through various stages:

> There we conversed, she and I alone, very sweetly, and "forgetting the things that were behind and straining forward to those ahead" (Philippians 3:13), we were discussing in the presence of Truth, which You are, what the eternal life of the saints would be like, "which eye has not seen nor ear heard, nor has entered into the heart of man" (1 Corinthians 2:9). But with the mouth of our heart we panted for the supernal streams from your fountain . . . so that if some drops of that fountain, according to our capacity were to be sprinkled over us, we might somehow be able to think of such high matters.
>
> And our discourse arrived at this point, that the greatest pleasure of the bodily senses . . . seemed to us not worthy of comparison with the joy of that eternal life. . . . Then with our affections burning still more strongly toward the Selfsame we advanced step by step through the various levels of bodily things, up to the sky itself from which the sun and moon and stars shine upon this earth. (*Confessions* 9.10)

It is important to notice that the material world is spoken of both negatively and positively by Augustine. The negative assessment of the cosmos, and the ascent through regions beyond the material is doubtless due to the influence of the celebrated neo-Platonic philosopher Plotinus who had so marked Augustine's early thinking. Yet the material world is not simply seen in *contrast* to God; it also takes on a positive role, since it is by means of contemplating the creation that two interlocutors came to understand more and more of God. There comes a point in the conversation, however, where Monica and Augustine experience, as it were, a leaving behind of this world, a momentary death, in which they "sigh," or ecstatically give up their spirit. Here they catch a visionary glimpse of truth and wisdom, before returning to themselves:

> And higher still we ascended, by thinking inwardly and speaking and marvelling at your works, and we came to our own minds and transcended them to reach that region of unfailing abundance where you feed Israel forever on the food of truth (Ezekiel 34:13). There, life is wisdom by whom all things come into being. . . . And while we were speaking and panting for wisdom we did with the whole impulse of the heart slightly touch it. We sighed and left behind "the first fruits of the Spirit" (Romans 8:23) which were bound there, and returned to the sound of our own tongue where the spoken word has both beginning and ending. (*Confessions* 9.10)

In the end, however, even this ascent in the intellect is seen as insufficient: not only is it temporary, in its reaching of the pinnacle, but that height itself is still "mediated" and therefore not the full presence of God himself. Even sublime words and thoughts are inadequate: so Augustine considers that there must be a point at which even the "mediation" of revealed words and visions will be left behind in silence. It is only then that God's greatest gift can be given —

> How is it [i.e. "the spoken word"] like your Word, our Lord, "remaining ageless in himself and renewing all things" (Wisdom 7:27)? We said therefore: If to any man the uproar of flesh grew silent, silent the images of earth and sea and air; and if the heavens also grew silent; if the very soul grew silent to itself, and by not thinking of self ascended beyond self; if all dreams and imagined revelations grew silent and every tongue and every sign and if everything created to pass away were completely silent — since if one hears them, they all say this: We did not make ourselves, but he who abides made us. Suppose that, having said this and directed our attention to him who made them, they also were to become hushed and he himself alone were to speak, not by their voice but in his own, and we were to hear his Word, not through any tongue of flesh or voice of an angel or sound of thunder or in-

volved allegory, but that we might hear him whom in all these things we love, might hear him in himself without them, just as a moment ago we two, as it were, rose beyond ourselves and in a flash of thought touched the Eternal Wisdom abiding over all. If this were to continue and other quite different visions disappear, leaving only this one to ravish and absorb and enclose its beholder in inward joys so that life might forever be such as that one moment of understanding for which we had been sighing, would not this surely be: "enter into the joy of your Lord" (Matthew 25:21)? But when shall it be? Perhaps when "we shall all rise again" (1 Corinthians 15:51) and "shall we not all be saved?" (*Confessions* 9.10)

The best service that the created order can offer, then, is to confess, "We did not make ourselves, but he who abides made us." Such wisdom mediates truth about God. Yet it is necessary, mused Augustine and Monica, to class even visions and revelations in the rank of created things, for they are not God *himself*. Though their brief visionary glimpse of Wisdom had, for a moment, rendered them speechless (they "sighed"), still they had not seen God himself. One does not want to worship even such a remarkable experience. Full satisfaction can only come when we see the greatest beauties of the created order grow pale before the Creator of all, and are ravished by that one joy. But this, Augustine says, will come only at the resurrection and transformation that we await during the dénouement of God's great drama.

Augustine's comments must be understood in the light of a lingering prejudice from his earlier philosophical training, that the "material" is somehow suspect: the mystery of the Incarnation has yet to make its full impact, even among God's children. Nevertheless, he has in this vision moved beyond the limiting vision of his pre-Christian "dualistic" worldview, which split the material and the spiritual. Thus he appreciates how it is that God acts both *in* the created order and *beyond* it to reach us. Wisdom is indeed to be found in the contemplation of God's creation; but there is more to be had in the sheer voice of silence, far beyond what we can ask or imagine. We should also take note of two pertinent warnings that the saint provides for our own idolatrous age. First, he makes it very clear that even the ineffable moment he shared with Monica was not to be worshiped — this is a strong corrective to the restless search of today's Christian for "worship experiences." Again, we are helped by noticing that Augustine's "vision," though extremely personal, is not wholly private: it takes place just after his baptism, in the company of his mother, and as they are thinking about the hope of all the resurrected. This is a strong reminder to those who would conceive of their spiritual journey as wholly private to themselves! Though a "time apart" has made its great impact upon this theologian, he does not conceive of this vision as separating him from the body of believers — this personal vision is intensely ecclesial, "of the Church." The "we" is dominant even in this stunningly intense confession.

Some might expect that the corporate life of the Church would be even more marked in the work of St. John Chrysostom, than in the personal writings of his contemporary St. Augustine. After all, much of Chrysostom's work has come to us from the period of 386 to 407, when he first became a preaching elder, and then the Patriarch of Constantinople. Like Augustine, Chrysostom's life was marked by the influence of a godly mother, whose death seems to have been the catalyst for his adoption of a strict monastic life prior to his ordination. There is a combined tenderness and demanding practicality in his writing, as well as an awareness of family life and the woes of womankind (at least as experienced in the fourth and fifth centuries) that is disarming. His pastoral concern for women is especially remarkable since the prophetic Chrysostom was tormented, like Elijah, by his own "Jezebel" — Eudoxia, pagan wife of the emperor. Time would be well spent reading Chrysostom's teachings concerning God's wooing of humanity, Christ's presence with us, and the illuminating life of the Spirit. These are to be found particularly in his sermons on John's Gospel and in his homilies for those on the verge of baptism (or "illumination," as it is aptly called). Here, we will look at some of the key moments in the Divine Liturgy (a service of Entrance into the holy Presence, Word, and Sacrament) that bears his name, and that is regularly used in Eastern Orthodox worship up to this day.

There is much scholarly controversy over the actual role that St. John played in the transmission of the "Divine Liturgy of St. John Chrysostom," which is by nature a family document, and not the work of a single composer. It would appear that his particular work included the editing and reformation of a longer original service by St. Basil. Nonetheless, to focus upon this liturgy as characteristic of the golden-tongued bishop is to honor what he himself privileged — the common praise to the Triune God of the one, holy, catholic, and apostolic Church. Indeed, the liturgy is important because of what God does, even more than because of what we do. As St. John insisted, "The priest only lends his hand and provides his tongue. Everything is brought to pass by the Father, the Son, and the Holy Spirit" (see Kallistos Ware, "Approaching Christ the Physician: the True Meaning of Confession and Anointing").

Comparison of this liturgy to other ancient rites discloses its characteristic flavor — a concentration upon the Triune God, through multiple invocations of the thrice-holy One, and an emphasis on the Holy Spirit's blessing of the communion elements and the worshipers. The liturgy begins with a declaration of the Trinity's blessed rule among us, and with petitions that remind the congregants of the fallen and needy nature of humankind. These initial petitions culminate by deliberately placing the congregation within the context of the entire Church, with reference to the *Theotokos* ("God-bearer") Mary and the other great followers of Christ, and by committing the worshipers to Christ. Then follows this prayer, where God's greatness in mysterious glory and ineffable mercy are invoked, for the faithful, and for all those in hearing of the prayers:

> Lord, our God, whose power is beyond compare, and glory is beyond understanding; whose mercy is boundless, and love for us is ineffable; look upon us and upon this holy house in your compassion. Grant to us and to those who pray with us your abundant mercy.

The service continues in a double movement that is both progressive and cyclical. There are many repetitions of prayers, but also a dramatic forward direction that recalls the salvation story. The repetitions and constant invocation of the Trinity gives the sense of a sacred time and space, or perhaps a stilling, and filling up of all time and space, in which God meets with his people: in praying along, we find ourselves with Isaiah's angels, crying "Holy, holy, holy." However, in the dramatic action of the liturgy we also follow on the way with God the Word as he comes to be among humankind to redeem and sanctify them by his Incarnation, life, passion, crucifixion, resurrection, and ascension. In mind of these two facets, timelessness and "timefulness," the priest prays for the congregation, and blesses the doors of the sanctuary that they might "enter" into the ongoing worship of the cosmos. Then he marvels at God's invitation to worship, offering petitions on behalf of the people:

Holy God, you dwell among your saints. You are praised by the Seraphim with the thrice holy hymn and glorified by the Cherubim and worshiped by all the heavenly powers. You have brought all things out of nothing into being. You have created man and woman in your image and likeness and adorned them with all the gifts of your grace.

You give wisdom and understanding to the supplicant and do not overlook the sinner but have established repentance as the way of salvation. You have enabled us, your lowly and unworthy servants, to stand at this hour before the glory of your holy altar and to offer to you due worship and praise. Master, accept the thrice holy hymn also from the lips of us sinners and visit us in your goodness.

Forgive our voluntary and involuntary transgressions, sanctify our souls and bodies, and grant that we may worship and serve you in holiness all the days of our lives, by the intercessions of the holy Theotokos and of all the saints who have pleased you throughout the ages.

Reference to the mediation of the saints may be troubling for some — yet this worship takes place within the context of heaven and the whole of salvation history. The ancient saints have pleased God not because of their own goodness, but through the gracious gifts of Jesus and the Spirit. So, as members with us of one family, they are pleased to pour their love upon God's pilgrim Church, as members of Christ's body pray one for another: throughout this point of the liturgy, petition predominates, with the refrain, "Lord have mercy." The Scriptures are read, Old and New Testament, culminating with the illuminating Gospel. Prior to its reading (which the people honor by standing), we hear this prayer:

Shine within our hearts, loving Master, the pure light of your divine knowledge, and open the eyes of our minds that we may comprehend the message of your Gospel. Instill in us, also, reverence for your blessed commandments, so that having conquered sinful desires, we may pursue a spiritual life, thinking and doing all those things that are pleasing to you. For you, Christ our God, are the light of our souls and bodies, and to you we give glory together with your Father who is without beginning and your all holy, good, and life giving Spirit, now and forever and to the ages of ages. Amen.

The key nouns that refer to humanity in this prayer are "hearts," "light," "eyes of our minds," "spiritual life," and "souls and bodies." Clearly, the "spiritual life" is not something that has only to do with those things that are non-material, for Christ, the incarnate One, illumines the body as well as the soul. The Master who shines within the "heart" (that is, the center of the being) does not bypass the mind, but speaks through the gospel, which gives its propositional "message" — that is, a message that communicates with ideas. The spiritual life, however, affects not only mind, but also the whole of the person, for it has lodged within the heart. This transformation is intended to give glory to God — Father, Son, and Holy Spirit — since it works within those who are in Jesus, who as Son, with the Holy Spirit, gives glory to the Father.

Prayers for brothers and sisters ensue, culminating with prayers for those who are preparing for baptism. In Chrysostom's time, these "catechumens" (those not yet baptized) were actually dismissed from the congregation prior to the third part of the liturgy, the Communion, as evidence of the reverence and mystery afforded this act. Though this is not practiced in most Orthodox churches today, the sacrament is still given and received in liturgical churches as a moment of great mystery, a time when heaven and earth meet. Congregants and celebrant enact the roles of a great drama, with the people placing themselves among the heavenly hosts, and the priest, all too aware of unworthiness, picturing the compassion of Christ as he offered himself for humankind. The vestments worn by the priest are meant to obscure his human identity and serve as a means of "speaking Christ" to the people, since "the priest only lends his hand and provides his tongue":

People: We who mystically represent the Cherubim sing the thrice holy hymn to the life giving Trinity. Let us set aside all the cares of life that we may receive the King of all . . .

Priest: No one bound by worldly desires and pleasures is worthy to approach, draw near or minister to you, the King of glory. To serve you is great and awesome even for the heavenly powers. But because of your ineffable and immeasurable love for us, you became man without alteration or change. You have served as our High Priest, and as Lord of all, and have entrusted to us the celebration of this liturgical sacrifice without the shedding of blood.

For you alone, Lord our God, rule over all things in heaven and on earth. You are seated on the throne of the Cherubim, the Lord of the Seraphim and the King of Israel. You alone are holy and dwell among your saints. You alone are good and ready to hear. Therefore, I implore you, look upon me, your sinful and unworthy servant, and cleanse my soul and heart from evil consciousness. Enable me by the power of your Holy Spirit so that, vested with the grace of priesthood, I may stand before your holy Table and celebrate the mystery of your holy and pure Body and your precious Blood. To you I come with bowed head and pray: do not turn your face away from me or reject me from among your children, but make me, your sinful and unworthy servant, worthy to offer to you these gifts.

For you, Christ our God, are the Offerer and the Offered, the One who receives and is distributed, and to you we give glory, together with your eternal Father and your holy, good and life giving Spirit, now and forever and to the ages of ages. Amen.

Here, again, we see two contrasting approaches to God. The created ones (people and priest) are "filled up" with God's goodness, so that they can represent angels and Christ to each other. Their ordinary lives thus become vehicles of God's grace. Yet, *nothing* and *no one* is comparable to the great majesty, compassion, and holiness of God himself, who is the only creator, redeemer, and sanctifer, and who meets the people in their gathering together. This tryst is possible only because of the ministrations of the Triune God, who gives Christ, the "unspeakable gift" (2 Corinthians 9:15) to us. Human beings are called to "lay aside" earthly care, and to receive what God has to offer them, here in the time of worship, but continuing with them into their "ordinary" lives. With Augustine, Chrysostom sees God as both unspeakably transcendent and tenderly *immanent*, that is, "indwelling" or "remaining with" those whom he loves. The love of the Trinity spills into our world in the Incarnation, crucifixion, resurrection, and ascension, so that God's people can receive the "King of all."

Confessional psalm, prayers, and the creed are followed by this responsive confession between God, priest, and people as the actual Eucharist begins:

Priest (in a low voice): It is proper and right to sing to you, bless you, praise you, thank you and worship you in all places of your dominion;

for you are God ineffable, beyond comprehension, invisible, beyond understanding, existing forever and always the same; you and your only begotten Son and your Holy Spirit. You brought us into being out of nothing, and when we fell, you raised us up again. You did not cease doing everything until you led us to heaven and granted us your kingdom to come. For all these things we thank you and your only begotten Son and your Holy Spirit; for all things that we know and do not know, for blessings seen and unseen that have been bestowed upon us. We also thank you for this liturgy which you are pleased to accept from our hands, even though you are surrounded by thousands of Archangels and tens of thousands of Angels, by the Cherubim and Seraphim, six-winged, many-eyed, soaring with their wings,

Priest: Singing the victory hymn, proclaiming, crying out, and saying:

People: Holy, holy, holy, Lord Sabaoth, heaven and earth are filled with your glory. Hosanna in the highest. Blessed is he who comes in the name of the Lord. Hosanna to God in the highest.

Notice the striking combination of sobriety and celebration that marks this action! The worshipers together wonder that God can receive their "lit-urgy" — literally, the "effort, or work, of the people" — since he is already hymned by the celestial angels. Yet they are invited by the priest to celebrate in joy; so they welcome Christ, as did the children when Jesus entered Jerusalem! Reverence and abandon come together in these prayers. This juxtaposition reminds us of the mixed life of St. John himself, a man of small physical dimensions but great of spirit, who knew both how to serve and to celebrate, and who was prepared, for the sake of integrity, to be exiled by a furious pagan queen at the twilight of his life.

The consecration of both the elements and the people is accompanied by many prayers, and culminates in this response between priest and people, which proclaims both the holiness of the Church, and the absolute holiness of the One being worshiped:

Priest: The holy Gifts for the holy people of God.

People: One is Holy, one is Lord, Jesus Christ, to the glory of God the Father. Amen.

Then ensues a confession that brings together Jesus' parable of the foolish virgins, the intimate imagery of the Song of Songs, and the repentance of the thief on the cross. The personal significance of being prepared, the mystical sanctity of the Supper, and the historical dimension of our salvation are thus brought together:

> How shall I, who am unworthy, enter into the splendor of your saints? If I dare to enter into the bridal chamber, my clothing will accuse me, since it is not a wedding garment; and being bound up, I shall be cast out by the angels. In your love, Lord, cleanse my soul and save me.
>
> Loving Master, Lord Jesus Christ, my God, let not these holy Gifts be to my condemnation because of my unworthiness, but for the cleansing and sanctification of soul and body and the pledge of the future life and kingdom. It is good for me to cling to God and to place in him the hope of my salvation.
>
> Receive me today, Son of God, as a partaker of your mystical Supper. I will not reveal your mystery to your adversaries. Nor will I give you a kiss as did Judas. But as the thief I confess to you: Lord, remember me in your kingdom.

All has been transfigured — people, words, bread, and wine — by the responsive coming of the Holy Spirit, so that the unique sacrifice of Jesus may be joined to the "bloodless" spiritual offering of gathered people. Each communicant then receives the elements of the Supper, in mystery joined to the real last supper, and to the crucifixion of the Lord. It is not the priest who offers communion to the people but Christ himself, for "forgiveness of sins and eternal life." This holy moment, a communion in the Father, Son, and Holy Spirit, is followed by a paean of praise and celebration:

> We have seen the true light;
> we have received the heavenly Spirit;
> we have found the true faith, worshiping the undivided Trinity,
>   for the Trinity has saved us.
> Let our mouths be filled with your praise, Lord, that we may sing of your glory. You have made us worthy to partake of your holy mysteries. Keep us in your holiness, that all the day long we may meditate upon your righteousness.
> Alleluia. Alleluia. Alleluia.

St. John's maturity of life enabled him to bequeath to the Church a liturgy that is solemn without calling attention to itself as a ritual. Prayers, actions, readings, responses become the means by which God gathers up Christ's own, including them in the drama of salvation, enlightening them by the Holy Spirit, and strengthening them for their lives. Nor would the Golden-mouthed be happy to claim this as his own "composition" — for the liturgy, though marked by John's insight, is nourished by all the Scriptures, by the very ancient prayers of Israel and Church, and by the Church's glimpse of the heavenly throne room, where the eternal liturgy is always being offered. No doubt the bishop's desire, in commending this liturgy to his people, was that they should be caught up into the divine glory as well. As he exults in Homily 12 on John's Gospel, "He in no wise lowered his own nature by his descent [in the Incarnation], but elevated us, who had always been in a state of ignominy and darkness, to ineffable glory."

Chrysostom, while glory-struck, is also well aware of theological and other human problems. So we see a practical cast to his work, even when he is providing a space for believers to be drawn up into heavenly worship. In this double focus, he is like Augustine, who during his philosophical speculations maintained a deep humility and modesty, so that the intellectual world is leashed in its rightful place before our wholly transcendent God. Both Fathers agree that God's people are meant to edify each other, and both yearn for believers to enter intimacy with God, whose compassion has crossed the barrier of our fallen nature. It seems that what Augustine anticipates as reserved for final beatific vision, Chrysostom hopes that worshipers may glimpse as they are caught up together with seraphim and cherubim at the time of corporate worship. For both, however, it is the life of the Trinity, coming from the Father in the enlightening Word, and through the enlivening Spirit, that renders human transformation more than an elusive dream. Neither philosophical speculation nor liturgy *force* God's hand; *theurgy* ("the manipulation of God") is not the Christian way, because it is an impossibility.

The God Seers: St. Maximos, St. Symeon the New Theologian, and St. Gregory Palamas

Some have spoken, however, as though mystics could "encourage" the Almighty to visit them. Careful reading of subsequent spiritual theologians will reinforce what we have learned from the anonymous author of *Aseneth*, as well as Sts. Gregory, Augustine, and Chrysostom: our God is sovereign and gracious, and has undertaken all on our behalf. "Do not say in your heart, 'Who will ascend into heaven?' (that is, to bring Christ down). . . . But what does it say? 'The word is near you, on your lips and in your heart.' . . . For, 'Everyone who calls upon the name of the Lord shall be saved'" (Romans 10:6-8, 13). We are well instructed by the utter humility of three beloved God-seers — Sts. Maximos, Symeon, and Palamas — who adopt a practical and *incarnational* approach to God's meeting with us.

Those who know something about the history of spiritual theology may be surprised that we are not going to tackle the work of the renowned St. Denys (sometimes called "Pseudo-Dionysius the Areopagite"). Though it is clear that he influenced many of those whose work we will taste, his work is by no means for the beginner. Moreover, the most poignant of his insights have been preserved, and made more markedly incarnational and trinitarian by those who followed him. St. Maximos the Confessor (ca. 580-662) is one of those by whose hand we receive the wealth of Denys, in a helpfully pastoral form. Though best known in the East, St. Maximos made a strong impact upon the entire undivided Church, through his insistence that the Son had a human as well as a divine will. This doctrine is no arcane matter, for "what is not assumed is not healed" — if the Son did not possess a will like ours, then our wills cannot be transformed and sanctified! His strong witness, so important for our full understanding of salvation, liter-ally cost him his tongue and his right hand, since the monarchs of his day sided with his enemies, and as an older man, he was savagely disciplined. Eighteen short years after his death, in the sixth ecumenical council at Con-stantinople, the Church vindicated his deep insights, and *monotheletism* (the doctrine that Jesus only had "one [divine] will") was quelled. The martyr was wise not only in creedal but in psychological matters — he declared "self-love" to be "the mother of all vices," and so his voice rings down the centuries, challenging our own arrogant and self-asserting age.

One of the great gifts that St. Maximos possessed was his ability to read critically, in the light of Scriptures and the whole apostolic council, and thus to transmit in his own work the best discoveries of his predeces-sors. Well aware of the distinction between Creator and creature, he was able to see a danger in the teaching of that earlier great spiritual theolo-gian, Origen, and so discarded as erroneous both Origen's teaching that our souls are "pre-existent," and the misconception that their embodied

good thing to devote ourselves to seeking God, as we have been commanded. For although in the present life we are unable to arrive at the limit of God's depth, yet at least by reaching in some small way his depth we would see the holier among holy things and the more spiritual among spiritual things. (*Chapters* 2.18, 19)

Maximos taught that worshiping together, in particular, enables human beings to come to know the light of the One God. When, at the verge of reception in the Eucharist, the communicant worshipers confess, "One is Holy, one is the Lord Jesus Christ, to the glory of the Father," they, as one, are in holy union with the angels and indeed, with the Trinity, God himself:

There they behold the light of the invisible and ineffable glory and become themselves together with the angels on high open to the blessed purity. . . . To them there is lacking nothing of this good that is possible and attainable for me, so that they also can be and be called gods by adoption through grace because all of God entirely fills them and leaves no part of them empty of his presence. (*The Church's Mystagogy*, 21)

To some this final statement may be entirely shocking, for the doctrine of "theosis" or "deification" sounds strange, even pagan, to western Christian ears. It is important to realize that this is not a teaching peculiar to Maximos, though he did articulate it very clearly, when he said "If the Word of God and God the Son of the Father became son of man and man himself for this reason, to make men gods and sons of God, then we must believe that we shall be where Christ is now as the head of the whole body, having become in his human nature a forerunner to the Father on our behalf" (*Chapters* 2.25). His words about our becoming "gods" and "sons of God" by adoption were anticipated in the Scriptures (Romans 8:19; 2 Peter 1:4) and by St. Irenaeus in the second century (*Against Heresies*). They were then explained unequivocally by St. Athanasios in the fourth century (*On the Incarnation*), by St. Augustine in the fifth century (*Sermon on the Feast of the Nativity*) and others, including St. Maximos. Particularly in the West (with the exception of some Wesleyan and holiness movements) "salvation" has come to be understood solely in terms of rescue from punishment, and not in terms of being visited and enlivened by the God of all life and light. In the climate of New Age religions, and in an epoch that tends to confuse Creator with creation, the doctrine of "joining in God's communion" must be retrieved with care. However, for those who retain a clear sense of God as the One who in essence is beyond anything we could attain, this promise of human glorification astounds, and leads to *deeper* adoration of our Lord. St. Paul cried out in Romans, "We have peace with God . . . and we boast in our hope of sharing the glory of God" (5:1-2). He is joined by St. Maximos, who exults,

> The one who keeps sacred *the whole meaning* of the Word of God's becoming incarnate for our sake *will acquire the glory* full of grace and truth of the one who for our sake glorifies and consecrates himself in us by his coming: "When he appears we shall be like him" (1 John 3:2). (*Chapters* 2.76)

The Incarnation means, in the end, nothing less than our complete illumination by the Trinity, and our being called no longer "servants" but "sons" and "friends" — this is God's gift, who draws us deeper and deeper into his fellowship.

St. Symeon (942-1022), called the "New Theologian," since he was matched with his ancient predecessor St. Gregory (Nazianzus) the Theologian, commended the way of light even more vigorously to the Christian community. After a rather wild youth, he became a monk at age 27, then priest and abbot of the monastery of St. Mamas in Constantinople. He reacted strongly against the formalism of the Church in his own day, upheld the charismatic authority of Spirit-filled spiritual directors, whether lay or ordained, and yearned for all believers to have the deep experience of light and love with which he himself had been graced. The personal quality of his writings, especially his "Hymns of Divine Love," recall the intimacy of St. Augustine; his reference to the "gift of tears" and "baptism in the Holy Spirit" anticipate the revivals of Wesley and others with whom the West is more familiar. A proponent of theosis, his writings disclose an acute awareness of his own need for transformation, and God's graciousness to accomplish this glory within the ones whom he loves:

> How shall I describe, Master, the vision of your countenance?
>
> How shall I speak of the unspeakable contemplation
>   of your beauty? . . .

As I was meditating, Master, on these things,
Suddenly you appeared from above, much greater than the sun
And you shone brilliantly from the heavens down into my heart . . .
At once I forgot the light of the lamp . . .
I said to you and now I say it from the bottom of my heart:
"Have mercy on me, Master . . ."
It was you yourself who said that it was not the healthy
    who had need of a physician, Christ, but the sick.
And I have a great sickness and have been so negligent,
    so pour out your great pity upon me, O Word!

But O what intoxication of light, O what movements of fire!
Oh, what swirlings of the flame in me, miserable one that I am,
    Coming from you and your glory!
The glory I know it and I say it is your Holy Spirit,
Who has the same nature with you and the same honor, O Word,
He is of the same race, of the same glory,
Of the same essence, He alone with your Father
And with you, O Christ, O God of the universe!
I fall in adoration before you.
I thank you that you have made me worthy to know as much as it is
The power of your divinity.
I thank you that you, even when I was sitting in darkness,
Revealed yourself to me, you enlightened me,
You granted me to see the light of your countenance
That is unbearable to all . . .

                            (Hymns of Divine Love 25)

The intensity of this visitation is such that Symeon has both a sense of light and of darkness: there is an ambiguity to his situation: he simultaneously knows that God has filled him with his light, while also sensing that he, in comparison to that great light, is in the deepest shadows. Knowledge of God makes him both sensible of his being other than God, yet transforms his darkness into light, so joining him with the Source of light:

You appeared as light, illuminating me completely from your total light. And I became light in the darkness, I who was found in the midst of darkness. . . . Likewise I am in the light, yet I am found in the middle of the darkness. So I am in the darkness, yet still I am in the middle of the light. (*Hymns of Divine Love* 25)

So seized is Symeon by the enormous implications of God the Son's Incarnation, that, with St. Maximos, he does not downplay the body — though, in the rapture of the vision, earthly things can become pale. All the same, he insists that the vision of God affects the body with the soul, because God has visited every part of humanity. Symeon does not leash God's visitation by speaking about a merely intellectual or spiritual vision, but is awed at God's utter condescension to us:

> O awesome wonder which I see doubly,
> With my two sets of eyes, of the body and of the soul!
> Listen now. I am telling you the awesome mysteries of a double
> God who came to me as a double man.
> He took upon Himself my flesh and He gave me His Spirit
> And I became also god by divine grace, a son of God by adoption.
> O what dignity, what glory!
>
> (*Hymns of Divine Love* 25)

God's transfiguring power remains a grace. Thus, despite Symeon's acute experiences of visitation by the divine light, the new theologian will not presume that he has *attained* and so can rest at ease, no longer dependent upon mercy. He is keenly aware of the One whom he has seen, but will not depend upon his experiences to safeguard his place with God in eternity. Rather, that future illumination and blessedness also depends wholly upon mercy. So he worships the One who can justify, and not the luminous visions that have come his way:

> Insofar as I am human, I have nothing of the transcendent
>   and divine realities,
> But insofar as I have received mercy through the kindness of God,
> I possess Christ, Lord, the Benefactor of all things.
> For this reason again, Master, I fall down before you
> And ask that I not fail in the hopes I have placed in you,
> As being my life, honor and glory and kingdom,
> But also as even now you have allowed me to look up at you, Savior,

So also after death grant me to see you! . . .
Do not totally shame me, Christ, in the day of judgment,
When you place your sheep on your right hand
And place me and the goats on your left.
But may your immaculate light, the light of your countenance,
Hide my works and the nudity of my soul,
And clothe me with joyfulness
So that with confidence without shame,
I may be placed at the right hand
With the sheep and with them
I may glorify you forever and ever.
Amen. (*Hymns of Divine Love* 25)

The joy of St. Symeon that God has come to earth, and continues to come to his beloved, in such a way that he can be perceived with bodily as well as spiritual eyes, struck many as too bold. We have seen that he was not alone in this emphasis upon the whole person, especially in the Eastern Church; the West, perhaps because of Augustine's overarching emphasis, tended more to speak about the intellectual or spiritual vision of God. In the thirteenth century, some God-seers who followed in Symeon's train (called *hesychasts,* or "those who practice sacred quietude") actually required defense against those who felt that reference to the body was impious. They were championed by a contemporary of St. Thomas Aquinas — the monk, archbishop, and leading theologian of the East, St. Gregory of Palamas (1296-1359).

In his *Triads in Defense of the Holy Hesychasts,* St. Palamas argued that the emphasis upon the whole body at prayer and as open to God's light was no novelty, but went back to the experience of the three disciples at Mount Tabor. St. Evagrius (fourth century), St. Macarius the Great (fourth to fifth century), St. John Climacus (sixth to seventh century), and St. Symeon had all spoken about this holistic enlightening by God through constant prayer and contemplation. By the late thirteenth century a tradition had evolved in order to help the one who prayed in intimacy with God. That tradition included the use of various meditative repeated prayers such as the well-known "Jesus Prayer" ("Lord Jesus Christ, Son of God, have mercy on me, a sinner"); bodily posture such as sitting with the chin directed down towards the heart; inhaling and exhaling in a rhythmic motion attuned to the prayer one was saying; or simply attending in silence to God. These practices, adopted by laity as well as clergy, were attacked by the Greek philosopher Barlaam, who had studied in Italy. He had fallen into a worldview that opposed nature to God's grace, and thus was convinced that the human mind could only be *approximately* enlightened through the mediation of creation, especially philosophical means. He was shocked by the claim of uneducated monks that they were *theodidaktoi* (taught by God alone), repulsed by their adoption of bodily means to pray, and shocked by their belief that the body as well as the mind could be transfigured by the light of God. In his view, these presumptuous and ignorant meditators were heretics who needed to be corrected — and silenced. They were, he scoffed, those who had their "souls in their navels" — their practices could hardly be of God!

St. Palamas, monk, priest, and theologian at Mount Athos, the ancient Eastern center for monastic meditation, had his work cut out for him. In the *Triads* (three groups of three sections, like the present work), he argued that Greek philosophy "cannot save," and that God's wisdom can indeed be rightly contemplated "in his creatures." Going back to the disciples' insight at the transfiguration, he argued that the illumination of the Lord, the descent of the Holy Spirit, and the cloud-like phenomenon were "clearly perceptible to the senses" — what the disciples saw was immediate *uncreated* light, over against philosophical knowledge, which is created.

It was not, however, God's *essence*, which remains God's alone to know, but God's *energies* that the disciples (and subsequent God-seers) were enabled, by grace, to see. These energies, themselves uncreated, manifest the presence of God himself; they are communicated to the prepared person, body and spirit, who then is, in turn, transfigured by them. The mind, incapable of attaining to the knowledge of God, can yet be "brought down" into the heart, so that the entire person can be visited by God's light, and so changed. While there is a "darkness" surrounding God, this darkness is not "empty": in this cloud, with the senses purified and mind stilled, the believer finds himself or herself in God's very presence, and so is changed. At the moment of the illumination, there may be a sense in which one transcends the body and mind, but the entire person, body-mind-soul-spirit, is touched, and participates in the "seeing." This results in the love of others, for it comes from the light and love of God.

The Greek philosophers, then, were wrongheaded when they thought that the mind had to abandon the body, or make itself blank, in order for

God to meet with them: "We recollect the mind not only within the body and heart, but also within itself," argued Palamas. All this is because the body is altogether important to God, the Creator and the incarnate One, who has "deified the flesh" and "grants to the body also the experience of things divine." The greatest gift that God can give, following upon the greatest gift of the Incarnation, is to grant to the believer the ability to love God "ecstatically" and so to *become* prayer:

> Thus, beyond prayer, there is the ineffable vision, and ecstasy in the vision, and the hidden mysteries. . . . It is in this dazzling darkness that the divine things are given to the saints. . . . Under the effect of the ecstasy, he forgets even prayer to God. . . . The mind does not pray a definite prayer, but finds itself in ecstasy in the midst of incomprehensible realities. . . . This most joyful reality, which ravished Paul, and made his mind go out from every creature but yet return entirely to himself — this he beheld as a . . . light without limit, depth, height, or lateral extension. He saw absolutely no limit to his vision and to the light which shone round about him; but rather it was as it were a sun infinitely brighter and greater than the universe, with himself standing in the midst of it, having become all eye. (*Triad* B.I.iii)

Palamas maintained, against Barlaam, that the Incarnation has made the unthinkable possible — that we should participate in the energies, the virtues, and the blessedness of God himself, even while God remains himself, and ineffable:

> The transformation of our human nature, its deification and transfiguration — were these not accomplished in Christ from the start, from the moment in which he assumed our nature? Thus he was divine before, but he bestowed at the time of his transfiguration a divine power upon the eyes of the apostles and enabled them to look up and see for themselves. This light, then, was not a hallucination, but will remain for eternity, and has existed from the beginning. (*Triad* E.III.i)

The disciples, who reverently fell on their faces before the eternal glory shown on Tabor, were astonishingly initiated into God's glory and life — their life was caught up into that of their Master, and so began their transformation. Palamas still urges us today: "Let us not turn aside incredulous before the superabundance of these blessings; but let us have faith in him who participated in our nature and granted in return the glory of his own nature, and let us seek how to acquire this glory and see it" (*Triad* B.II.iii).

The Making of All Things Well:
Julian of Norwich and Thomas à Kempis

Julian of Norwich (1342–c. 1423) and Thomas à Kempis (1380-1471) are the first of our mystical theologians to bring us to areas beyond the Mediterranean and the Tigris-Euphrates cradle of civilization. The first English, and the second German, these two have become beloved for their homely yet astute ways of describing the spiritual life to their Christian brothers and sisters. Though both were able to speak in imagery that communicate well to the common person, they were also well educated, both formally and by the Spirit of God. As might be expected, both had the uncommon gift of humility. Despite her training in English, Latin, rhetoric, and the Fathers, Julian called herself "a woman, ignorant, weak, and frail"; Thomas was educated by a celebrated teacher as a youth, but opposed the fashionable humanism of his day, and wrote the great classic that has come to be known as *The Imitation of Christ*.

Dame Julian's revelations came in three forms: visions of the imagination; "locutions" or *words* formed in her understanding; and imageless and wordless visions that she called "spiritual" or "intellectual." Her "Showings" (a series of sixteen revelations) were experienced over a period of only a few days: written first in brief, they were finally expanded after 20 years of theological and scriptural meditation upon them. Like the three Eastern God-seers that we have considered, she does not play off the spiritual and the material, but sees God displayed in all of creation, and considers that our "substance" and "sensualyte" (that is, our soul/body aspects) are meant to be harmonized by God, though our capacities have been disordered by the Fall. She is perhaps best known for her "hazelnut vision," in which she saw "with the eye of understanding" that everything exists, even the smallest creation, "because God loves it," made it, and preserves it. Nothing that God has made is to be despised, not even the tiniest thing that one can hold in the hand; it exists through God, and can teach us about the creator, since "he is in everything that is good."

Especially, however, we come to understand God through Jesus himself, says Dame Julian, since "where Jesus appears, the blessed Trinity is understood" (First Showing). This theme is struck again in her Second Showing, where she sees Jesus and comes to understand this truth: "If God wills to show you more, he will be your light. You have need of none but him." God communicates not simply in vision, but also in word, and so, in an age of innumerable troubles and plagues, and during a time when Julian herself had a near-fatal illness, he promised to this dear servant, "I will make all things well, I shall make all things well, I may make all things well, and I can make all things well." This promise, taken from her Thirteenth Showing, is expounded in terms of the omnipotent Trinity, who acts so as to rescue and glorify the creation.

Julian's emphasis upon the crucified and glorified Christ, and upon the Trinity, is astonishingly practical. She is well known for perceiving, without the use of pictures or words, but by what she calls the intellect or spirit, revelations of God that show the Trinity (and particularly Christ) as our nourishing and protective Mother.

In speaking of the "true motherhood" of God, Julian uses a poignant and important metaphor. It is unfortunate that some contemporary hymnodists and liturgists have mistaken her devotional intent, and coopted her meditations as the foundation of a novel movement in naming God. We should be clear, however, that Julian herself is not *naming* the ineffable God, or seeking to replace Father, Son, and Spirit — the name given by Jesus and the Church to this One above all understanding — with "Father, Mother, and Spirit." No, in these showings she is speaking of the *work* of the Trinity (especially of the Word), and its characteristics in our human sphere (what theologians call the *economic* Trinity), not of the Trinity in its inner relationship between Father, Son, and Spirit. Indeed, even in the midst of the maternal language, she consistently uses the masculine pronouns "he" and "him." As we draw on her piety and insight, we must be careful not to misunderstand them as attempts to amplify or correct the creeds! But let us listen to her:

> I contemplated the work of all the blessed Trinity, in which contemplation I saw and understood these three properties: the property of the fatherhood, and the property of the motherhood, and the property of the lordship in one God. In our almighty Father we have our protection and our bliss, as regards our natural substance which is ours by our creation from without beginning; and in the second person, in

knowledge and wisdom we have our perfection, as regards our sensuality, our restoration and our salvation, for he is our Mother, brother, and saviour; and in our good Lord the Holy Spirit we have our reward and our gift for our living . . . out of his great plentiful grace. . . .

And so our Mother is working on us in various ways . . . in mercy on all his beloved children. Therefore he must need nourish us, . . . feed us with himself . . . with the blessed sacrament, . . . lead us easily into his blessed breast [and] say "See how I love you." (Tenth Showing)

Thomas à Kempis as the unwitting author of a centuries-old bestseller, matches the ardor of Julian, and commends a warm heart to others. In a time of cold, scholastic approaches to the faith, Thomas, with his characteristic unassuming air, modeled what was called the "new devotion" that had been adopted in his monastery. This movement, in its emphasis on Christ's human nature and passion and its devotional reading of Scripture, was instrumental in helping many to return "to their first love." Since then, the *Imitation* has introduced countless readers to the riches of Scripture and the Fathers, and to a way of practicing the presence of Christ that has fostered both intimacy with the Lord and the "ecstatic" way. It is best read slowly, in prayer, and with a Bible in hand. Here is a taste of what will be found by the one who journeys with Thomas.

In a series of interior dialogues with the Lord, Thomas alludes to scriptural passages including Luke 10:21-24, Colossians 3:1-2, Revelation 3, and Romans 8:12ff. In his hunger to know God, he asks what to do with his "indifferent" and "lukewarm" heart, and yearns to have the burning faith of those who broke bread with Jesus after the Emmaus walk and dinner revelation (Luke 24:13-32). Jesus answers the praying Thomas that one must only "open" the door of the heart to him, and he will visit, console, and love the one seeking him. Thomas senses this love of Christ as that of a "beloved spouse" and "pure lover" who can give to the seeker "the wings of true liberty to fly and repose" in him. The dialogue is marked by both warmth and quiet confidence:

O Jesus! The brightness of eternal glory, the comfort of a soul in its pilgrimage, my tongue cannot express the sentiments of my heart, but my silence itself speaks to thee. . . .

O light eternal! Transcending all created lights, dart forth thy light from above, which may penetrate the inward parts of my heart.

Cleanse, gladden, enlighten, and quicken my spirit with its powers that I may be absorbed in thee with ecstasies of joy. Oh, when will this blessed and desirable hour come when thou shalt fill me with thy presence and become to me all in all? (*Imitation of Christ* III, 21, 34)

The heart's yearning for Christ's presence is assured as Thomas passes on the quiet assurance of the Lord: "Son, as much as thou canst go out of thyself, so much wilt thou be able to enter into me." This interior life, however, does not issue in quietism, or lack of concern for others. Thus Thomas prays, prompted by the Holy Spirit, "Let me love Thee more than myself and myself only for Thee, and all others in Thee, who truly love Thee as the law of love commands, which shines forth from Thee." The light of Christ shines upon the one who loves him, and this light then shines forth on others.

Love's Flame: Sts. Teresa of Ávila and John of the Cross

The flame of love cherished by Thomas was fanned into a flame by the Spanish reformers of the Carmelite movement, St. Teresa of Ávila (1515-1582) and St. John of the Cross (1542-1591). Despite her lack of formal education, Teresa is one of three women who have been given the title "Doctor of the Church" by the Pope. (The others were Catherine of Siena, 1347-1380, and St. Thérèse of Lisieux, 1837-1897.) Anyone reading her *Book of God's Mercies, Meditations on the Song of Songs, Way of Perfection,* and *Interior Castle* will agree that she is a writer of great profundity and devotion. Teresa's work is marked by an intimate knowledge of Scripture and of human nature, for despite her cloistered life, she experienced much sorrow and temptation, even abandoning the life of prayer for an entire year. Teresa's *Interior Castle* is organized around a brilliant picture of the human life, reminiscent of the ancient visionaries' understanding of the "realms" of heaven, each encircled within the other, and each more holy as one proceeds inward. (For a glimpse of this apocalyptic view of God's holy realms, consider 2 Corinthians 12, which speaks of three heavens; or the elaborate writings included in *1, 2,* and *3 Enoch,* where there are even more layers. It would seem that this view of increasing realms of holiness corresponds to the Jewish Temple, with its various courts, which culminated in the center with the "Holy of Holies.") Teresa's castle includes seven concentric "mansions," each with innumerable rooms. The King visits each of these, but is to be found supremely within the heart, that Holy of Holies by which the human person is destined in herself or himself to be a "temple" of the Almighty.

Contrary to what we might expect of a "spiritual" writer, Teresa meditates, in the penultimate, second to most inward mansion (the sixth dwelling place), upon the *humanity* of Christ and his passion. Yet utter silence is necessary within the final, seventh dwelling, since in this "prayer of union" "the Most Blessed Trinity, all Three Persons," reveals himself through an "intellectual" (that is, wordless and imageless) vision, "enkindling in the Spirit in the manner of a cloud of magnificent splendor." The three Persons are distinct, yet there is "one substance and one power and one knowledge and one God alone" and "all three Persons communicate and explain those words of the Lord in the Gospel, that he and the Father and the Holy Spirit will come to dwell with the soul that loves him" (*Interior Castle*, "Seventh Dwelling Place," I). At this point, the favor of "spiritual marriage" is granted to the beloved worshiper, since "His Majesty desires to show himself to the soul through an imaginative vision of his most sacred humanity . . . in the form of shining splendor, beauty, and majesty, as he was after his resurrection" ("Seventh Dwelling," II). Beyond this approaching vision of the imagination, the believer is caught up into the most intimate "intellectual vision," in which the Lord appears "in this center of the soul." It is clear by Teresa's words that she does not intend the term "intellectual" to conjure up ideas of great feats of rationality, since she is speaking of a completely inward vision that requires *no* media, either of the senses or of the reason. Rather, the Lord himself comes "delicately," entering the person without passing through flesh or mind, "as he appeared to the apostles without entering through the door when he said to them *'pax vobis'* ['Peace to you']."

This union she likens to the joining of two wax candles, so melded that "the flame coming from them is but one, or that the wick, the flame, and the wax are all one." This ultimate spiritual marriage, she supposes, is what Paul meant when he said to the Philippians, "For me to live is Christ and to die is gain" (Philippians 1:21). For "The King is in his palace," meeting with the believer in the Holy of Holies, without need of word or image. As might be expected given her humble spirit, Teresa ends by "laughing" over the analogies that she has used, because they do not satisfy: yet they are, she affirms, true.

One of Teresa's protégés was St. John of the Cross, who, through many complicated twists in his monastic life, worked to extend Teresa's female reform of the Carmelite movement into the male monastery. His writing began at a critical point in his life when he had been snatched away by hostile clergy from Teresa's order, and actually imprisoned in another religious house in Toledo, Spain. While incarcerated he wrote the poem "One Dark Night":

> One dark night,
> fired with love's urgent longings
> — ah, the sheer grace! —
> I went out unseen,
> my house being now all stilled.
>
> In darkness, and secure,
> by the secret ladder, disguised,
> — ah, the sheer grace! —
> in darkness and concealment,
> my house being now all stilled.
>
> On that glad night
> in secret, for no one saw me,
> nor did I look at anything
> with no other light or guide
> than the one that burned in my heart.
>
> This guided me
> more surely than the light of noon
> to where he was awaiting me
> — him I knew so well —
> there in a place where no one appeared.
>
> O guiding night!
> O night more lovely than the dawn!
> O night that has united the Lover with his beloved,
> transforming the beloved in her Lover.
>
> Upon my flowering breast,
> which I kept wholly for him alone,

there he lay sleeping,
and I caressing him
there in a breeze from the fanning cedars.

When the breeze blew from the turret,
as I parted his hair,
it wounded my neck
with its gentle hand,
suspending all my senses.

I abandoned and forgot myself,
laying my face on my Beloved;
all things ceased; I went out from myself,
leaving my cares
forgotten among the lilies.

On dramatically escaping the sanctified prison and the city, he returned to the Order, and wrote his twin works, *Ascent of Mount Carmel,* and *Dark Night of the Soul.* These works were actually commentaries and expansions of the initial poem, and aptly depict John's life, which itself was, on the whole, a dark night. He died in loneliness, rejected by his fellow Carmelite brothers, but with the light of Christ.

Even a reading of the short poem, without further study of his larger pieces, shows that John traces the mystical path in three stages — purification, illumination, and union with Christ. One is to "leave" and to "still the house," learning to wait for God in the darkness, and engage in "exercise of spirit" even when one feels dry, and is no longer aware of God's presence while praying:

> When God sees that they [the beginning prayers] have grown a little, He weans them from the sweet breast so that they might be strengthened, lays aside their swaddling bands, and puts them down from His arms that they may grow accustomed to walking by themselves. (*Dark Night* I.8)

This first stage of purification concerns the senses (for one can no longer find any sweetness in prayer, and must still be disciplined); following this, there is an even deeper purging that God desires to do of the inner person, preparing it for union with him. St. John wonders about the paradox, and cries out — "Why, if it is a divine light (for it illumines souls and purges them of their ignorances), does one call it a dark night? . . . The brighter the light the more the owl is blinded; and the more one looks at the brilliant sun, the more the sun darkens the faculty of sight, deprives it, and overwhelms it in its weakness" (II. 5). During this time when we seem to be abandoned by God, patience and perseverance in prayer are instead working within us, for we are learning to be attentive to God, even when we are not being delighted by the process. It is in this time when we are prepared to renounce any sensations, or any rationally restricted understanding of God, that God can enkindle love, and eventually exalt us. The dark night is actually a process of illumination, and will foster within the one who perseveres "a certain feeling and foretaste" of himself. Thus "a living flame of love" makes its mark upon us, and creates a thirst that can only be satisfied by One.

Perhaps one further word should be said of these two. Though their meditations are extremely personal, and they stress interiority, both retained a devotion to their brothers and sisters in the faith, even during times of great duress. Their writings are not private diaries, nor memorials to self-indulgence, but have the practical purpose of explaining the spiritual pilgrimage to others who may benefit from their own growth in the light. So Teresa interrupts herself throughout the Castle meditations to address her sisters in the convent; so John, amidst his personal trials, speaks with tenderness to the "beginner" in prayer, exhorting that one to continue until the flame is kindled.

The Marriage of Practical Theology and Song: The Wesleys

In the West, we are accustomed to thinking of mystical or spiritual theology as being largely the domain of Roman Catholicism. Yet, it would be impossible to speak of the "flame of love" that has enkindled the Church without reference to the two Wesley brothers, who from their youth were devoted to the Lord, but whose formal faith was warmed through an encounter with a fervent group known as the Moravians. John (1703-1791) was the theologian, and Charles (1707-1788) the hymnodist; yet both were spiritual theologians, and their writings and songs were infused by the insight of those who had gone before. Those who have assumed that the Wesleys' work was purely spontaneous, an utter "new" development in the Church, do well to remember that they were self-consciously joined to the apostolic Church, and that they had interpreted their experience of God in the light of such greats as Ignatius, Polycarp, Justin Martyr, Irenaeus, Origen, Macarius, and Ephrem of Syria. Indeed, John lists these names (which include the "mystics" Origen, Macarius, and Ephrem) in his "Plain Account of Genuine Christianity," not because he considers them the most *learned* of saints, but because they were blessed by a love for God, and a life of integrity. So, they are worthy of our "reverence" — their writings "direct us to the strongest evidence of the Christian doctrine." As we go on to read the hymns and theology of these two brothers, the spiritual light of the early and historic Church becomes obvious, even though some might object to the looser ecclesiology that came in their wake.

One poem from Charles Wesley will serve as an emblem of their work, his "Wrestling Jacob":

> Come, O Thou Traveler unknown,
> Whom still I hold, but cannot see!
> My company before is gone,
> And I am left alone with thee;
> With thee all night I mean to stay,
> And wrestle till the break of day.
>
> I need not tell thee who I am,
> My misery or sin declare;
> Thyself hast called me by my name,
> Look on thy hands, and read it there.
> But who, I ask thee, who are thou?
> Tell me thy name, and tell me now.
>
> In vain thou strugglest to get free,
> I never will unloose my hold;
> Art thou the Man that died for me?
> The secret of thy love unfold:
> Wrestling, I will not let thee go
> Till I thy name, thy nature know.
>
> Wilt thou not yet to me reveal
> Thy new, unutterable name?

The Flame of Love

Tell me, I still beseech thee, tell:
To know it now resolved I am:
Wrestling, I will not let thee go
Till I thy name, thy nature know.

What though my shrinking flesh complain
And murmur to contend so long?
I rise superior to my pain:
When I am weak, then I am strong;
And when my all of strength shall fail
I shall with the God-man prevail.

Yield to me now — for I am weak,
But confident in self-despair!
Speak to my heart, in blessings speak,
Be conquered by my instant prayer:
Speak, or thou never hence shalt move,
And tell me if thy name is *LOVE*.

'Tis Love! 'Tis Love! Thou diedst for me;
I hear thy whisper in my heart.
The morning beaks, the shadows flee,
Pure Universal Love thou art:
To me, to all, thy bowels move —
Thy nature, and thy name, is *LOVE*.

I know thee, Saviour, who thou art —
Jesus, the feeble sinner's friend;
Nor wilt thou with the night depart,
But stay, and love me to the end;
Thy mercies never shall remove,
Thy nature, and thy name, is *LOVE*.

The Sun of Righteousness on me
Hath rose with healing in his wings;
Withered my nature's strength; from thee
My soul its life and succor brings;

My help is all laid up above:
Thy nature, and thy name, is *LOVE*.

Contented now upon my thigh
I halt, till life's short journey end;
All helplessness, all weakness, I
On thee alone for strength depend;
Nor have I power from thee to move:
Thy nature, and thy name, is *LOVE*.

Lame as I am, I take the prey,
Hell, earth, and sin with ease o'ercome;
I leap for joy, pursue my way,
And as a bounding hart fly home,
Through all eternity to prove,
Thy nature, and thy name, is *LOVE*.

This, one of Charles Wesley's most imaginative and personal poems, is thoroughly informed by Scriptures, as are his hymns intended for more corporate use. Though the first person singular is used, the use of the Scripture invites any Christian to enter into the story. We take our point of departure from Genesis 32:22-32, but soon meet other biblical images and ideas such as the power of the Name, the Psalmist's joy of the hart, the Isaianic prophecy of the Sun of Righteousness, and the special revelation of God's character in Jesus, the Loving one. Retold in a Christian accent, Jacob's struggle with the man at night is transformed into the Christian's encounter with the heretofore unknown God-Man, Who has the power (and mercy) to name the human one with whom he wrestles. The poem is immersed in creedal Christianity common to all believers; it is also poignantly aware of the *intimate* communion that God has with his own. This Christian "Jacob" is privileged to give a name to the unknown one — but it is a *revealed* name, the "name" of Love, which binds the wrestler to the Lover. The wrestler is, like countless spiritual theologians who seek the Merciful One, "wounded" by love — yet that very weakness (the "limping" thigh) becomes a strength for life and for eternity, enabling the seeker to find the way home, leaping. Like Paul, who saw unutterable mysteries (2 Corinthians 12), the wrestler learns that "when he is weak, then he is strong" — for his strength is in the One who died and rose for him.

In this poem we see that same great paradox, that same tension, encountered in others insistent on knowing God — a great striving for this communion, yet a discovery that fellowship is, after all, a gift of the One who is seeking them! It is only when "Nature's strength" is recognized to be withered, that the new name, and divine strength, can do God's transforming work. Perhaps this is something learned only in the praying, and not well communicated, though this poem comes as close to transmitting the truth as one can imagine.

Wesley, in the spirit of Ephrem and Macarius, and resting firmly upon the foundation of Chalcedon and Nicaea, spent his life urging his flocks to *orthodoxy* of the fullest sort — full *belief,* full *practice,* and full *worship.* In some cases, the legacy that he left seems to have miscarried. Some who claim Wesleyan heritage concentrate more upon the experience than on the God who meets us. In theological terms, this means that some now are exalting "experience" as a fourth source of authority (alongside Scripture, tradition, and reason) for making doctrinal decisions in the Church, rather than as a life communion into which all of God's people are called. In some cases, Wesley's celebration of "pure love" was frozen into a "second blessing" formula of perfectionism that tantalizes and frustrates, rather than sounding a clarion call for full Christian living. Yet in our day, as Catholic, Eastern, and Protestant Christians have learned more about each other, Eastern Christians have seen in Wesley some of their beloved Maximos and their bracing Symeon, and Catholics have wondered if Wesley had encounters like their beloved mystics. Similarly, Wesleyans have seen in their tradition's hymnody and John's theology the imprint of the "great tradition." Indeed, some have wondered whether the Eastern language of *theosis* bears a family similarity to their hope of entire sanctification. In the East, Maximos envisages our final goal: "Thus, we will be found giving worship in every way in imitation of the angels in heaven, and we shall exhibit on earth the same manner of life as the angels" (*Chapters* 2.21). In Western Catholicism, Julian rejoices, "in him and by him we are . . . gloriously brought up into heaven, and blessedly united." The ecstatic Wesley rejoins:

Finish, then, thy new creation,
Pure and spotless let us be.
Let us see thy great salvation
Perfectly restored in thee,

Changed from glory into glory
Till in heav'n we take our place,
Till we cast our crowns before thee.
Lost in wonder, love, and praise.

Depth in a Shallow Age:
John of Kronstadt, Thomas Merton, Evelyn Underhill

Though the contemporary age brings its own challenges, there are many in the past century who have sought to learn the ancient lessons of humility and hope, and so approved themselves within the Christian family. Though we are perhaps too close to the twentieth century to be certain of its "greats," we will take as representative of three traditions the Orthodox priest John of Kronstadt, the Roman Catholic monastic Thomas Merton, and the Anglican spiritual director Evelyn Underhill.

The oldest and least well known (for Western readers) of this trio is Fr. John of Kronstadt (1829-1908), *staretz* (that is, spiritual "father" and advisor) to many in Russia. He came from a poor family, and as a child had difficulty learning to read — he speaks of a "miracle of enlightenment" at age nine, when he finally did pass this hurdle. The government paid for his seminary education at the Academy of St. Petersburg, and after he had married his wife Elisabeth in 1855, he was ordained, serving at Kronstadt for fifty-three years as their curate and rector. He combined his busy time as a priest with cat naps and early morning walks, was personally generous to strangers beyond all reason, and seems to have struggled with both depression and fatigue. He celebrated communion on a daily basis — an unusual act in Orthodoxy for his age — and his conservative approach to the faith brought him many enemies. So many thousands flocked to him for confession and guidance that he improvised, introducing general confession during the liturgy — all the members confessing aloud one to another. This novelty (though in fact it goes back to the primitive church!) was confirmed by a vision revealed to one of his congregants, who saw the Lord himself extending the blessing of peace to the confessing congregation. John was prophetic, and so, at times, engaged in startling activities — for example, offering communion to a harried but loving Anglican governess during a house-call, and refusing it to her spiritually arrogant (but Orthodox) employer! Indeed, in 1907, he spoke prophetically against Russia, a judgement which many faithful believe came to pass in the national catastrophe of 1917, when the royal house fell and the nation was propelled into chaotic unrest. When John died in 1908, there were 60,000 in attendance at his funeral — those who had been moved by his sacrificial compassion, nourished by his insight as a spiritual leader, and touched by the miracles he had performed.

Amongst the Orthodox, his most beloved work is *My Life in Christ*, which begins with the Incarnation and the necessity of prayer, moves on to liturgy, the saints, the doctrine of the Church, and the practical life. We will concentrate upon his pastoral and strong spiritual counsel, which are laced through with the Scriptures and the devotional tradition of the Church, and offered by one who knew the Lord in intimacy. His words are practical, taking account of our human weakness, but putting our frailty in the context of God's strength:

> When you are praying alone, and your spirit is dejected, and you are wearied and oppressed by your loneliness, remember then, as always, that God the Holy Trinity looks upon you with eyes brighter than the sun; and so do all the angels, including your own guardian, and all the saints of God. Truly they do; for they are all one in God, and where God is there are they also. Where the sun is, thither also are all its rays. Try to understand what this means. Bear in mind with whom you are conversing. Men often forget with whom they are conversing during prayer, and who are the witnesses of their prayer. (IV, 4)

Again, in commending his flock to worship together, and reminding them of God's plan for the Church to be glorified *together*, not individually, Father John is most astute:

> If during service your brother does anything irregularly, or negligently, do not become irritated with him, whether inwardly or outwardly, but be generously indulgent to his faults, remembering that you yourself commit many, many faults, that you yourself are a man with every weakness, that God is long-suffering and all-merciful, and that he forgives you and all of us our offenses time without number. (VI, 3)

Or again, in speaking about the need for us to grow in knowledge, he commends with great vigor both Bible study and the study of the ancient theologians — all Christians, and not simply pastors and teachers, need to learn from these sources:

> The writings of the fathers . . . express the Mind, Word, and Spirit of the Holy Trinity, in which the spirit of the more spiritually advanced of mankind partakes. . . . If you read worldly magazines and newspapers, and derive some profit from them, as a citizen, a Christian, a member of a family, then you ought still more and still oftener to read the gospel, and the writings of the fathers. . . . Of those who do not read the gospel, I would ask: Are you pure, holy, and perfect, without reading the gospel? Is it not needful for you to look in this mirror? . . . Every word of Holy Writ . . . bears in itself the power corresponding to it. . . . How attentively and reverently, with what faith, must we therefore pronounce each word! For the Word is the Creator himself, God, and through the Word all things were brought into existence. (VI, 4)

Again, in speaking of how to order our daily lives, he directs us to the wonder of God's image in each human being, pulling the eyes of his congregants towards that beauty above all others. This positive approach to chastity is not only more effective than a simple judgement against licentious thoughts, but puts human beauty in the context of God's whole creation:

> Do not forget yourself in looking upon the beauty of the human face, but look upon the soul. . . . Do not admire the magnificence of the house, but look upon the man who dwells in it, and what he is; otherwise you will offend the image of God in the man, will dishonor the King by worshiping his servant, and not rendering unto him even the least part of the honor due to him. When you see a beautiful girl or woman, or a handsome youth or man, lift up your thoughts at once to the supreme most holy beauty, the author of every heavenly and earthly beauty, God himself; glorify him for having created such beauty out of mere earth. Marvel at the beauty of God's image in man, which shines forth even in our fallen state; imagine what our image shall be when we shine forth in the kingdom of our Father, if we become worthy of it; picture to yourself what must be the beauty of God's saints . . . imagine the unspeakable goodness of God's countenance. . . . (XI, 7)

Father John's practicality and ecstatic joy in the One who is all Beauty and Goodness is infectious. Though he would be embarrassed by this tribute, we could say that he is himself ample evidence of the adage found in his closing pages: "The simpler, the better and more unselfish a man is, the more blessed he is inwardly." The blessing of this man is that he directed others to the Giver of all blessings.

John of Kronstadt's prophetic mode, though not his pastoral simplicity, is also seen in the well-known works of Thomas Merton (1915-1968), whose parentage brought together New Zealand and the United States. He was raised in France, becoming motherless in his early childhood and fatherless by age sixteen. He left France to study at Columbia University, and in his early twenties, became a monastic at Our Lady of Gethsemani in Kentucky. His spiritual autobiography *Seven Storey Mountain* was immediately celebrated, then followed by many other writings, not all limited to the internal life, but all informed by his faith. Merton did not himself claim to have reached "illumination," but wrote about God's desire for intimacy with us, and about the significance of the faith in every area of life, blending the monastic life with the prophetic vocation. He emphasized the *exilic* nature of the Christian pilgrimage, and was not afraid to face the wilderness experience in his contemplations, since Christ's passion has taken the sting out of hell. This realism spoke strongly to a generation that had seen the atrocities of two World Wars, the drab senselessness of Vietnam, and the emptiness of self-love, so popular from the sixties onward. Amidst the noise and pragmatism of North America, he writes:

> We are living through the greatest crisis in the history of man; and this crisis is centered precisely in the country that has made a fetish out of action and has lost (or perhaps never had) the sense of contemplation. Far from being irrelevant, prayer, meditation, and contemplation are of the utmost importance in America today. (*Contemplation in a World of Action*, p. 178)

Contemplative prayer, or listening in quiet, is countercultural in our frenzied world, and so he tried to recover for the Christians of our day the awareness of those ancients who learned to rest in God's presence, to see the value of "unknowing" and to pray so as to become unaware of even their action of prayer. In his work, he cites Pseudo-Dionysius, St. Anthony of the Desert, and others. He commended to those who would listen the "holy indifference" that those who walked with God possessed, because God was their defender and God was their reward.

The great humility of this man is seen in his warning that those who have grasped something of God's holiness and love, never see ourselves as "teaching contemplation" to others — that is for God to do. We might want to add, that God teaches not simply personally, but through the assembly of the Church, in worship. Some have worried (and perhaps with reason) that Thomas sometimes blurred the distinctions between Christian and other (especially Buddhist and Sufi) forms of meditation. Nevertheless, his most powerful insights come from the heart of Christianity — one must love God solely for his sake alone, not for peace, nor transformation, nor for any other gift; and once one has been "wounded" by joy, this love overflows to others:

> We do not see God in contemplation — we know him by love; for he is pure Love. . . . God does not give his joy to us for ourselves alone, and if we could possess him for ourselves alone, we would not possess him at all. Any joy that does not overflow from our souls and help other men to rejoice in God does not come to us from God. (*New Seeds of Contemplation*, p. 268)

No doubt those who seek God with this desire for the Lord enshrined in their heart will find (or be found by!) that true God of love, the Father, Son, and Holy Spirit, whom Merton describes as leading the cosmos in the great "dance," that ecstatic movement in which we "forget ourselves on purpose" for the sake of joy.

Evelyn Underhill (1875-1941), a slightly older contemporary to Merton, is exemplary for bringing together the *doxa* of creed and worship. (Let us recall that *orthodoxy* means "right belief" and "right worship.") Her writings are bracing for the mind, and seductively warming for the heart, as she was one who insistently kept heart and mind together. An Anglo-Catholic, her work was nourished by her years as a retreat leader, lay theologian, and founder of the Fellowship of St. Alban and St. Sergius (in which Anglicans and Eastern Orthodox met together). She was educated at King's College, Oxford, converted and married in her early thirties, and wrote her well-known book on *Mysticism* several years later. Some may find her little book *The Spiritual Life* even more helpful. She begins by warning,

Any spiritual view which focuses attention on ourselves, and puts the human creature with its small ideas and adventures in the center foreground, is dangerous till we recognise its absurdity. So at least we will try to get away from these petty notions [that spirituality is about myself; that it is for special people] and make a determined effort to see our situation within that great spiritual landscape which is so much too great for our limited minds to grasp, and yet is our true inheritance. (*The Spiritual Life*, p. 12)

To a busy age, so consumed with action, she cried out: "We mostly spend [our] lives conjugating three verbs: to Want, to Have, and to Do . . . forgetting that none of these verbs have any ultimate significance, except so far as they are transcended by and included in, the fundamental verb, to Be" (p. 20). Indeed, it is God's action, God's initiative, that is the key to our life: "All takes place within him. He alone matters, he alone is. Our spiritual life is his affair; because, whatever we may think to the contrary, it is really produced by his steady attraction, and our humble and self-forgetful response to it. It consists in being drawn, at his pace and in his way, to the place where he wants us to be; not the place we fancied for ourselves" (p. 35). What happened with the great spiritual theologians was that they caught glimpses of God himself, and God's love, and responded: "A spring is touched, a Reality always there discloses itself in its awe-inspiring majesty and intimate nearness, and becomes the ruling fact of existence; continually presenting its standards, and demanding a costly response" (p. 49). This same communion is God's delight to give every one of us, because "each human spirit is an unfinished product, on which the Creative Spirit is always at work" (p. 44).

Underhill followed the simple spiritual path of the seventeenth century Cardinal de Bérulle, who pictured our pilgrimage towards God in the three actions: Adoration, Adherence, and Cooperation. This dynamic can be seen, for example, in the encounter and transformation of Isaiah during his "thrice-holy" vision: first, the glory of the Lord dazzles; then Isaiah adheres to reality, acknowledging his sinfulness and the state of the world; finally, Isaiah is given his commission. With wit and prophetic fire, Underhill explains the difference in perspective that comes about through adoration:

What really seems to you to matter most? The perfection of his mighty symphony, or your own remarkably clever performance of that difficult passage for the tenth violin? And again, if the music unexpectedly requires your entire silence, which takes priority in your feelings? The mystery and beauty of God's orchestration? Or the snub administered to you? Adoration, widening our horizons, drowning our limited interests in the total interests of Reality, redeems the spiritual life from all religious pettiness, and gives it a wonderful richness, meaning and span. And more, every aspect, even the most homely, of our practical life can become part of this adoring response, this total life; and always has done in those who have achieved full spiritual personality. (*The Spiritual Life*, pp. 64-65)

To be a full person of this sort, adoring the Lord and adhering to reality, not to one's fond dreams of self-importance — to this she incites us, with a light but accurate hand. Face to face with the Lord, and soberly aware of the world as it truly is, we, with Isaiah, may well find ourselves responding "Here am I, send me!" — without regard for the results. Each time we pray "thy Kingdom *come*" there is an urgent note of cooperation sounded, as we are called to "costly collaboration with the Spirit in whom we believe" (p. 83). The kind of self-giving which Underhill here envisages produces in the human being a rare threefold quality, commended first by St. John of the Cross — "Tranquility, Gentleness, and Strength" (p. 93). For *"we ourselves form part of the creative apparatus of God"* (p. 104). We are parts of that real world God has created, instruments forged for its re-creative healing; or, if you like, we are musical instruments, that in our own turn, are being repaired, tuned, or made true to middle C, and perfected by him for his own creative purposes.

Along with this great mercy, and heady calling, come some practical and sobering thoughts — that we must have formed within us the particular shape that God has in mind, which means "selecting in order to achieve." We have "a whole psychological zoo living within us" (p. 115) — and from the multiple opportunities may come chaos, rather than character, unless we both allow God to prune us and cooperate with this process by self-discipline. (This pastoral wisdom speaks to our own age, which has seen first the midlife crisis, born of wistful second thoughts, and now the "twenty-something" crisis, catalyzed by the paralyzing range of possibilities made available in a self-gratifying age.) At first, our life duties may seem a distraction from God's purpose, but indeed, he works within them, if we turn our work to prayer, and if we allow some devoted time to the work of the Spirit within us. Here again is to be found that "tension" seen time and time again — that God is present in all of our life, yet calls us to intimacy set aside for him alone. Creation can mediate his love, power, and mercy to us; yet we long to be touched directly by the Creator and Re-Creator. As we consider this longing for maturity, Evelyn Underhill reminds us of the way that our spiritual life proceeds, and sums up, it seems, what we have learned from all these, our older brothers and sisters in the Lord: "there is nothing of the self-made person about the saint":

> So you see, our inheritance of heaven, eternal life, the life of prayer, the full, all 'round development of our Christian vocation means just this: the secure possession and enjoyment of God in proportion as we are unencumbered of ourselves. It does not mean to be clear of jobs, troubles, or sufferings, but merely to be clear of self-regard in every form. We are not self-made, but we are inheritors. What a difference! There is nothing of the self-made person about the saint. There is no grim struggle for their own success. So, too, everything worth having is given to us — not fought for or earned. Thus it may include things we would never have chosen. It may take a form we would never have guessed. Yet is it given by love, and when received by love it brings us to God. That is heaven: the love, joy, and peace of the Spirit harnessed, humbled, and unencumbered of itself. . . . (*The Ways of the Spirit*, p. 240)

With the gift of God in our mind's eye, and imprinted on our hearts, we finish this all-too-brief tour of God's own remarkable household, praying along with one of the youngest in the roll of God-seers:

> . . . O Lord, *thou* art my heritage, the companion of my pilgrimage. . . .
> God is the soul's country. Real prayer must always bring us to that.
> (*The Ways of the Spirit*, p. 240)

Further Reflection

The things that have come into being have received from the Creator their proper place, their beginning and, in some cases, their end. But there is no boundary to virtue. The psalmist says, "I have seen the end of all perfection, but Your commandment is very broad and is without limit" (Psalm 118:96). Now if it is true that some good ascetics pass from the strength of action to the strength of contemplation (cf. Psalm 83:7), and if it is true that love never fails (1 Cor. 13:8), and that the Lord will guard the coming in of your fear and the going out of your love (cf. Psalm 120:8), then love has no boundary, and both in the present and in the future age we will never cease to progress in it, as we add light to light. Perhaps this may seem strange to many. Nevertheless, it has to be said . . . that even the angels make progress and indeed that they add glory to glory and knowledge to knowledge. (St. John Climacus, ca. 579-649)

The true source-books of Christian spirituality are the Psalter and the New Testament; but this fact is not always appreciated by beginners. The dependent literature is enormous and should be approached with discretion, as advanced books merely confuse and delay those who are not yet ready for their teaching. (Evelyn Underhill, *The Spiritual Life*, p. 127)

Attuned to us is the Deity, like a nursing mother to an infant, watching the time for his benefits, knowing the time for weaning him, both when to rear him on milk and when to feed him with solid food, weighing and offering benefits according to the measure of his maturity. (St. Ephrem the Syrian, *Hymns on the Church* 25.18)

FURTHER READING

All of these readings are excerpted in the section above, and are listed here in chronological order.

Joseph and Aseneth. Translated by C. Burchard. In *The Old Testament Pseudepigrapha* II, edited by James H. Charlesworth, pp. 177-247. Garden City, N.Y.: Doubleday, 1985.

St. Augustine of Hippo. *The Confessions*. In *Augustine of Hippo — Selected Writings*, translated by Mary T. Clark. Mahwah, N.J.: Paulist Press, 1984.

St. John Chrysostom. *The Divine Liturgy of St. John Chrysostom*. Available online at http://www.ewtn.com/library/LITURGY/DILITSJC.TXT. The

Divine Liturgy is available in many printed editions, including *The Great Book of Needs* I. South Canaan, Pa.: St. Tikhon's Seminary Press, 1998. On St. John and the liturgy, read the April 1999 lecture by Bishop Kallistos Ware, "Approaching Christ the Physician: the True Meaning of Confession and Anointing," available online at http://www.incommunion.org/kal3.htm.

St. Gregory of Nyssa. "Sermon Six on the Beatitudes." In *The Lord's Prayer; The Beatitudes*, translated by Hilda C. Graef. Westminster, Md: Newman, 1954.

————. *Life of Moses*. In *Gregory of Nyssa: The Life of Moses*, translated by Abraham Malherbe and Everett Ferguson. Mahwah, N.J.: Paulist, 1978.

————. *Commentary on the Song of Songs*. In *From Glory to Glory: Texts from Gregory of Nyssa's Mystical Writings*, translated by Herbert Musurillo. Crestwood, N.Y.: St. Vladimir's Seminary Press, 1979.

St. Maximos the Confessor. *Chapters on Knowledge* and *The Church's Mystagogy*. In *Maximus Confessor — Selected Writings*, translated by George Berthold. Mahwah, N.J.: Paulist Press, 1985.

St. Symeon the New Theologian. *Hymns of Divine Love by Symeon the New Theologian*. Translated by G. A. Maloney. Denville, N.J.: Dimension, 1976.

St. Gregory Palamas. *The Triads*. Edited by J. Meyendorff. Crestwood, N.Y.: St. Vladimir's Seminary Press, 1983.

Julian of Norwich. *Showings*. Translated by E. Walsh. Mahwah, N.J.: Paulist Press, 1978.

Thomas à Kempis. *The Imitation of Christ*. Translated by J. J. Gorman. Brooklyn, N.Y.: Confraternity of the Precious Blood, 1982.

St. Teresa of Ávila. *The Interior Castle*. In *The Collected Works of St. Teresa of Avila* II. Translated by K. Cavanaugh. Washington, D.C.: Institute of Carmelite Studies, 1980.

St. John of the Cross. "One Dark Night" and *The Ascent of Mount Carmel — The Dark Night*. In *The Collected Works of St. John of the Cross*, translated by K. Cavanaugh. Washington, D.C.: Institute of Carmelite Studies, 1976.

John and Charles Wesley. "A Plain Account of Genuine Christianity" and "Wrestling Jacob." In *Selected Prayers, Hymns, Journal Notes, Sermons, Letters, and Treatises*, edited by F. Whaling. Mahwah, N.J.: Paulist Press, 1981. For a meeting of Western and Eastern minds, and on similarities and differences between Orthodox and Wesleyan spirituality, see S. T. Kimbrough, Jr., *Orthodox and Wesleyan Spirituality*, Crestwood, N.Y.: St. Vladimir's Seminary Press, 2002.

Fr. John of Kronstadt. *Spiritual Counsels: Select Passages from* My Life in Christ. Edited by W. J. Grisbrooke. Crestwood, N.Y.: St. Vladimir's Seminary Press, 1967.

Thomas Merton. *New Seeds of Contemplation*. New York: New Directions, 1962.

————. *Contemplation in a World of Action*. Garden City: Doubleday, 1973.

Evelyn Underhill. *The Spiritual Life*. New York: Harper and Bros, 1936.

————. *The Ways of the Spirit*. New York: Crossroad, 1993.

FURTHER DISCUSSION

1. Which of the spiritual theologians or mystics intrigues you the most and why?
2. Which parts of the Scriptures seem to be emphasized most often by these writers? Can you see why these passages are particularly helpful in the cultivation of the life of the Spirit?
3. Which of these writers seems the most alien to our culture, or to the thinking of our generation? What can be learned from this strangeness?
4. What common themes or ideas run throughout the writers?

C

Icons of Love — Communion in Friendship, Family, Marriage, and Church

Our last foray led us into that strange country of the mystic; yet in the midst of the pilgrimage, perhaps we had an unexpected sense of familiarity, as though we had been there before. Now let us spend some time inhabiting the all-too-familiar world of human relationships; here it may be that we will find things stranger, deeper, more "mystical" than we had expected! "True mysticism is to discover the extraordinary in the ordinary," is the insight of the French theologian Olivier Clément. After all, are we not always remarking upon the oddness of our encounters with other persons — "How wise that baby's eyes look!" "Doesn't she look strangely like her father?" "It is bizarre, as though we have always known each other. . . ." "I never knew he had it in him!" Moreover, just when we feel that we have understood someone, or nailed down their personality in our mind, we discover some new strength, weakness, endearing quality, or frustrating quirk that we never expected. We might have anticipated what the God-seer has discovered, that God's essence exceeds the bounds of human understanding, yet this Mysterious One calls us to share in communion with him. What we may not have accounted for is the depth of mystery implanted within those who bear his image, with whom we naturally expect to have concourse.

This means that though we share together in the human mode of existence, there is a definite sense in which every human being I know is remarkably and pleasingly "other" to me. Indeed, because I am ultimately God's creature, and not my own, there is also a sense in which I remain, so to speak, bracingly "other" even to myself. As one who is in the process of becoming, I can hardly understand all that I am to be. As a complex being in which God has brought together spirit, soul, and body, I am continually startled to find, within myself, things that bind me to other creatures.

We are not speaking here only about the estrangement between human beings, or the barrier to self-understanding, that comes as a result of the Fall. Certainly prejudice and blindness regarding other human beings, and even within our own psyche, mark our fallen existence. The answer to such human walls comes when we acknowledge those sort of humanitarian truths uttered by, among others, the Latin poet Terence: "I consider nothing human alien to me." Rather, we are considering here that delightful "otherness," that intriguing depth in the mate which is an essential ingredient of true human communion — as anyone who has been in love, or had their first baby, or joined a church, or found their "kindred spirit" discovers. There are whole worlds, then, made even more complex by our fallen condition, to discover within anyone whom we love, and within ourselves, too. As St. Macarius, spiritual theologian of the fourth century, puts it,

> Within the heart are unfathomable depths. . . . It is but a small vessel: and yet dragons and lions are there, and there poisonous creatures and all the treasures of wickedness; rough, uneven paths are there, and gaping chasms. There likewise is God, there are the angels, there life and the Kingdom, there light and the Apostles, the heavenly cities and the treasures of grace: all things are there. (*Homilies* 15.32; 43.7)

It is essential to realize that Macarius is *not* saying that the spiritual life is simply "a state of mind," so that there is no actual existence of God, angels, and the New Jerusalem outside of our own thoughts and feelings: that would be a concept only possible in our psychologically-oriented and solipsistic age. Rather, he is remarking upon the distinctive nature of human existence, the fact that our all-wise God has created us as mediating, or "go-between" creatures, who each and together portray a "microcosm" of reality.

A glance back at Genesis, at the foundational first Act of the human drama, reminds us of this. God creates the world, and then crowns it with his masterpiece: "So God created man in his own image, in the image of God he created *him*; male and female he created *them*." We are one, yet we are male and female. We are in the image of God, yet we are corporeal, sexual beings along with the animals. And God blesses this state of affairs, giving the command to both be fruitful and to wisely govern the rest of creation. The sixth day ends on a high note. Not only does God note that it was good: *it was very good* (1:31). For in the human being, God has made a creature that is, as C. S. Lewis has put it, "amphibious" — at home in the realm of matter and in the realm of spirit. The great act of the Incarnation, in which God assumed humanity, offers the highest confirmation of this wonderful mode of being.

That we are created in God's image means that we should expect to find, in our fellowship with each other, echoes of God's own communion. Our human relationships are important in themselves, but remain holy and beautiful exactly in the proportion that they truly mirror the life of the Trinity, and indeed, point us to the One from whom all communion springs. We can, then, look at the mystery of human relationships from two different ends — that mystery is contingent upon the God of Love; and it magnifies our loving God. It is in the latter sense that we can understand rightly ordered human liaisons, true but differing forms of communion, as *living icons* of the Trinity. That is, when a human being truly communes with another or others, we see not simply a symbol, or metaphor, but a remarkable theological picture, a solid love infused with God's glory, that directs us *through* it *to* the One who is Real Love in himself.

Some, among them the theologian Karl Barth, have been nervous of theology that is based upon a presumed "analogy of being," that is, when we trace a trajectory *from* the created order *to* God. They argue that we should never make an easy link between the natural realm and the divine mystery, because revelation of the truth comes from God to us, not because of what we can extrapolate from our human situation. Their caution is salutary, especially for those who speak too glibly of God's nature, and forget that God remains, as Creator over against creature, totally other. Not only our weak human nature, but also our condition as *fallen* creatures should make us shy of reasoning from our experience to God. That would be for the tail to wag the dog — or, rather, to try to wag the Maker of dogs and tails!

However, by the Incarnation, God the Son assumed human nature: dogs, tails, and human eyes to love them, have been visited intimately by the One who has all things in his care. So every part of our life is informed by, and indeed, may direct us to, the God of life, light, and love, *so long as we are in Christ, and remain there.* The great spiritual theologians discovered this, as we have seen, when (astonished!) they caught the grandeur of God in the tiny microcosm of an acorn, or the image of God stamped upon even the most debauched human face. Yet it is not by means of the individual, but through human beings in communion, that God's glory is seen, and that God most characteristically touches his people. Certainly our human fellowships are strained, distorted, and frequently the locale of great pain. Certainly they are in need of healing and nurture from the One who is communion itself. Yet our fragile human liaisons are able, in their feeble way, and in the light of the Christian story, to direct us Godward. Because God's nature has been, in part, revealed to us, and because we have been caught up into the drama of God's action, we can understand our various forms of human communion as bound up with God's own being and action.

Hidden among my cookbooks, relegated there by my embarrassed teenage daughter, is a small, framed photograph that used to sit beside the bust of Beethoven on our piano. It is the photo of a young girl, perhaps seven years of age, playing the violin with utter abandon. She stands jubilantly, one foot up on the piano stool — good thing her instructor did not see this posture! — like Tevye's fiddler on the roof. The picture is not only a paradigm of ecstasy, but of intimacy as well. For the girl child is dressed only in undies, and has the family's budgie perched atop her head at a rakish angle, a kind of hat to her bobbed hair. Eleven years later, as an adolescent, she perhaps considers the photo a kind of intrusion, a violent capture of a "private" moment in her life. Yet all the details of the frozen scene scream out that this was not private, but a time of communion — though intimate communion for an inside group. Consider the levels of fellowship: rapture with the musician whose music has whisked her away; delight in the bird, who may have been chirping along; shared fun with the maternal photographer, who knows what the instructor would say about this unorthodox practice scene, and whose usual place is at the seat of the piano, accompanying her. All this is going on in the living room, the place where the family plays, works, and entertains. In this homely moment, we see a symbol of life at its best, where there is an intersection of numerous relationships, coupled with a shared joy between two family members, and the photographic promise that the joy will overflow to others. Here is a classic example of ecstasy and intimacy: the

Alexandra with her violin

episode is significant in itself, while it also acts as a pointer, a light, to the One who gives us all this, and more.

It was contemplation of my daughter Alex's photo, indeed, and remembrance of that poignant moment, that served as the initial catalyst for this study on *Ecstasy and Intimacy*. God provides many ways to draw us to himself, one of them being the wonder of human conviviality. So then, we move on to consider human interconnection as a facet of Christian spirituality, looking at the interrelation between friends, parents and children, spouses, and siblings, both natural and spiritual. In following this pattern, we begin with the least "physical" and most deliberately chosen tie, move on to the strong natural link between parent and child, and inward to the passionate communion between husband and wife, before broadening out to consider the sibling tie which by its nature is bound up with others, whether in the family or in the Church. We take our cue from God's own dictum: "It is not good that Adam should be alone."

Friends

Tragically, friendship, which was an object of great fascination to our learned ancestors, is little discussed today. This does not mean, of course, that people no longer value friends. However, of all the connections in which human beings find themselves, deep friendship seems to be the union least practical, least obviously necessary, on the physical plane, for our actual survival. Romantic love, for example, is connected with the bearing of children, parental love with the nurture that young ones require, and contractual liaisons (rather than actual friendship) are sufficient to ensure the continuation of a family, community, or nation. Again, the great mobility of today's society militates against the development of long-term friendship, and our frenzied pace does not afford us the leisure either to cultivate real friendships, much less to contemplate the importance of friendship. Indeed, the egalitarian or democratic ideals of our age may actually lead us to regard solid friendship with a jaundiced eye. Gathering with one or two others inevitably leads to the exclusion of those not embraced in the fraternity, sisterhood, or class. Add to this the current obsession with romantic and/or sexual love; the suspicion of many today who would reduce any same-sex intimacy to the homoerotic; and the pragmatic, cynical, and self-absorbed tenor of our age, and we can understand why this significant form of human concourse has been so eclipsed.

As C. S. Lewis remarks, "To the Ancients, Friendship seemed the happiest and most fully human of all loves; the crown of life and the school of virtue. The modern world, in comparison, ignores it" (*The Four Loves*, p. 69). The ancients, we will see, were not far off the mark in giving such honor to this form of communion. Although inevitably connected with utility and pleasure, true friendship is distinguished, said Aristotle, because it is not entered into for these reasons. Most other human relationships are entered into for either advantage or pleasure, whereas the friend is loved for what he or she is in himself or herself. So, then, authentic friendship combines a great devotion, or esteem, of a person, with a frank disinterest in personal gain, and a non-pragmatic attitude. It is not a relationship that is strictly necessary, but is characterized by its *discretionary* quality. Though all friendships are asymmetrical, in that no two persons are complete peers in every respect, all of us know the difference between an alliance based on need or duty, and a truly free bond in which friends delight in each other as well as in mutual deep-seated interests.

As Christians, we would no doubt want to qualify the absolutism of the Confucian proverb, "Have no friends not equal to yourself," for we have been called to consider each other "better than ourself" (Philippians 2:3). The saying points out rightly that "equality" or "matching" seems inherent to friendship, though we will want to admit that there are different strengths in different people. Because we are many-faceted, I may have a deep friend who cannot be yours, because this person answers to something in me — a quality, a temperament, a keen interest, a perspective — that he or she does not quite match in you. She is my *peer* in a sense that she cannot be yours; yet this should not mar the friendship that you and I have together. Friendship, then, grows best in the soil of reciprocity, and sometimes can include several, rather than simply a pair, who enjoy mutual esteem and share a similar outlook on life, or concern, or love, or whose interests intersect.

When we consider a good friendship, mutuality is definitive: both must be friends of the other, or all of the others. Curiously, friendship has by nature *both* an exclusive and inclusive property. Not everyone is my "friend," though as a Christian, I strive to be at peace with all, must practice the unconditional love of Christ even to the enemy, and can often be a companion to many. To recognize someone as a friend, and to be so recognized, means that there is a quality very particular about this conjunction, something that is not entered into with others: immaturity is not the only reason that the elementary school-aged child recognizes a "best friend." In the sense that friendship is directed towards the particular person, and preferential when it discovers and responds to the "saltiness" of that one, the conjunction is exclusive, even "jealous."

Yet, because friendship is initiated, or deepened, as the friends focus upon something outside of their own togetherness, there is an inherent inclusivity here, for the passion or subject matter is a third factor in the network. Indeed, because of the regard that each friend has for the other, and especially because of the shared object(s) of interest, friendship also has the potential for drawing in others: a true friend will be at least curious about the other friends of the comrade, and open to seeing in them what the other sees; especially wonderful is when a pair encounters that "Aha!" experience regarding a common concern with a third, or fourth newfound friend. The symbiosis of an authentic circle of friends, based not on pride or exclusion of others, but on true respect and shared concentration upon something beyond the group, is a phenomenon unto itself; yet what the group has together is not exactly the same thing that a pair of friends within the group possesses. Indeed, one member of the circle may be the "glue" between the other members, that one whose characteristics overlap and draw together two very different people, who would not themselves be easy friends without the ministrations of the go-between: yet when he or she is there, an intimate affection and group ecstasy are inevitably released.

Though some have remarked upon the progression within the Christian tradition, where *agape* (altruistic love) has tended to replace *philia* (friendship), amity is indeed exalted not simply by pagan philosophers, but also in the Bible, both in narrative (as in, for example, Jonathan and David) and in adage:

Friends always show their love. What are brothers for if not to share troubles? (Proverbs 17:17)

Some friendships do not last, but some friends are more loyal than brothers. (Proverbs 18:24)

Forsake not an old friend; for the new is not comparable to him: a new friend is as new wine; when it is old, thou shall drink it with pleasure. (Sirach 9:10)

An honest answer is the sign of true friendship. (Proverbs 24:26)

A friend means well, even when he hurts you. But when an enemy puts his hand round your shoulder — watch out! (Proverbs 27:6)

A faithful friend is a sturdy shelter; he who finds one finds a treasure. (Sirach 6:14)

Iron sharpens iron; so a man sharpens his friend's countenance. (Proverbs 27:17)

In case we think this is simply an Old Testament preoccupation, we recall one of Jesus' parting statements to his disciples: "I no longer call you servants, but friends." It is interesting to notice that in the biblical witness, friendship is seen as not simply enjoyable, but also *salutary*, in a two-directional sense — the true friend is honest even when this is not convenient, and ready to sharpen his friend, or shelter her when necessary. Typically, friendship was understood in ancient societies as something that occurred between members of the same sex, both because of conceptions of equality, and because of possible complications due to romance or social skepticism. However, we can trace, beginning in the ancient Christian world, the opening of a possibility for heterosexual friendship — though the virtue of this was usually safeguarded by assuming either a sibling or parental relationship (spiritual brother and sister, father and daughter, mother and son). During the monastic period, the parental relationships flourished, whereas in contemporary times, we see the example of the Quaker "Society of Friends" in which members name each other as sibling. In early Christian centuries, we can note the amity between Paul and Junias (first century), the fellowship between the martyrs Perpetua and Saturus (late second century), the affection between the martyr Sabina and the priest Pionius (late second century), the closeness of Basil to his pupil and canoness Theodora (third century), and the regard of Gregory Nazianzen for "*my* Theosebia," a godly woman who was the sister of Gregory of Nyssa (late third century). No doubt, despite their disparate ages, St. Teresa and St. John also enjoyed a friendship in which both delighted in the other, and in their common passion for Christ and for those things that fostered the internal life of the Spirit. In each of these cases, the New Testament declaration that there is no longer "male and female" provided a new matrix so that a common bond of disinterested affection, and common affection for an interest, could be pursued in holiness of intent.

Friendship, then, has a double focus — the friends' regard for each other, and the common interest shared. These two aspects mean that friendship is, by nature, both intimate and ecstatic. There is a going out from person to person, and their common rapture with something else, which creates the environment for an intimate tie; or, perhaps the process goes the other way, with intimacy between person and person creating the ability for an increasing going out both to each other and to the shared thing. With regards to the internal and external foci of friendship, women appear to place more weight upon the concern for each other (intimacy) and men upon the shared interest (ecstasy). It is not clear whether this is a feature of nature or of socialization, or even whether these two "causes" can be so easily divided. We are not surprised, however, that women, who commonly give pride of place to the personal aspects of life, find themselves in close concourse with other women who are very different: if they are mothers. It may be the playing children in the playground that play the role of their "common interest," but soon they will know much about each other's "private" lives; later in life, such women, originally thrown together by duties they had when they were younger, will maintain a most unlikely connection! Alternately, men frequently forge deep friendships through a shared passion, and yet sometimes know almost nothing about each other's lives. However, with time and a growth in the bond, both ecstasy and intimacy will deepen. The friend who has been similarly absorbed will surely take on significance for his or her own self; the one whom I find so dear in his or her own self will entice me to join in a new diversion.

If I trust my friend, then, I will not be reserved in disclosing to her (or him) my own enthrallment in something — there will be no fear of "pearls before swine." Or, if we are commonly bound up in a matter of significance, I may trust this companion with a close secret of my heart. We have already, after all, come together around common affection for the other and a shared attentiveness to an outside concern or activity: we have had that surprising confluence of intimacy and ecstasy, and hope that this can proceed in a new direction. This does not mean, of course, that there is no place for reserve in friendship, for friends live in a fallen world, and are forging a specific form of intimacy that must remain true to its own shape. It is probably unwise, for example, for Christian friends, male and female, to go backpacking alone together for a month in the Rockies unless they are prepared for their affection to take a different form! And it is certainly unwise for friend to tell friend something that belongs strictly within the privacy of another bond, for example, something of concern to one of the friends and his or her marriage partner. Even where confidences are perfectly legitimate, the discerning friend will become aware of the other's predisposition and limits, and not force the alliance in a way that is uncomfortable, or tedious, for his or her companion. Friendship includes courtesy and boundaries.

Friendship appears difficult to define in concrete terms, because it emerges in conviviality between friends: each friendship has its unique contours. We have seen, however, that there is a constellation of common characteristics that we recognize as proper to friendship. Friends concern themselves with each other and with a shared passion; they are not fixed upon the usefulness of the conjunction; there is an easy communion that they share which is distinguished from other alliances, such as romance. (However, some have indeed found that friendship can be combined with another type of bond.) Because ecstasy and intimacy are inherent in friendship, friendship is also tied up with our spiritual life, the locale of total ecstasy and intimacy. As Christians, we have seen that spirituality participates, through the incarnate Jesus and the Spirit, in the Triune God, the source of love, light, and life. How, then, does the life condition of friendship serve as both a light by which we can understand more of our loving God, and also as a focal point for God's refracted light, a conduit of God's very own love?

We can approach our answer to these two questions by way of the characteristics that we have seen in friendship — mutuality, "equality," exclusivity, inclusivity, and absorption in something shared. Each aspect of human friendship, through parallel and contrast to the life of the Trinity, helps to enlighten our understanding of God; each is also capable of mediating God's love and light to us. The reciprocity or mutuality of friends, for example, is a faint echo of the *perichoretic* dynamism that we have been told of (though can hardly grasp) between Father, Son, and Spirit. Nevertheless, because of our human condition, our "boundedness," there is a sense in which the mutuality between friends is always partial — friendship retains a growing edge, a fragility, in which total intimacy can never be assumed or forced, else it ceases to be friendship. Even while we disclose ourselves personally to the other, there remains the "mystery" of the other, which a good friend will learn to cherish, and not try to obliterate. (And, we should remind ourselves, friendship ceases to be friendship when physical boundaries, or — more elusive, "desire" boundaries — are overstepped, and *eros* enters the picture. The ease of friendship yields then to the desire to possess and be possessed.)

Though we must tread carefully here, it would seem that it is otherwise with the Persons of the Godhead. Father, Son, and Spirit share one essence, "co-inhere" or indwell each other, and share characteristics through *perichōresis:* we conclude, though tentatively, that their bond excludes mystery, with nothing hidden one from the other, even while they remain distinct in some ineffable way. *Their* utter mutuality is matched with an eternal quality, something not experienced in the temporary nature of our friendships, which always have a beginning, and sometimes (through circumstances or death) have an end — even though St. Jerome declared that "the friendship that can cease has never been real." Perhaps, for those in Christ, the doctrine of the communion of saints gives us hope that this *reality* to friendship, its enduring quality, is by God's gift eternal. Even this, however, is not in the bare nature of friendship, but something forged because we are in Christ. Where human beings are concerned, the contingent quality of friendship must ever be acknowledged, because we are not *settled* in who we are, and so can both surprise and be surprised in our alliances with others. While growing apart is a sadness that many of us have undergone, outright infidelity, given or received, brings anguish. The psalmist laments concerning the great pain of being betrayed by "my equal, my companion, my familiar friend [with whom he] used to hold sweet converse together [while walking] within God's house in fellowship" (Psalm 55:13). Such perfidy came the way of the perfect human, Jesus, who among us all, possessed the qualities necessary to keep friendship sound — his affliction at the hands of his brother Judas, with whom he ate and shared all things, shows that none of us is exempt from the vicissitudes of friendship. This intimate alliance is indeed a hard school of virtue, as Aristotle remarked, and the breaking of it excruciating. Only God has the wherewithal to create light in this dark shadow side of human communion. Paradoxically, it is even through the betrayal of the Son by his human family that God brought about our healing. In taking on, or assuming, human friendship, inevitably accompanied by that dark moment of violent disloyalty, God the Son rescues us. For Jesus, our brother as well as our friend, the "dark night of the soul" had no purpose other than to bring us into the light. So God's wholeness thus floods our partial communions, and heals them.

Both the similarity and dissimilarity of our amities to the communion of the Trinity thus become instructive: a vibrant friendship can teach us something about the wonder of God, but also serves to remind us of how far short we fall of the divine bond. This is particularly true with regard to the factor of equality that the ancients so prized among friends. Of course, they, like us, expected, in the rough and tumble of life, that equality in friendship would be mitigated by disagreements, correction, and reproof — that is, times when one or the other partner takes "the high ground" in the relationship. Because of the frailty of human nature, we also experience this lack of symmetry whenever one party of a friendship is in need, and the other is called upon to help. Such moments are commonly experienced as a disruption of the free association of friends, a momentary bump in the true business of enjoying each other and the friendship's common interest. However, the biblical writings do not themselves uphold our visceral feeling that friendships are best, freest, when they do not require succor: in the wisdom tradition, we see that the elements of "salt" and "light" are part and parcel of comradeship. For the most part, however, we cherish free exchange over dependency, empathy over sympathy, rapport over discord. So we thrill to the words of Jesus when he says, "I no longer call you servants, but friends," yet perhaps recoil when we hear his mold-breaking words, "The greatest love a person can have for his friends is to give his life for them" (John 15:13). Jesus will not allow us the fantasy of independence, for indeed, we *need* our friend to bear our burden, and must, if we are Christians, be prepared to be burden-bearers, as well. Only the Father, Son, and Spirit have the kind of disinterested love, unencumbered by need, to which friendship aspires, because only these have the equality that such an association requires. Again, Jesus will not allow us the fantasy of preference, for, contrary to folk wisdom, human beings do not sovereignly choose their friends — "friendship happens." Only God has the prerogative of freely choosing humanity to be his friends!

The tension between exclusivity and inclusivity in friendship remains fascinating. Emily Dickinson suggests a natural difference between our inclinations and the generosity of God in this regard. She admits, with bracing candor, "My friends are my estate. Forgive me then the avarice to hoard them. They tell me those who were poor early have different views of gold. I don't know how that is. God is not so wary as we, else he would give us no friends, lest we forget him." Not all "exclusivity" in friendship springs from the fallen nature, however. Again, we can only suggest how it may be with the Godhead, for their "friendship" is known to Father, Son, and Spirit alone. Yet it is helpful to remember how the church theologians have described their communion, based on the revelation of Scripture. Father and Son have a correlation of begetting and begotten that they do not share with the Spirit; and the Spirit, if the Eastern view is correct, "proceeds" from the Father and not from the Son, at least not in the same way. (Even if the Western version of the creed — "proceeds from the Father and the Son" — is accepted, most theologians agree that Spirit proceeds eternally from the Father in a unique manner, and secondarily from the Son. At any rate, the West likewise tends to distinguish the Spirit as the One who binds together the Son and Father in their self-giving: neither the Son nor the Father have this binding quality. The principle that the modes of connection differ between Persons remains secure.)

So then, even in the utter communion that seems not to have any "mysteries" obscured by or from the three Persons, there is a sharing between pairs that distinguishes Father, Son, and Spirit. Their relations, though mutual to an extent that we can hardly imagine, are not wholly symmetrical in every respect. This means that exclusivity is not by its very nature a product of our created limitations or of the Fall, though frequently in our human context it becomes such. That very subject matter which joins human beings together naturally can, sadly, become a shibboleth, a weapon by which others are summarily dismissed from our fellowship. With God, such pettiness is unthinkable — we are not, by *nature*, a part of the friendship of the Trinity, yet God's very generosity sweeps us up into that communion, as we are baptized into the Triune name. It is out of the divine essence of the Trinity that God's astounding offer of friendship comes. Were the exclusive, special nature of the Trinity to be forgotten, our amazement at God's overflow to us would be lost as well (as, for example, in Mormonism, where all are asserted to be in the process of becoming gods). Whenever the amicable unity of two is secure enough, big enough, to truly admit another without fear of violation or diminution, we are, it seems, refracting the light of the Trinity.

Yet the boundaries themselves give friendship its characteristic form, and remain essential. If I expect my friend to appreciate my other friend in precisely the same way that I do, and if I become jealous of some "life music" that they come to "hear," to which I am tone-deaf, our mutual friendship may be mortally wounded. The nature of friendship as exclusive can well be destroyed by lurking jealousy and exclusivism. One of the benefits of such adventures, if negotiated with prayer and vulnerability, is that I come to understand myself (as well as the others) better: as the seventeenth-century poet George Herbert put it, "The best mirror is an old friend." In the end, these negotiations and short-falls in intercommunication are intended to make of us solider persons, to school us in the art of love, and to drive us to the One from whom all good liaisons come.

Perhaps the closest link to the trinitarian life is seen when we consider how friends are, by nature, caught up into something shared. Certainly this is part of Jesus' meaning when he calls his apostles (and by extension, us) "no longer servants but friends, *because a servant does not know what his master is doing*." Most often throughout John's Gospel, the intimacy of Son with Father and Father with Son is described by the use of the term *agape*, or the verb *agapao* — that altruistic love also enjoined on the Christian community in 1 Corinthians 13. Yet, a few times, the term for friendship (noun *philia*, verb *phileo*) is used. This occurs, significantly, at points where Jesus is explaining the common interest, common will, or common work of Father and Son. So, in John 5:20, we read: "The Father loves [as a friend] the Son and shows him all that he himself is doing."

It is, therefore, out of the sense of mutual concern, or effort, that the friendship of the Trinity springs, and it is when the Son's followers are made cognizant of God's effort that they can themselves be called friends — all this dependent upon what the Father is doing in the Son through the Spirit. It is in this sense that we can understand how it is that the Trinity, without need of anything, and totally self-sufficient, comes to create, and then to re-create and sanctify — or even, in the patristic sense, to divinize! The entire creation is God's common project. In God's case, however, it is not that common work which *constitutes* the trinitarian fellowship, for that is already formed by the communion of Father, Son, and Spirit. Yet we are astonished at the way in which the creation can express or mirror that Mystery, first in hidden terms, and finally with the curtain pulled back in the Incarnation of the Son and ensuing Re-creation of God's own.

In all these things we see "through a glass darkly." But for the Christian who is growing increasingly into the mind of Christ, the common association of friendship, which is today all too uncommon, reveals, through cautious analogy, God's mystery, and in itself can partake of it, especially when lived in the light of the Trinity. Albert Einstein declared, "The most beautiful thing we can experience is the mysterious; it is the true source of art, science, and friendship." Christians will want to rephrase this, saying that there is a most beautiful One with whom we are called to be friends, that Mysterious One, who is indeed the source of true friendship.

Parents and Children

God's first commandment to his creatures, beyond the bare organization of the created order, was that they should "be fruitful and multiply" — this command is given both to the animal kingdom and to humankind. It is in the multiplying that species are established, and in the human sphere that families are born. If the natural beginning of a friendship is in twos, the clearest origin of a human family is in threes — two parents, and their first child. This is not, of course, to say that a married couple is not, at least *in embryo*, a family. But until the most recent times, childless couples considered that they were not realizing their natural potential, one of the major reasons for which marriages were instituted. In most societies, children have been considered the good fruit of a godly marriage — "your children will be like olive shoots around your table" (Psalm 128:3). However, this "fruit" is no mere reward, or possession, to belong to the couple. He or she is created in the image of God, and therefore a potential "friend" in the Lord to the parents!

What, then, of the affinity between parents and children, and its connection with our spirituality? Of all human relationships, we might expect this to provide the most easily retrieved echo of the Holy Trinity, for we are extremely accustomed to hearing God titled "Father" and humankind given the name "children." We discover, however, that this is one of the most misunderstood topics of our day. With the Athenian poet whom St. Paul quoted while evangelizing in the common square, we have frequently reverted to assuming that humankind in general, by virtue of its creation alone, is the "offspring" of God (Acts 17:29). Though the apostle could *use* the poet as a springboard for the gospel as he spoke to the Greeks, the fatherhood of God that he proclaimed was a much deeper truth than any pagan might have imagined. That is, when Paul and other New Testament writers used the term "Father" for God, they were not appealing to an analogy that explains God's creative and sustaining patronage of humanity. Instead, they were declaring that a startling new state of affairs had come into being as a result of the Incarnation. The true Son of God, who became the human being Jesus, has come into solidarity with us, making us his brothers and sisters. So he has opened a way for us to become, in a deep manner that goes far *beyond* analogy, the children of God. The biblically-minded Christian should not think that we are to reason from *our* understanding of human fathers in order to grasp this paternal character of God. It is exactly the reverse. Indeed, every human father is meant to derive his name and character from *God;* every human father and every human family needs to be measured in the light of God, from whom all *fatherhood* and every *family* spring (Ephesians 3:14).

What, then, of mothers? The Hebrew and Christian witness is more muted when it comes to picturing God as mother, though it does so from time to time in metaphor and simile. We have seen how this potential in Scripture is expanded in the devotion of Julian of Norwich (without seeking to replace the normative or revealed name of Father in the Christian creeds). With care, too, the Christian tradition, especially in the East, has understood the *energies,* or outward print of the Holy Spirit in a feminine mode. This insight is to be found especially in the fourth-century poems of St. Ephrem the Syrian, and enshrined in the sixth-century Church of *Hagia Sophia* ("Holy Wisdom") in Istanbul. The understanding seems to go back to St. Paul, who in Romans 8 figures the Spirit as a midwife, helping creation and humanity in their labor pains of the re-creation.

On the whole, however, biblical use of feminine imagery for God is "shy." In our different climate of New Age religion and eclectic goddess spirituality, we must especially heed this reserve. The reasons for it are twofold. First, the role of mother is more naturally assumed by the city of Zion (Isaiah 66), or by the people of God as a whole (Revelation 12), or in Catholic and Orthodox tradition, by Mary, the mother of the Son, because she is understood as embodying God's promise to all redeemed humanity. Second, there is a distinct possibility of misconstruing God's parentage as an emanating, quasi-biological affair, which the close connection between the maternal womb and offspring, nursing mother and babe, might suggest. The late Elizabeth Achtemeier cautioned us that the use of "Mother" as a proper name for God tends to foster an unchristian kind of panentheism (a view that God is in everything) because in using womb language, we are apt to confuse Creator with creature. Liturgies that have explored in this vein frequently end up sexualizing the image of God in a bizarre manner. Here is one prayer that throws caution to the wind:

> Elder woman, from the wine of your womb-love, You create the universe and bring healing to the sick and rejected ones. Pour out upon us the elixir of your divine mercy: that, touched in the innermost parts of ourselves, we are restored as your beloved to wholeness and joy: One whose splendour gave birth to the angels, Eye of wisdom, Holy Sophia, Goddess Three in One. Amen. (Mary Kathleen Speegle Schmitt, *Seasons of the Feminine Divine*)

What worshiping body would accept a parallel prayer that used masculine terminology (e.g., "the seed of your penis-strength") as blatant as the feminine imagery used here? It should be noted that where such feminine sexualized language is being adopted in Christian circles, the catalyst frequently comes from non-Christian sources — as in the above prayer, influenced by Barbara Walker's 1985 book on pagan goddesses, entitled *The Crone*.

Finally, in considering this matter of God's name, we keep in mind the central thrust of this entire book — as Christians we are trinitarians, who have been *given* the name of Father, Son, and Holy Spirit, the Triune God. "Father" is the proper name for God, not simply a title. Jesus gave us the "Our Father"; it is through Jesus we come to know about Father, Son, and Spirit. Though the Old Testament used metaphors, including that of father, to speak of God, in the New Testament "Abba Father" is a name taken up by Jesus, a name that goes beyond a mere picture. As the theologian Pannenberg so aptly marvels, "On the lips of Jesus, 'Father' became a proper name for God. It thus ceased to be simply one designation among others." For us this revealed mystery is meant to be a source of joy, not embarrassment or exclusion of women: "No one knows the Son except the Father, and no one knows the Son and those to whom the Son . . . reveals him" (Matthew 11:27). So then, as trinitarians and incarnational Christians, we believe God *has revealed* himself to us. His mysterious self-revelation will go on and on for eternity, of course — but there is a *givenness* to the truth of what we know now. While we accept the insights of "negative way" mystics, hoping to ever learn more of God's nature, we do not in fact need to struggle to name God, for he has himself given us his name. We cannot avoid or tamper with this revealed name without doing great violence to our understanding of God and our understanding of reality, or, indeed, to our relationship with God and with each other.

With this strong brake in place, we need yet to acknowledge that all good gifts come from the "Father of Lights" — including motherhood itself. It is clear that the gift of human motherhood is eloquent to speak about the Almighty, who helped Eve bear her firstborn (Genesis 4:1), whose life-giving quality is mirrored in Eve, "the mother of all living," and who promises to "take up" the orphan when forsaken by father *and mother*. The close physical connection of mother with suckling child, her fierce and comforting protection of the weak child, her intuitive sense of the child's unspoken need, her "alongside" but wisely reserved mode of presence as the child matures, her painful "holding back" when the child must learn by trial and error, her generosity of giving even when the child does not demonstrate gratitude, her traditional place at the birthing-bed of her grown daughter (now a young woman), her ability to "interpret" young women to her perplexed and courting son — all these actions are redolent of the God who is not only supreme, but humble enough to be *with* and even *in* his people and his creation.

The Bible itself acknowledges all these aspects, from the psalmist who celebrates the calm of the "weaned child" with a God teaching him to grow up and yet remain God-dependent (Psalm 131:2), to the cry of Jesus as a mother hen over Jerusalem, to the New Testament's description of the activity of the Spirit, called alongside, leading us into truth, giving voice to our stalled prayers, participating in our pain, and interpreting Christian to Christian. God as Father stands transcendent and sovereign, source of our being, standard of justice and truth, hope of our own glorification, object of our awe and love; when God acts maternally, we are touched on the inside, so that our capacity for life, light, and love grows. "For all who are led by the Spirit of God are sons of God. . . . Likewise the Spirit helps us in our weakness. . . . [I]n everything God works for good with those who . . . are called according to his purpose" (Romans 8:14, 26, 28). The Spirit within us, redeemed Christians interceding on behalf of their unredeemed friends, humankind giving voice to the labor of the fallen world — we form a set of concentric circles that will issue in glory

(Romans 8:18-25). We, with all creation, become all that we are meant to be. It is by the prophetic and wooing Spirit that, in Christ, "he will turn the hearts of fathers to their children and the hearts of children to their fathers" (Malachi 4:6). For God's deepest desire is to bless and transform, not to smite the land with a curse. Like an ever-hopeful mother, God is *for us* — God is good and loves humankind.

God, then, has freely entered into connection with us, nurturing us and adopting us as his children, so that the "family life" of the Trinity comes to illumine our own sphere. Parents and children do not *choose* their nexus, however, but, in God's economy, find themselves there, willy-nilly. Even while the parent-child bond mirrors God's eternal love within the Trinity as well as God's love for humanity, it also reminds us forcibly of our finite nature. Together and singly, parents stand in an ultimately unavoidable interconnection with their children — this is true biologically, emotionally, and psychologically. Because this contact is particularly susceptible to change through time, it is both a deep-seated and unstable, or malleable, kinship. As many have said, the major purpose of a parent is to make himself or herself redundant, to bring his or her children to a point where they no longer require parenting, but can care adequately for themselves and their own families. Moreover, from our tiny human perspective, this transformation occurs unevenly, but in a relatively short period of time, adding the extra burden of adaptability to the required vigilance of a wise parent.

Typically, fathers and mothers disagree concerning the extent or type of attachment and detachment necessary for child-rearing. Though not always the case, it is safe to say that parenting styles tend to be a source of contention, with some parents insisting that detachment allows children to take responsibility for actions, and others desiring to protect the child against himself or herself. Often, but certainly not always, fathers find themselves taking the former point of view and mothers the latter. These differences in parental styles may either be "natural" or caused by the unbalance of the Fall, or both; regardless, if negotiated well, the complementarity can work for a fruitful situation, with parents making up for one another's shortcomings, for both hands-on and hands-off parenting styles have their strengths and weaknesses.

When the road is not smooth — and often it is not — there is an inbuilt danger for the continuing strong affection between children and parents. After all, while we choose our friends, we do not choose our children, nor do they choose us. However, this sense of "givenness," especially in the choice-crazy climate of our day, tends to magnify any difficulties, whether encountered by the dutiful parent of a difficult child, or by the yearning child of a careless or abusive parent. This relationship is for keeps, though it is intended by its nature to develop and change entirely, even to the point of reversal, in cases where the child becomes the caregiver of the aging parent.

It is in the family that we are most vulnerable, and thus, when sin reigns, that we can be most hurt. We should therefore not be surprised to see that there have been many tortured attempts to avoid the permanence and depth of family life. The absentee father; the resentful mother who has discovered, contrary to what her high-school counselor told her, that she cannot "have it all" without seriously compromising her health or that of her family; the child whose psyche is destroyed by her indulgent parents who neglect to erect boundaries for her or for themselves; the gifted child who is prized as a "possession" and extension of his parents' desires; the billions of throwaway aborted babies whose presence is simply not convenient — none of these scenarios has enabled us to escape the natural relation of parent and child. These are only distortions and tragedies. The stubbornness of an abused child's love for an undeserving parent or the depth of reactive hate harbored by a loved one whose communion with a parent is irrevocably broken both testify to the foundational nature of this bond. Family conviviality finds a dim echo in the animal world, but its human representation is unique, and pregnant with the meaning of who we are, personally and together. Family is where we see, it seems, the best and the worst of human passion and patience.

So, then, despite the snide comments of some biblical scholars regarding the "household code" parts of Paul's letters, Christian instruction regarding families is no pagan additive to the gospel. Rather, the incarnate God, who deigned himself to have a mother, and adopted a human father, whose way was prepared by a cousin, and of whose siblings at least one became a leader in the church — this incarnate God has, by his entry into our world, sanctified the family, and made it a major place where we are to grow up in him. We could have expected nothing other from the God whose Ten Commandments to Israel included the law that children respect parents, and who offered a reward for this obedience! So, then, the love, duty, and courtesy enjoined in Ephesians 6 and Colossians 3 are utterly significant and entirely in order. They do not simply mimic the customs of an ancient time, but include a few Christian surprises — for example, the dismantling of the Roman ideal of an omnipotent *paterfamilias* ("father of the family"), and the caution that fathers not dishearten their children. The Incarnation affirms family sodality in totality, rendering the relationship between parent and child a holy icon of God's love for humanity, and for each one of us.

At the same time, however, the Christian story is *iconoclastic* with regard to our fond assumptions regarding the composition and given nature of family members. So, for example, in 1 Timothy, we hear about the unnatural "fatherhood" over a church of a young man, who is told not to allow his congregants to despise his authority, because "prophetic utterances" have been spoken over him. Again, the disruptive quality of the gospel must sit uneasily alongside instruction to keep families intact: Jesus reminded his followers that being on the Christian way might involve being rejected, or having to "leave" (at least in lifestyle) a father, mother, or even child who will not answer to the higher calling of Christ. "Who are my mother and brethren? Those who do the will of God."

The new creation also means that we have been adopted into a newly constituted family, and so there will be frequent astonishments for us. I may find myself being "fostered" by a Christian mother or father in the Lord not of my choosing, when I am by nature an independent person, for whom humility is not easy. Or, a private person who is embarrassed to be in someone else's business, I may discover that, in the Church and in the community, I am called to nurture or sacrifice for "children" I never expected to have. Paul, with the Corinthian and Galatian churches, found himself paying the price of emotions and energy that he might not have expected when he first preached the gospel to them. He likens his concern for them to that of "parents" who lay up what is necessary "for children" (2 Corinthians 12:14), taking on the role both of a father eager to "present" his church "as a pure bride to one husband [Christ]" (2 Corinthians 11:2) and of a mother to his "little children, with whom [he is] again in travail until Christ be formed in [them]" (Galatians 4:19).

In Protestant circles, the likening of a spiritual mentor to a mother or a father has been resisted as (literally!) too "Popish," with the words of Jesus "Call no man father" ringing in the ears. It is true that the new covenant has created a direct communion of the Holy Spirit, and that believers are each and all children of the Father. God has no grandchildren.

So then, even churchly parentage needs to feel the radical edge of the gospel, with a father in the Lord extending liberty to the ones he is offering spiritual guidance, and the children or recipients of such care not resting upon the abilities and holiness of their spiritual guide. However, the Holy Spirit also indwells and glorifies human mentoring relations, and the Scriptures do indeed speak of spiritual fathers and mothers *in the Lord.* The real joy of a spiritual parent is to find himself or herself outstripped by the spiritual depth of a protégé. The greatest legacy any leader can pass on is to render the follower able to walk side-by-side, and to become himself or herself a leader to newcomers on the path.

So parental pain and concern is not something exacted only of church leaders. All Christians who walk by the Spirit are likely to have similar demands made on their affections from their extended spiritual family, even while they may, on the literal family level, be ridiculed for their faith, or kept at arm's length by the wary or jealous family member who does not understand their loyalty to the "household of faith." The role of parenting a child in this confused age may exact an enormous price, both emotional and physical, as the Christian parent stands against the currents of the times, and comes to understand the anguish of the waiting father for a prodigal. Or, contrarily, the Christian parent may, in great pain, find it necessary to cease fruitless rescue attempts, and allow a wayward adult child to go his or her way. This would be to adopt God's style of offered freedom in Romans 1, so that the child feels the full weight of wrong choice and turns, of his or her own will, to the Divine Father who waits with open arms, and runs to see the prodigal returning. For children who are Christians, there are equal demands, since this age does not give much credit to the virtues of humility and obedience. It is a delicate affair for young Christians to seek to mature so that they can, themselves, be taught by the Lord, while at the same time respecting and honoring their parents. This is perhaps a psychologically difficult thing in a Christian household, since the healthy adolescent needs to learn how to "break away" as a person, while not adopting the individualistic lie that each person has only to answer for himself or herself. It is also difficult for a Christian child in a non-Christian household, where respect to mother and father must be balanced by a careful detachment from their unchristian values. Here, the family of the Church and the nurturing guidance of the Holy Spirit are our allies.

For the Christian, then, family relations present a double joy and a double burden — the joy of having a spiritual as well as natural family to participate in as well as to receive nurture from; and the burden of caring for those outside one's natural family, while perhaps being rejected by those family members who do not yet know the truth. The work of the Spirit in this regard is both broadening and deepening: broader as we acknowledge our participation in a large family that crosses geographical, racial, and temporal boundaries; deeper as we participate in God's ultimate complex calling of our own family members, and not just our fond and common aspirations for their success and happiness.

Husband and Wife

We move from parent and child to the "holy of holies" of the family, the spousal bond. Here our spirituality and our sexuality come together, as we consider that which makes us both distinct and inherently interrelated as male and female. Sexuality is as difficult a concept as spirituality, including but not limited to physical aspects. Since we are physical, social, and spiritual beings, it is not likely that we can understand our sexuality, nor our spousal relationships, by considering only one of these spheres. Several clues to the complex nature of our sexuality are given in Scripture itself.

There we see that male and female, masculine and feminine, are considered in various genres and from different angles, from the narratives of creation to the metaphor of God's relationship to Israel (in the Old Testament) and the church (in the New). From the creation narrative or narratives we learn that our created sexual differences are key to our identity as human beings. The solemn declaration of Genesis 1:27 stresses both diversity and unity: "So God created *adam* in his image, in the image of God he created *him*, male and female he created *them*" (my translation). Again, in the more homey stories of Genesis 2 and 3, God creates Adam and Eve with equal dignity, in a complementary but asymmetrical relationship. They are intimately connected for good or ill, in blessing and in deprivation. Taken as a whole, these chapters say that sexual distinctions are part of God's good (very good!, 1:31) creation. It is not good for Adam to be alone: the first and greatest answer, on the human plane, was Eve.

Yet sexuality and the spousal relationship, along with other facets of human life, have been deeply affected by sin and by divinely imposed limitations. The judgment declared for disobedience — "You shall surely die" — is partly fulfilled in the less-than-spontaneous and complicated inter-relations in which humans, even in their most intimate bonds, now labor. Yet the bond created in the beginning between husband and wife still retains its original stamp of goodness, for in it Eve becomes the "mother of the living" and in their harsher surroundings human beings learn the marvel of interdependence and dependence upon the One who has made them in two sexes. This interdependence is presented as part of the initial and perfect will of God. "It is not good for Adam to be alone" finds an answering exultation by Adam — "This is bone of my bone and flesh of my flesh!" Jesus comments upon the divine decree and Adam's agreement — "Therefore a man leaves his father and his mother and clings to his wife, and they become one flesh." The innate relationship, however, is distorted or exaggerated as a result of the limitations imposed by the Fall (3:36-37), so that healthy interdependence can become, in our experience, something else, such as codependence.

Thus the initial stories of Genesis present dynamically the relationship between the sexes, showing that sin complicates an already intricate relationship. This complexity has caused great difficulty as commentators of various ages and backgrounds have struggled with the text of Genesis. Some ancient Christian writers seem to have been overly influenced by their own contemporaries' low view of the physical. Thus, they sometimes understood the physical sexual act as in itself sinful, and engaged in special pleading to explain how the injunction to "multiply" given before the Fall might have been obeyed without erotic desire — or even in a non-genital manner! These teachers of the church allowed the plight of humankind in Genesis 3 to obscure the goodness declared in Genesis 1 and 2 — at least, with regard to sexuality.

Contemporary thinkers have tended to err in the other direction, taking seriously the first stage in the drama, the good creation, while denying the deep implications of the second, the Fall. Yet this tendency ignores the way in which distorted human sexuality is implicated in the ongoing traditions and stories of the Hebrew Bible. We see this in the temptations and dangers faced by the patriarchs and matriarchs (for example, the tensions experienced by Sarah, Hagar, and Abraham in polygamy), the careful legislation of appropriate sexuality in Leviticus, the stories of David and Solomon (whose sins and indiscretions are not whitewashed, but used as examples for the faithful), the severe sanctions against intermarriage after the exile, and finally the teachings of Jesus and Paul on marriage and celibacy.

Quite clearly the intimacy of the marriage bond is not tangential to human experience: in our divinely protected but vulnerable world it must be understood as both a great gift and a dynamic instrument for good or ill. It provides the scene for healing fidelity and looming destructive faithlessness. Here, in our most common and most demanding relationship, we see a powerful symbol of the intimacy that God desires with us as the body of Christ. Single and married people alike know that the relationship between male and female is a "given" in life, but also that it is difficult. So the epigram: "Marriage is the only war in which you sleep with the enemy."

Today's recognition of a "war of the sexes" sits uneasily side by side with expressions of the "religion of love" found in practically every age and tirelessly promulgated in contemporary popular culture. The one view grasps disharmonious sexuality without acknowledging its fundamental integrity. The second lays on human love a burden it cannot bear, granting romantic love the status of a religious experience, and blithely ignoring human fallibility. Among other scriptural witnesses, Hosea, Ephesians 5, and Revelation 21–22 teach us that the highest purpose of human sexuality is to serve in marriage as an icon of God's relationship with his people. That is, the union of husband and wife is meant not to be simply a symbol, or metaphor, but a theological picture infused with God's glory that directs us through it to his greater reality. This is lost in the popular culture, where romantic sexual encounters are seen as the be-all and end-all of human existence.

In summary, the Bible presents marriage as a divinely prescribed mode of being for human beings, valuable in itself and in its iconic representation of divine-human relations. From the beginning, it entailed interdependence, companionship, and procreation; the distortion and strained fulfillment of these good things, subsequent to the Fall, has not completely thwarted the original intent. So in the Song of Solomon, human love is celebrated, and in the New Testament, marriage is explicitly blessed, both by Jesus' presence at a wedding in John's Gospel, and by the teaching regarding marriage in the Gospels and the letters.

That the loving union of husband and wife is a powerful thing is seen in its use within the biblical story of redemption, beginning with the Old Testament. The prophets frequently use the profound lessons

taught by interdependent spousal relationships to declare God's covenant plan and redemptive will for Israel. The books of Judges, Hosea, Jeremiah, and Ezekiel portray in explicit terms God's deep "desire" for Israel. For example:

> You grew up and developed and became beautiful. Your breasts were
> formed and your hair grew, you who were naked and bare. Later I
> passed by, and when I looked at you and saw that you were old enough
> for love, I spread the corner of my garment over you and covered your
> nakedness. I gave you my solemn oath and entered into a marriage
> covenant with you, and you became mine. (Ezekiel 16:7-8)

This positive use of marriage imagery is balanced in the Old Testament by passages that describe the infidelity of God's people and their
breaking covenant. The use of such metaphors in the Old Testament assumes that faithful marriage between husband and wife is a great good in
itself, but not that the marriage relationship is in itself redemptive. Jewish
rabbis subsequent to the Old Testament period sometimes understood
the physical union of husband and wife as a means of restoring an original, undifferentiated human being, an "androgynous" Adam, but this notion has not been followed in the Christian tradition. In Gnostic writings,
celibacy was frequently enjoined for similar reasons, in an effort to recover a primal identity that was neither male nor female. The *Gospel of
Thomas,* a noncanonical book which some scholars suggest should be
placed alongside the Gospels of Matthew, Mark, Luke, and John, makes
this strange pronouncement: "When you make the two one, inside like
the outside, and outside like inside . . . and when you make the male and
the female one and the same, so that the male not be male nor the female
female . . . then you will enter the Kingdom" (*Gospel of Thomas* 22). Authentic Christianity, however, does not demand that women become
other than women, or men become other than men.

Moreover, the New Testament and ongoing Christian tradition has
never seen our state as male and female to be irrelevant in the story of redemption. There are some surprises in the New Testament, but marriage
remains important. So, although celibacy is offered a new dignity, both
by Jesus and Paul, this is not because sexuality is understood as inferior
or as a block to spirituality. Rather, celibacy becomes an *atypical* sign that
our human sexual relationships are less than the final or ultimate good:

our need to be in communion with God is even more foundational than the marriage bond. Even while Jesus affirms the validity of a human life that foregoes marriage ("Some become eunuchs for the sake of the Kingdom"), he also affirms the normative goodness of monogamous marriage — "What God has joined together let no one put asunder." In the single person, the sacrificial foregoing of erotic love has a particular value (witness Jesus' own pattern of life), while the symbolic import and fundamental goodness of marriage is never questioned. Paul echoes this double understanding both in his personal comments and his teaching on singleness and marriage (1 Corinthians 7). Marriage is honorable, and may even play a part in salvation, when an unbelieving partner is influenced by a godly spouse. Singleness is also a gift to the family of the church and has its place in the healing of humanity.

If anything, the New Testament deepens the use of marriage as an image of the relationship between God and his people. No longer is the communion between husband and wife a simple pictorial reminder of God's desired intimacy with his people; rather, it takes on a "sacramental" or iconic significance. This difference between Old Testament symbol and New Testament sacrament follows the same pattern as Old Testament talk about Wisdom personified, as compared to the New Testament declaration that God's Wisdom has *actually taken flesh* in Jesus (John 1; 1 Corinthians 1:30). The Incarnation, the coming of God himself as one of us into our world, has made what was only metaphor a living reality. Similarly, the relationship between believing husband and wife *tangibly* indicates the life of Christ with his beloved Church; indeed, each marriage relationship that is in Christ itself partakes of this divine mystery. In blessing a marriage, the Church gives thanks to God for the couple, and declares that together they are a picture or icon of God's love — that they display in a certain mode the salvation story, that in their marriage they are glorified or taken up into God's own actions and being. It celebrates their significant and fruitful part in creation, seeing the liveliness of marriage as a symbol of the inbreaking and coming rule of God, and the sanctity of the bond as participating in the holiness of Christ, in which the Church now shares and in which we will eventually participate fully. As a believing community, we "bless" or "speak a good word" (Greek *eu-logein*) concerning the relationship, and mark it out as a condition in which the way of the cross and the way of new life come together. In doing this, believers commend marriage as a special state that is conducive to repentance, healing, growth, and glo-

rification for the couple involved. Precisely here, we say, one can see a refracted picture of the wholeness, the holiness, the love of God in human
form, and the glory of humanity. Here is a sacramental mode of living, an
occasion where the holy God meets us.

In this sense, acts of toil and sacrifice, such as a husband's toil for his
partner, and a woman's pain in bearing children, themselves take on a glorious role in God's saving work: they are sub-creative acts, dignified and
glory-tinged by the toil and pain of Jesus. The curse has been reversed by
the last Adam, Jesus. Sin, sorrow, pain, and death have lost their sting: the
plumbing of the depths of our condition, and the victory of resurrection
seen in Jesus, give us a living hope. Thus, amid other signs of healing and
reconciliation, the barrier or strain between the sexes is lifted in Christ
("there is no male and female"). Yet we still await that new age in which
there will be no mourning, pain, or death. Until that new age arrives, our
lives (in fullness and in deprivation) are being worked into God's plan, and
this happens, sometimes in the ordinary mode, sometimes with great
drama, in the family, as spouse communes with spouse. It is (to use Eugene Peterson's happy phrase, startlingly borrowed from Nietzsche) this
particular "long obedience in the same direction" that God uses to transform and transfigure both together, and each personally.

Our married state, indeed, aids our growth as Christians, for in marriage we are placed in a demanding yet fulfilling relationship, where we
learn that dependence and trust are essential to our being. Though the
dangers of our self-indulgent age are clear, we are privileged in our society to be able to choose our spouse, and so the probability of spousal
friendship accompanying romance is much greater. However, the same
opportunities for choice mean that some will be tempted to default when
the relationship offers discomfort. Few of us find it easy to discover that
the "knight in shining armor" has flaws, or that the "lady" has a less lovely
side, or that our "companion" has lost interest in what was once a shared
passion. Even fewer of us find it pleasant to see our own faults emerge as,
for the first time, we find ourselves in an intimate but mutual liaison. I remember my shock as a young wife at discovering that I had a great tem-
per. This had been muted during my childhood because my parents were
strict disciplinarians, requiring respect even in the free 1960s, and I was
an only child, desperate for friends, and uncomplaining regarding most
things that my companions wanted to do. We had been home from our
honeymoon one week when I became so infuriated with Chris that I pro-

pelled my loaded dinner plate his way, with beef and vegetables slopping into his lap. He had the grace to laugh, which infuriated me even further. I was face to face with a characteristic I never dreamed to possess, brought out within our atmosphere of comfort and intimacy. Chris's presence had become a mirror, or catalyst, for my own character. So our spouses, if we live with them deeply, and over time, bring to our attention those things that must be handled. Truly living in their presence is like practicing the presence of Christ, and being still in the Spirit — we may be told things about ourselves that we are not prepared to hear.

Because we are fallen creatures, such lessons will involve pain. Sometimes, we will be taught truths inversely (that is, as our spouse does not exhibit fidelity, and as we find it impossible to trust and threatening to remain vulnerable). God, however, is the author of creation and resurrection, and so aims to turn such situations to our good and to the good of others. As with our membership in God's Church, it is lethal to approach marriage simply as a "voluntary association." Rather, God's unconditional love for his people shows that marriage is an inviolable covenant, unless the other steadfastly refuses to pursue a life of fidelity. I will say little about the pain of separation and divorce, having not suffered that wound myself, except to offer the truism that this is a blow even more devastating than the termination of a friendship. It is, indeed, a kind of amputation, to be enacted in extreme situations only. In a marriage where both are trying to follow God, however, we learn to express love (which includes straight talk, patience, and sometimes anger) in good times and in trouble, when the other is strong and when he or she is weak. Similarly, a faithful decision to be celibate, devoted as spouse only to God, frees those who are not married to enter into dynamic and life-giving relationships with persons of both genders. In our highly sexualized age, both marriage and celibacy are arduous callings of great benefit to the community of God, and to the world at large. It is time for us to recover in the Church a sobriety regarding romantic intimacy that does not degrade celibacy, and a commonsense approach to marriage that does not require continued "fireworks." Couples rather should anticipate and foster a deepening and changing love that adapts to new and unforeseen situations. Godly lifestyles, when lived out consistently, are potent expressions of the surprising truth that in Christ God has done something about "hardness of heart" (Matthew 19:8, 11-12). Faithful marriage and celibacy are creative and complementary adventures in which God's grace is enacted; neither of them ought to be viewed as lifestyle choices that impinge upon our freedom.

On the most basic level, our unity and differentiation as sexual beings mirror God's tri-unity. Within the arena of a fallen world, our complicated interrelationships may become part of God's medicine, though by foreclosing on relationships we do not always allow this medicine to do its healing work. Neither an uncommitted heterosexual relationship nor a same-sex union can ultimately fulfill this role, although "in its early stages it may have an appearance of particular beauty and spirituality" (Karl Barth, *Church Dogmatics* III.4). This is because both the uncommitted liaison and the attempt to find fulfillment in one of the same sex are expressions of autonomy, "trying to be human in the self as sovereign man or woman" (again Barth, *CD* III.4). However, self-controlled sexuality (kept within the limits of monogamous marriage, or expressed in the choice of celibacy) shows forth to the Church, and to society, which looks on, the glories of faithfulness and self-sacrifice.

The Scriptures teach that the physical dimension of sexuality is both under the authority of the person (1 Corinthians 6:18) and a gift for the benefit of one's spouse (1 Corinthians 7:2-4). So our sexuality, expressed appropriately in a monogamous physical union, or expressed chastely by single persons in means other than those that are erotic, becomes a powerful factor in helping us to be healed, and to grow up into what we are meant to be. It is intimately involved with our whole being, and thus connected to the spiritual life. The married couple will be surprised to find how it is that their growing intimacy, yieldedness, and vulnerability to each other indeed transfers to their relationship with God, the lover of all. The celibate Christian will discover how his or her intimacy with the Lord can give great insight and intimacy (though not of an erotic sort) in relations with others. There is, therefore, a crossover between our embodied condition and our spiritual life that we might never have expected. Amidst current assumptions that sexuality is for the purpose of self-gratification, the Church's different attitude towards this great gift is bound to be a strong sign in the world of God's love and righteousness. For two Christians who are married, it becomes the dearest school in which we grow up, as God's own adopted children (and therefore as spiritual brother and sister). It is, if you like, our serious "make-believe," in which we "play house" in preparation for that day when, together with others, we take our destined place as the Bride of Christ.

Siblings in Nature and in the Faith

If the link between husband and wife is complex, then the first chapters of Genesis should forewarn us regarding siblings. There never was a brother or sister relationship not marred by the fallen nature of humanity. This is poignantly pictured in the trouble between the first two brothers, with the elder taking the life of the younger out of envy. There is, it seems, a note of surprise in Psalm 133, suggesting that harmony between siblings is frequently elusive: "Behold, how good and pleasant it is when brothers dwell in unity! It is like the precious oil upon the head, running down upon the beard, upon the beard of Aaron, running down on the collar of his robes!" (vv. 1-2).

Sibling love has a character of its own, and opens the door to great demonstrations of mutuality, generosity, and humility. Bound up with such consanguine affection is a kind of triangulation, since siblings always presuppose the presence of parents — certainly in terms of genes, but also often in terms of physical or imaginative presence. Again, as one commenting upon this phenomenon, I am simply an observer (at least on the natural level) since I was an only child. However, I have three daughters, whose relationship almost exactly matches the descriptions in the "birth-order" books. Moreover, even an only child can come to understand the beauty and depth of sibling affection through its spiritual form in the Church.

Like the relationship between parent and child, there is something involuntary about being a brother or a sister, or having a brother or a sister. One doesn't choose one's siblings, although they may also become friends, if they share interests and natural affiliation. Even when the sibling is too different to be a friend, however, the conjunction can run very deep. So sisters and brothers can be appalling to each other, but fierce as tigers when someone outside the family criticizes one to the other.

I am told, however, that the specter of parent is nearly always present. For the younger child, being in the company of the older one elicits thoughts of deserved or realized equality, and concerns regarding parental approval or otherwise, depending on which "mature" activity is being pursued. Either younger or older child can assume the role of a substitute parent, if need be. However, when one sibling is in danger, and in need of correction, succor, or rescue by the other, there is frequently a momentary flash of "what mother (or father) will think." Sometimes this strikes in a less-than-altruistic mode, when one ambitious child anticipates being exalted because of his or her rescue or correction of the other. However, in extreme circumstances, the attention is almost wholly focused on the sibling in trouble; but in the back of the mind, there is the question as to what mom or dad would do if they were present in order to act. The family unit, though not always physically together, seems all-pervasive where brothers and sisters are concerned, even more than with husbands and wives, who come together before there are children, and usually end their common life with children "graduated."

The illness of a sibling, or the loss of a sibling by death, is, as any who have encountered it know, particularly distressing, because this has happened on a "parallel" level, and so invites questions: "Could this be me? Why was it not me?" Despite the fragmentation of our society, counselors and those in professional health care increasingly are recognizing the importance of sibling bonds. Groups such as Alcoholics Anonymous have recognized the deep impact that an alcoholic, for example, has upon his or her brother or sister; there is a recognition of the importance of placing siblings together in adoptive homes; and there are newer psychological studies regarding the importance of sibling ties in the health of one who is in older middle age. The solidarity of siblings is an important feature of our psychology as human beings, and so those who are only children frequently look to lifelong friends, or to congenial in-law siblings to fill the gap. Like that between parent and child, the connection between brother and sister reflects our needs as frail human creatures, for the family, extended in ancient cultures to the tribe, is the most basic unit that offers us shelter and protection, and the place where we learn the necessity to give and take.

Certainly the biblical narrative is well aware of this bond as foundational. Jesus implies that he has forged such a bond with us when he speaks with Mary Magdalene on the resurrection morning, commending her and the disciples to "my Father and your Father." The letter to the Hebrews, quoting the psalm, says that our brother Jesus has "brought many sons to glory":

> For he who sanctifies and those who are sanctified all have one origin. That is why he is not ashamed to call them brethren, saying, "I will proclaim thy name to my brethren, in the midst of the congregation I will praise thee." (Hebrews 2:11-12)

Of course, in a strange way, Jesus is more than our brother, for the verse goes on to envision Jesus, with the psalmist, saying to God, "Here am I, and the children God has given me." Jesus is indeed our "brother, kind and good" — and more. As the eldest child, he takes on the parental role, as well, working in concert with his Father, but never with the kind of jealousy or spite that common human triangulation frequently exhibits. As we are reminded in the hymn to Christ, "he did not cling to his privilege" (Philippians 2:5).

Sibling relations, then, often present themselves in hybrid form. Age or infirmity of one sibling, coupled with duty on the other's part, may forge a quasi-parental bond; common interest and affection, plus the maturity of the younger sibling, may bring about an authentic friendship, something that goes beyond the "accident of birth." Yet the sibling tie is peculiar to itself, and in multiplied families, is something naturally shared between more than a pair. Within the household of faith, the tie between spiritual brothers and sisters is something that naturally invites addition — every new family member brings a new joy, along with a new challenge. In a relatively stable situation, the sibling relation may well be the longest familial bond that someone can know: between two healthy and well-disposed siblings, it can be as long or longer than seventy years, and so easily outstrip both the marriage bond and the parent-child bond, so far as longevity is concerned. Its significance, then, on the natural level, is indisputable. If we will allow enough time and longevity in our Church relations during this frenetic and unstable age, we will learn the truth that iron sharpens iron. May the natural level of sibling ties remind us that we cannot pick and choose our spiritual siblings; may the extra-natural solidarity of our brother Jesus remind us that we are required, each of us, to *choose* to take on the burdens of our brothers and sisters in the Lord.

Light Refracted through Human Communion

We have seen that our communion with each other, on various levels, leads us to understand more about God. We have also seen that God's light is essential to form and inform our human relationships so that they grow with proper roots, and in the only soil possible — that of God's very own love. Paul says that "When we cry, Abba! Father!", the

Holy Spirit bears witness that we are indeed "small-c" christs, little anointed ones — as the Bible puts it, "sons of God" (Romans 8:15-17). What a tremendous gift, what an immense privilege, that we have been adopted as the very children of the Father, and so have become "co-heirs with Christ!" This inheritance, though, comes with the presupposition that, as those walking in the Way, we will "suffer with him in order that we may also be glorified with him" (8:17). In all our relationships, we meet the strange paradox that we are called to strong effort, even while the Spirit works within our different bonds to make us what God has in mind for us to be. We are promised by the Seer John that Jesus is seeking his pure Bride — we are promised to him, have even now an intimacy, and await the consummation of this bond. How can we be guided by these various forms of intimacy in our everyday lives, remembering that they are valuable in themselves, and that they derive their worth from that ultimate ecstasy, the movement towards God himself, to which we are called?

It is not easy. It is never easy. We have a desperate need. The crisis of authority is everywhere — how are children and parents, husbands and wives, church boards and members, church leaders and congregations, to dance or work together? Left to ourselves, we simply do not know. The authoritarian model has been tried and found wanting. The radical egalitarian model is being tried and found impracticable or self-destructive. Our age both yearns for heroes and scorns them. Can we learn from the actions of Jesus, from the hints that we have of the nature of God, signified in the name of Father-Son-Spirit, a great secret? Here it is: order, submission, and headship are not the enemies of liberty and mutual honor.

Can we learn that our roles do not have to be identical, or rigidly symmetrical or exactly the same in order for us to be true persons? Can we learn, by practicing submission and leadership at the right times and in the right places, that it is in doing these very things that our identity, our personhood, is forged? In the pattern of Jesus, Son of the Father, and Lord of all, we come into communion with each other: but such communion requires self-sacrifice. We are called, like Jesus, to identify fully with our siblings, to lay down our lives for our friends. We will never be one in the ineffable way that God is one, but we are called to echo God's life in our interconnections, and within the Church family to become one body. We need the name of Father, Son, and Holy Spirit, to safeguard the characteristic idea of our faith, the idea of "otherness-in-relation." Or, we could say, it is only as we mirror the ordered and communicative Life of the Trinity, that we find our own life.

What would happen if we steadfastly turned our backs on rights- and power-language when we spoke with each other? What would happen, when faced with injustice, if we sought the mind of Christ, who did not claim equality with God? What would happen in our families, if as parents we took the painful and unpopular step of fostering obedience in our children, while still admitting our weaknesses and apologizing to them when we fail to be the parents we yearn to be? What would happen in our spousal relationships if we refused steadfastly to enter into the war of the sexes, but sought creatively to show forth the mutual love between Christ and the Church? Could we embrace the principles of headship and submission, all the while making room for freedom and mutual play? Could we freely accept a rule, or order, in our relationships, but at the same time moderate human rule by the knowledge that we are all of us, including those naturally in the leadership position, weak human beings who need checks and balances, and sometimes help? Would we be prepared to accept the fallout, the danger, of such vulnerability to each other, knowing that others, like us, are fallen, and that we may get hurt?

Those with seeming power might be called to show weakness and restraint; those with seeming weakness might be called to speak like the mouse that roared. Honoring others above ourselves is a daring and re-creative stance; it is, in fact, an action only God can foster, for it is his own very mode of being. If we open our ears and eyes, and do not give in to the world's flat way of thinking ("I'm just as good as anybody else"), God will show us more and more of this adventure. We are to be transformed together, as parent and child, as husband and wife, as priest and priesthood of believers, as brother and sister, as leaven within the world. The beauty of unity, enacted in our baptism, and the delight of diversity, released by the anointing Spirit, are to be formed in us, for it is God's joy to call us into his fellowship. We have been given peace through our Lord Jesus Christ, and we can rejoice in the hope of sharing the glory of God. If the road to that glory involves being slighted, marginalized, or hurt, we should not be disappointed — for "God's love has been poured into our hearts through his Holy Spirit" (Romans 5:1-5).

In the early days of the Church, faithful Christians had to argue with well-meaning but confused philosophers who played off the male against the female, the spiritual against the material, the body against the soul. Christians pointed to the Incarnation, and said that these radical divisions could not stand. Our true identity is affirmed and explained by Jesus, born of a woman, who lived our life as it was meant to be, died our death, was raised in power (body and all) and ascended for us to the Father's side. We are brought into God's Kingdom in a way that affirms our full identity: male and female; body, soul, and spirit; personal and corporate. The human body is no prison; though it is now mortal, it dies. It is by our physical genetic makeup that we are, on a natural level, linked to each other in families, in a manner that is deeper than most of us acknowledge. It is by the body that those who do not share genetic bonds come together as husband and wife to begin a whole new nexus of interconnected persons. Moreover, our body is noble enough that the very God of gods could assume it as a kind of holy tent, and transform it into a risen, undying temple. God's purpose is not to spirit us away from the space-time world, but to heal and fill it up, so that his glory may be seen in his whole creation. Our body can be hallowed so that it becomes a "temple of God" (1 Corinthians 6:19), so Paul warns his congregation against hurting that temple. The whole body of God's people can also be spoken of in a corporate sense, and it is this idea which Paul moves on to in his sixth chapter of 2 Corinthians: "For we are the temple of the living God, as God said, 'I will live in them and move among them, and I will be their God and they shall be my people'" (2 Corinthians 6:16). Jesus is the head of this body, the temple of the living God, up into which we are built and joined together (Ephesians 2:21).

The solid and sober reality of inter-human connections within family and society keep us from being seduced by vague ideas of spirituality. For we have God's own life-giving Holy Spirit to give us voice, as we cry, "Abba! Father!" "Beloved . . . test the spirits to see whether they are of God" (1 John 4:1). Let us not confuse the Creator and creation as we marvel at God's graciousness in binding us together, while including us in his glory and in his presence! Let us be grateful for our creation, and not play off our body and our spirit, as though the body were unimportant: "Jesus Christ has come in the flesh." As the new creation, we are called to live within the ordering and mutuality of God's own creation, and re-creation — male and female in the family, shepherds and sheep in the Church. Remember that order and mutual regard one for the other are both possible: that is the way of God — Father, Son, and Spirit. Those who are leaders should lead, remembering that to be a shepherd is to lay down one's life for the sheep. Those who are congregants should honor those who lead them, knowing that God lifts us all up together, and has made of each of us his children. Each of us should consider the other better than ourselves. For the Son, the One who was highest, became lowest for our sake. "Herein is love . . . that he loved us and gave his son for us" (1 John 4:10). And finally, let us understand what true love is. Like the Trinity, we are called to understand who we are not as isolated individuals who have to make contracts to protect ourselves, but as persons with faces turned towards God and towards each other. "There is no fear in love, for perfect love casts out fear" (1 John 4:18).

Yet what about the times when our human situation, when our Church, does not reflect the order and mutuality of the Trinity? What about when the hearts of the children are not towards the parents and when the parents disregard the children? What about when those in authority distort or suppress God's truth? What about when obedience to godly authority is scorned and flouted? What about when those Christians lack the necessary courage to stand against evil or dishonesty? In such painful moments, if we continue to look to our Savior, and encourage each other, he will help us know what to do. We have the Holy One within, teaching us truth: *his sheep hear his voice*. We have the pattern of others in relationship, from whom we can derive light and wisdom. And we have the godly admonition of each other, across the globe, as we hold to the apostles' teaching. Always there is a witness to the One who is truth and love. He will teach us how to remain both bold and humble in times when family, friendship, and Church are under fire, confused within, in danger from without.

He has two treasures that he has unlocked for us. First, there is his Incarnation by which we ourselves are made God's treasure: he has scooped us up, body and all, into his divine presence. Then, there is that other mystery, his Triune nature, which he has allowed us to glimpse. The glory of that Three-in-One spills upon us even now; and we will gaze at him eternally, as he shows us more and more. These treasures he has imparted to us, that we might, today, in these very earthen vessels, be keepers of the greatest wonder of all: his presence, love, and power. By his Spirit, he has betrothed us to himself until the day when our bodies are redeemed and we have faces that show us to be brothers and sisters of Jesus himself. So in these hard, cold, and confusing days, we do not lose heart.

My song is love unknown,
My Savior's love to me;
Love to the loveless shown,
That they might lovely be.
O who am I, that for my sake
My Lord should take, frail flesh and die?

He came from his blest throne
Salvation to bestow;
But men made strange, and none
The longed for Christ would know:
But O! my Friend, my Friend indeed,
Who at my need his life did spend.

Sometimes they strew his way,
And his sweet praises sing;
Resounding all the day
Hosannas to their King:
Then "Crucify!" is all their breath,
And for his death they thirst and cry.

Why, what hath my Lord done?
What makes this rage and spite?
He made the lame to run,
He gave the blind their sight,
Sweet injuries! Yet they at these
Themselves displease, and 'gainst him rise.

They rise and needs will have
My dear Lord made away;
A murderer they saved,
The Prince of life they slay,
Yet cheerful he to suffering goes,
That he his foes from thence might free.

In life, no house, no home
My Lord on earth might have;
In death no friendly tomb

But what a stranger gave.
What may I say? Heav'n was his home;
But mine the tomb wherein he lay.

Here might I stay and sing,
No story so divine;
Never was love, dear King!
Never was grief like Thine.
This is my Friend, in Whose sweet praise
I all my days could gladly spend.

(Samuel Crossman, 1664)

FURTHER REFLECTION

For the joy of human love,
Brother, sister, parent, child
Friends on earth, and friends above,
For all gentle thoughts and mild,
Lord of all, to thee we raise,
This our sacrifice of praise.

(F. S. Pierpoint, 1864)

If bodies please you, praise God for them and turn your love back from them to their maker, lest you should displease him in being pleased by them. If souls please you, love them in God, because by themselves they are subject to change, but in him they are established firm; without him they would pass away and be no more. . . . So you must love them in him. . . . For he did not make things and then go away; things are from him and also in him. (Augustine, *Confessions* 4.2)

Friendship is not a reward for our discrimination and good taste in finding one another out. It is the instrument by which God reveals to each the beauties of all the others. They are no greater than the beauties of a thousand other men; by Friendship God opens our eyes to them. They are, like all beauties, derived from him, and then, in a good Friendship, increased by him through the Friendship itself, so that it is his instrument for creating as well as for revealing. At this feast it is he who has spread the board and it is he who has chosen the guests. It is he, we may dare to hope, who sometimes does, and always should, preside. Let us not reckon without our Host. (C. S. Lewis, *The Four Loves*)

Friends have all things in common. (Plato)

Into this solid basis underlying every friendship worthy of the name, there must enter also some deep community of interests. (Henry Churchill King)

We are called to be our best to our friend, that he may be his best to us, bringing out what is highest and deepest in the nature of both. . . . If we choose our friends in Christ, neither here, nor ever, need we fear parting, and will have the secure joy and peace which come from having a friend who is as one's own soul. (Hugh Black)

Friendship gave being, awareness, hope: being, because man exists fully only in relation to others and to love is to admit that another exists; awareness, because the pain of separation and the frustration of otherness keeps one aware of reality; hope, because the likeness seen in the other is the Image of God and the union between the friends is a restoration of Eden's peace and a foretaste of the heavenly paradise. (Adele Fiske)

Eros, honored so far as love of God and charity to our fellows will allow, may become for us a means of Approach. . . . It is as if Christ said to us through Eros, "Thus — just like this — with this prodigality — not counting the cost — you are to love me and the least of my brethren. (C. S. Lewis, *The Four Loves*, p. 126)

God's love is to our love, our natural affection, as the soul is to the body, as form is to matter, as the life breathed into Adam's body by God: 'for the love of God, or God, the Holy Spirit, who is love, pouring himself into the love of man, transforms it into himself.' . . . God is the 'place' of the birth of love. (Adele Fiske, on William of St. Thierry)

O Lord and Master of my life, take from me the spirit of sloth, faintheartedness, lust of power and idle talk. But give rather the spirit of chastity, humility, patience and love to thy servant. Yea, O Lord and King, grant me to see my own errors and not to judge my brother or my sister, for Thou are blessed from all ages to all ages. Amen. (The Pentitential Prayer of St. Ephrem the Syrian, fourth c.)

As the angels in heaven live together in accord with each other in the greatest unanimity, in peace and love, and there is no pride and envy there, but they communicate in mutual love and sincerity, so in the same way the brethren should be in themselves. . . . He who reads should regard the one praying with love and joy with the thought, 'For me he is praying.' And let him who prays consider that what the one working is doing, is done for the common good. (Pseudo-Macarius, *Homily* 2.3.1 and 2.3.2)

FURTHER READING

Achtemeier, Elizabeth. "Female Language for God: Should the Church Adopt it?" In *The Hermeneutical Quest*. Allison Park, Pa.: Pickwick, 1986.

Black, Hugh. *Friendship*. Chicago: Revell, 1903.

Clément, Olivier. *The Roots of Christian Mysticism: Texts from the Patristic Era with Commentary*. Translated by Theodore Berkeley. New York: New City Press, 1993. An excellent introduction to Clément's remarkable work, as seen through his thoughtful commentary on the Fathers.

Evdokimov, Paul. *The Sacrament of Love: The Nuptial Mystery in the Light of the Orthodox Tradition*. Translated by Gythiel Steadman. Crestwood, N.Y.: St. Vladimir's Seminary Press, 1985.

Fiske, Adele M. *Friends and Friendship in the Monastic Tradition*. Cuernavaca, Mexico: CIDOC Cuaderno, 1970.

Florensky, Pavel. *The Pillar and Ground of the Truth: An Orthodox Theodicy in Twelve Letters*. Translated by B. Jakim. Princeton, N.J.: Princeton University Press, 1997. An intriguing, though problematic study that blends theology, philosophy, and psychology. The chapter on friendship (pp. 284-330) is helpful in showing the glory of that bond, though not entirely convincing in its elevation of *philia* to the level of (or even beyond) Christian *agape*.

Lewis, C. S. *The Four Loves*. London: G. Bles, 1960.

Meilaender, Gilbert. *Friendship: A Study in Theological Ethics.* Notre Dame: University of Notre Dame Press, 1981.

(Pseudo-) Macarius. *Pseudo-Macarius: The Fifty Spiritual Homilies and the Great Letter.* In *Collection II of Pseudo-Macarius,* translated by G. Malone. Mahwah, N.J.: Paulist Press, 1992.

Van Leeuwen, Mary Stewart. *Gender and Grace: Love, Work and Parenting in a Changing World.* Downers Grove, Ill.: InterVarsity Press, 1990.

FURTHER DISCUSSION

1. Which human connection seems to you most like God's love for humankind? Most like the love shared by Father, Son, and Holy Spirit? Why?

2. What are the possible theological dangers encountered when we try to liken our human communion to the intercommunion of the Trinity?

3. In what ways has a human bond helped you to grow as a person? In your love for God?

4. Have there been times when your love for another human being has detracted from your devotion to Christ? What can be done in the face of such a temptation?

LIFE

O Heavenly King, O Comforter, the Spirit of truth,
Who art everywhere and fillest all things,
The treasury of blessings,
And Giver of life,
Come and abide in us.
Cleanse us from all impurity
And of thy goodness
Save our souls.

When Spirituality Goes Wrong

The Distracted Human Condition

We begin by contemplating Raphael's well-known painting (reproduced on the cover of this book) of the patron saint of music, St. Cecilia, depicted in ecstasy, surrounded by her siblings in Christ. There she stands, in the midst of a worship scene, clutching her instrument, though interrupted in the playing of it. Indeed, she is heedless of the few pipes now slipping out of their lashings, and other instruments lie strewn at her feet. Up she gazes, in rapture, at the scene of the worshiping heavenly beings. Who are the saints who surround her? St. Paul and St. Mary Magdalene, to her extreme right and left, we readily recognize. St. Paul, apostle of the Spirit's sword, looks down, his weapon at rest, Bible at his feet, in an attitude of deep contemplation; St. Mary, ointment in hand, stands to the left of St. Cecilia, and looks straight ahead, as befits the "apostle to the apostles." Some have said that she is looking at us, but I don't believe so. Rather, she seems to me wholly absorbed, as though seeing and adoring the very One to whom the worship is directed.

Some say that the two figures slightly behind St. Cecilia are St. John the Evangelist and St. Augustine. If so, this is a strange scene. The worship of heaven proceeds, three angels sharing one book, one angel indicating to another where they are in the score: St. Cecilia is enraptured by their domestic homage. St. Paul theologizes throughout the event; Mary sees, though we do not. And what do John and Augustine do? They exchange knowing glances, behind Cecilia's back. Here is John, the beloved apostle who saw the Lord with physical eyes, communing with Augustine, that wistful recorder of the intellectual vision, that confidential confessor who yearned for the beatific vision. Is the evangelist quoting from his own final pages to the father of the personal *Confessions*, "Blessed are those who have not seen and yet believed"? Could it be that John is indicating to that great western theologian of the intellect that, through worship and music, he may *indeed* become a God-seer? Perhaps just as Augustine's mother Monica was his mentor in the vision of the intellect, Cecilia is being invoked as the mentor of true flight in the spirit.

True to Raphael's style, the painting is no icon: that is, it is not a transparent window through which we can see God. As a faithful work of art, it is significant, but is marked by just a touch of romanticism. It instructs, yet also leaves us smiling at the sentiments, causing us to objectify the painting — do angels really use manuscript music? Do they need coaching? Would celestial worship, once glimpsed, kindle deep theological questions? Have the worshipers forsaken the human-made instruments in favor of the celestial voices? Does the scene of (slightly cherubic) worshiping angels serve as a distraction?

Well, the painting might not be an avenue to ecstasy for us, its viewers, but it is indeed human. Here, it seems, is a typical snapshot of human liturgy caught in a moment, on canvas — complete with worshipers all in different attitudes, and a glance at the heavenly sanctuary to which our feeble efforts are joined. Here is the high, the deep, and the domestic, all in a jumble together. The painting may well reflect our usual experience of worship, but it is not, as we could say, "in order." After all, St. Cecilia herself takes center stage, so that hymnody itself is immortalized in the painting, rather than the Lord of the music. Only Mary, it seems, "gets it." Her straight gaze is remarkable, indeed, out of sync with the sentiment, the distraction all around. In contrast to the attention of the others, she is "caught out" like a child in a class photo, with her gaze out of line. Yet it is not this Christ-seer, this woman who was apostle to the apostles, who is actually wayward — but all the others in the painting! Even their undisciplined actions and stances are instructive, however. The glance of Cecilia towards the heavenly angels, the unspoken communication of John and Augustine, the rapt contemplation of Paul — all these actions, in their human quality, have the potential to lead us beyond the busy scene to the One who is hymned, if we recognize that they are appreciating a created joy, and not the ultimate source of life. Our hope (and experience) as Christians is that, in the Spirit, we will be "recollected" and healed, rather than distracted and broken.

Misdirected Spirituality

So, then, we move on to speak about life itself — though we have already considered some of its nitty-gritty in our discussion of human communion. Raphael's painting reminds us that even the noblest actions of humankind can be misdirected, not quite hitting the mark. Because the spirit of a human being is connected with the center of who we are, spirituality has the potential of going very wrong indeed. This has been true since the very beginning of the human drama, when the serpent tempted Eve to seize control so as to become "like God," when Adam blamed God for giving him Eve as a soul and body mate, and when Cain, overcome with anger because his offering was not acceptable to God, committed the first murder. The "flesh," wrongly indulged, can lead humankind to devolve into a brute beast; the "spirit," when deformed, can make someone into a demon. St. Paul taught that it was the privilege of everyone in Christ to be transformed so as to take on, more and more, the image of Christ; the shadow side of this is to be seen in his denunciation of the so-called "super-apostles" who prided themselves on spiritual perceptivity and special religious experiences. Their spiritual exploits had been accompanied by a spiritual change, albeit a deceptive one: like Satan, they had "transformed themselves in a counterfeit manner as angels of light" (2 Corinthians 11:14-15). All that is "spiritual" is not holy.

The problem of false spirituality is not new, then, and is not always found outside the people of God. In the first century, Paul was concerned, in the first place, to woo his pagan contemporaries away from the slavery of idol-worship, and to direct them to the living God. Yet he also worried that his converts, once redirected, could be swayed by those who preached a distorted picture of Jesus (a different "Jesus") and who imparted a different "spirit." Some of these tried to impose the Torah's legal requirements on the new Christians as a means of "perfecting" their faith, while others appealed to spectacular spiritual experiences and gifts as a sign of true knowledge.

Every age presents its peculiar challenges. Ours today bears similarities to that of Paul, but we encounter a further problem: it is not simply that there is a smorgasbord of ideas out there, and that within the Church a different "Jesus" is sometimes being preached. It is that some who still reside within our churches have come to believe that there is no one Jesus at all, and that Jesus himself is one among a number of human mediators of life, or that even that the enlightened individual requires no mediator except for his or her own spirit. We see those outside the Church, and even some of our brothers and sisters turning away from the fountain of life and seeking water in cracked and empty cisterns. Or, worse, they are being misled by teachers who misuse Christian forms, traditions, and language as a shrine for blasphemous worship, as they attempt to revitalize a religion from which they are actually, it seems, departing.

The first situation is one of desolation: non-Christians and Christians alike are searching for spiritual integration in empty wastelands, where there is no sustenance to be found. The second may be labeled, following the biblical apocalyptic tradition, "an abomination of desolation." Here we see those who deliberately use true insights about God and the human spirit, but against the grain of the biblical story. (I borrow the term "abomination of desolation" from the prophet Daniel and from Jesus himself, both of whom spoke of upcoming upheavals that would include social and political sacrileges against the holy place of the Temple. Many Jews believed Daniel's prophecy about an abomination of desolation was fulfilled in the time of the Maccabean brothers, when Antiochus Epiphanes IV offered swine's flesh to the pagan god Zeus upon the altar of the Lord; Jesus later adopted the term to anticipate the judgment against the Temple in A.D. 70, when the standards of the Roman legions, sporting the devices of the pagan deities, provided ready-made images to insult the honor of the living God. Israel had not recognized "her day of visitation" and so the Lord allowed Rome to visit the city in destruction.)

Today, then, we are faced with spiritualities that have "gone wrong" — both desolations and abominations of the spirit. How can we continue to know God, and commend this true God to others in an age that is not simply plural or multi-faceted, but pluralistic? We must, besides understanding our faith, understand better the day in which we live. This means that we will pay careful attention to those things that are drawing people away, or blinding them to the One who gives life. Inevitably we will find that there is a confused perspective, a misconstrued pattern of the over-arching human story, an inadequate principle, or an unworthy person — or a combination of these four elements. With the grounding that we have been given through the biblical and ongoing witness to God's Love and Light, let's analyze some examples that show forth the spiritual maladies of this age — taking note of their perspective, pattern, principle, or central person — and respond to these.

Desolations of the People

We turn first to a clear example of popular searching for the spirit in desolate places. Nearly every bookstore today has a section on spirituality, full to the brim with books that could be called mystical, even apocalyptic in the technical sense of the term. Apocalypses were very popular in the centuries just before, during, and after the time of Jesus. They were a type of literature that presented visions within a narrative framework, so as to disclose mysteries: mysteries having to do with time (past, present, and future), with space (especially heaven and hell), and with identity. In a time of flux and disorientation, they offered visionary and authoritative answers to the big questions of life. They gave to their readers a way of seeing their own troubles within a cosmic picture, and gave insight into what God had done, was doing, and was about to do. In this way, they sought to place social and political turmoil into a larger arena of cosmic conflict, and called upon their readers to reconstrue their identity as the people of God.

We face similar tensions today, and so we should not be surprised to witness the resurgence of this kind of writing; unfortunately, most of today's apocalypses are of the shallowest sort. Most commonly, identity is a dominant fixation among pop visions. Books such as James Redfield's *The Celestine Prophecy* (which spent more than three years on the *New York Times* Bestseller List and which is now being made into a film) focus upon the esoteric, and offer first-person accounts of tours of other worlds. Frequently they downplay organized religion, preferring to focus on individuals who claim to have been enlightened and so can offer "new" ways to understand past, present, and future events. In the appetite for such writings, we can see our generation's hope that the esoteric, or the latent and forgotten power within, can disclose a path for the individual to feel integrated or whole, frequently by taking a detour around specific systems of belief, Christian or otherwise.

Living in a day when religious and political ideology has inspired acts of terrorism, we should expect to see this emphasis upon "spirituality as opposed to religion" increase. Paul may have promised that the gospel's effect is to unite male and female, Jew and Gentile, slave and free, but many people today have the notion that creeds and specific religious practices can only divide the human family. Behind many contemporary popular routes to transcendence lies lurking a misguided perspective — that is, an assumption that a creedal and communal faith is enslaving and destructive. For the man or woman who has been disappointed by experiences in the churches, or who can only identify religion with acts of violence, this array of new custom-made spiritualities is enticing, and enables the seeker to avoid having to deal with human sin within the family of those who call themselves Christians.

Let us consider an example of this fashionable spirituality. Christine Bearse maintains a Web site, Awakening Rainbows (www.awakening rainbows.com), on which she posts messages she claims to have channeled from celestial beings. Hear now a selection attributed to the Archangel Metatron, dated May 11, 2000:

> Beloved brothers and sisters of light, congratulations on the successful integration of the Christ Ray!! For it was through the desire of your valiant and steadfast hearts that a change occurred upon this earth. All that is, all that lives, and all that inhales and exhales, has been affected by the tremendous in-pouring of Divine Light, Divine Love, and the Divine Feminine. Know that a change has occurred upon and in your world.
>
> The light codes that you are have been charged with an abundance of Christ Ray energy. The surcharging of energy produced a higher frequency within all your cells. You are all undergoing the integration of this energy now as these words are written, and will be fully integrated by the end of the month of June. The peak of this integration occurred during the time of the planetary alignment. . . .
>
> You and your higher self have been co-creators, adventurers. . . .
>
> My blessings to each of you as we ALL continue forward. I am here and available for assistance 24 hours a day, no matter where you are. Be at peace . . . you are never alone.

When I was in graduate school, I had hoped to devise a series of tests that could be applied to various apocalypses in order to determine whether they reflected actual visionary experiences or whether they were artificial. I never worked this out in detail, but I suspect that the above revelation would fail any such examination. To begin with, it was quickly rendered outdated: in the light of 9/11, just a few months later, its optimism rings decidedly hollow.

The revelation is also highly individualistic: the supreme guide Metatron is at times identified with individuals' "inner self," and those same individuals are credited with a kind of divine power and invincibility: "For it was through the desire of your valiant and steadfast hearts that a change occurred upon this earth." Too, it borrows indiscriminately from various religious traditions. For example, the name Metatron comes from Jewish mystical texts (especially *3 Enoch*), in which the glorified patriarch Enoch comes to be associated with the archangel seated closest to God, who is dignified with the title "the lesser YHWH." The talk of planetary alignment is drawn from astrology, and the concluding promise of peace is reminiscent of some of the words of the risen Jesus. Even the Trinity is recast as "divine Light," "divine Love," and "the divine Feminine," and there is the assurance of a Paraclete alongside the venturer "24 hours a day"! To readers steeped in the Christian tradition, this selection may seem bizarre; but the truth is that it is all too common fare today.

We might be tempted to cringe at such creations, but we would do better to look within them for the needs to which they respond — the desire for integration within the self, for intimacy with others coupled with radical freedom, for drama in life, for serenity and the capacity to play or create. Even this latter urge, the desire to "create," is not entirely un-Christian, though we should think carefully whenever we hear the word *co-creator* used for a human being. Our creative impulses should never be described in such a way as to encroach upon the utter holiness of the one Creator. Yet the words of J. R. R. Tolkien are instructive. He speaks, as a writer, about the role of humanity as *sub*-creator under God ("On Fairy-Stories"). Our desire to go outside of ourselves in ecstasy is, as we have seen, a facet of our reflection of the image of God, part of who we are. The above "revelation" has muddled up the distinction between the Creator, the God who is the "I AM," and the human being. Yet it articulates a real desire, to which we should pay attention. Those who are concerned for Christian orthodoxy in the last century have frequently done well in correction and reaction, but far less often have appreciated this sub-creative role of humanity as a gift of God. Frequently we type ourselves as the watchdogs of a decadent society; less frequently do we engage in positive, creative action.

As God's very own, whom he has, through Jesus, called "friends," we have God's own life, or energy, to offer to those who listen to and seek to dwell within the many desolations found on the Internet which share the strange worldview of the Awakening Rainbows universe. (Indeed, the avid "spiritual" surfer may well happen upon the Web site Celestinevision.com, which is related to the book *The Celestine Prophecy*, where she can gaze meditatively at a representation of the galaxy, which morphs into a globe, solar system, and wave of light. Alternately, she can click on a representation of linked human hands in order to "actively build a kind of community — an association, if you will, of those who see the vision.") Instead of a computer-generated virtual cosmos, Christians are ushered by God into a living story. This story, into which we are invited by God's Spirit, has the power to respond to human needs for solidarity, drama, serenity, and the creative impulse. To live as part of the great drama God has initiated, to hold fast against seeing ourselves individualistically, to submit to each other in love when we work within the Christian community, to come out of the fear and the frenetic bustle of the "purpose-driven" world for silence, contemplation, and prayer, to listen to God's word and know his presence, to foster and enjoy (though not uncritically) the arts where they acknowledge our Creator — all of this is the Church's answer to desolation. Here is relief from contractual or power-based relationships, from muddled and idiosyncratic mysticism, from self-advertisement and blasphemous artistic expression. The answer to desolation is not simply to reject it, but to build new homes for those who are desolate.

Abominations of the Intellect

Some leaders of the Church are endeavoring to do just that. However, in some cases the "building project" is a dead end, a mode of building that will not last, but which is seductive to intellectuals. Here we move from the shallow desolation of popular religion to what would seem to be a sophisticated abomination. For within the broader Christian community some have joined the growing trend to forge one's own approach to spirituality in an eclectic manner rather than being guided by the wisdom of the Christian tradition. This seems to be true even in the relatively "conservative" context of Canada, where (as Reginald Bibby demonstrates through convincing figures in his *Fragmented Gods*) almost 90% of Canadians typically continue to consider themselves as affiliated with a particular communion, or denomination — although they may have little deep experience or knowledge of their own specific tradition, or even of the Christian faith in general. Many approach their "spiritual journey" as artisans working on a *bricolage* — "a little bit of gospel language here . . . a little bit of celtic wisdom there . . . a little bit of karma in the sun. . . ."

We need to take care against flippancy, of course, and also to guard against the uncharitable assumption that truth is never found in non-Christian writings. Christians are not the only ones with insight into the human spirit, and different human traditions may have wisdom to offer us on the subject. God's Spirit blows according to God's will. Yet, Christians should be on guard against a simple drift into the contemporary consumer mindset, represented by, for example, Andrew Walker, who declares, "Nobody forces a version [of religion] on us any more. There are varieties on sale vying for our attention, but we, the consumers, have the absolute power. . . ." (Bibby, *Fragmented Gods*, pp. 111-12). So, too, should we be concerned about erudite attempts at spiritual truth that play off the *content* of the Christian faith (as it is expressed in verbal, or propositional form) against personal "spiritual" experience.

An obvious example is the popularization of a certain approach to the human spirit by the Bishop of New Westminster, Michael Ingham, in his 1997 book *Mansions of the Spirit*. Ingham follows Swiss theosophist and philosopher F. Schuon (*The Transcendent Unity of Religions*, 1993) in distinguishing two basic personality types, those who are "exoteric" and those who are "esoteric." Exoterics get "stuck" at the particulars, consider the world to be real, understand truth as concrete and practical, see God's personal mode as his only mode, ground their faith in doctrine, and aim to love God. Esoterics, on the other hand, treat form as a vehicle for substance, are drawn to the universal, consider the world to have only a qualified reality, see God as an absolute that cannot be spoken, recognize numerous ways of revelation, and seek to know the transcendent. For the exoteric, religions are mutually exclusive; for the esoteric, they all meet whence they have sprung — in the final Reality. Ingham, and others with him, are deeply committed to the concept of "God's unfolding revelation," the evolution of religions, and humanity's "emerging God consciousness." All this, it is hoped, will lead "noble spirits" beyond a God who makes himself known only personally, and beyond beliefs expressed primarily in creed, to a transcendent point where all faiths meet.

At this point we need to pause and think carefully about what it means to hold the faith of Jesus Christ. Surely such a search for a mystical point where all religions meet is an "abomination" — that is, a use of Christian language to shelter a way of thinking that does not fit with our identity. Of course, an appeal is made to the Bible. Where the Bible is discomfiting, imaginative adjustments are to be made. So, for example, Bishop Ingham suggests that in dealing with such disturbing statements as John 14:6 ("I am the way and the truth and the life. No one comes to the Father except through me") the esoteric will employ his or her "supple . . . capacity for spiritual abstraction," and understand "me" as "the Logos." Jesus thus is displaced for a spiritual abstraction, a mystical idea, and the problem of Jesus' particularity is neutralized. This is justified on the basis of a certain construal of the pattern of the Bible, traced according to the principle of increasing inclusivity. Here is a combination of mistaken pattern and misplaced principle.

This is, of course, a common version of the biblical narrative that is recounted in many seminaries today, and offered to us by those who preach the gospel of "coloring outside the lines" and "drawing the circle wider." Many priests and ministers continue to leave the seminary with a certain view of the "biblical" story that goes like this: As we consider the Bible, we note a progression in the human understanding of God. The Hebrew people began their sojourn with God by understanding themselves to be unique; later prophets taught the Hebrews to move beyond elitist rituals that protected their identity and stressed the importance of a more universal ethic; in books such as Job, the insight went beyond mere ethics to stress mystery, awe, and the importance of faith in a reality beyond human understanding; Jesus stands in the tradition of the prophets and of Job, showing a God who cared not for legalism but for righteous living, and a God who cared mysteriously for all of creation. Through a selection of various moments in Israel's history, a pattern is discerned, a pattern that demonstrates "the historical evolution in human understanding of God."

The principle of discerning a pattern in the Bible is a good one. But of course, we must get the story, or the pattern, right, and we must know the major character of the story, if we are not to walk right out of the biblical narrative into a world of our own imagination in our attempt to respond to the urgent. The story in which a pattern of widening circles is detected is actually quite selective. What about the call to purity associated with Nehemiah and Ezra? What about Jesus' own words that his mission was first to the lost sheep of Israel? What about the centrality of the cross and the resurrection? What about the continued "exclusion" of certain behaviors and attitudes from the New Jerusalem in the final chapter of the Bible? The New Testament surely *is* concerned to show how God has revealed himself more and more. It is clear that in the gospel God's faithful love is seen as extending beyond Israel to those previously outside of the covenant. But never once do the Gospel writers or the letters speak about this widening call without reference to what God *has done* historically. There is a progression, but it is an active progression in history, not a simple opening of God's purposes to those with more and more spiritual maturity. God did something in Israel, God did everything in Jesus, God is now intimately active in his extended people, through the Holy Spirit who makes Jesus known.

With the songs of two sirens singing in the ears of those both inside the ark of the Church and floundering in the water, those who are manning the boat must do their work with diligence. This will mean holding the compass of the creeds (the short form of our Christian story) in one hand, while we hold firm with the other to the "sheet" (i.e., the rope attached to the sail) of Christian tradition, allowing the sail its rightly angled contact with the wind of God's Spirit. Let us again recall our family story. It is about the ecstasy of the Triune God, moving out to us in God the Son (incarnate, obedient, crucified, resurrected, and ascended) and the new intimacy made possible in the subsequent coming of the Holy Spirit. It is about the healing, restoration, and glorification of humankind, made possible through the decisive acts of a God who created, called Israel, came in Jesus, and now woos us by the Spirit. It is a story that must be plotted along two axes — the horizontal axis of time, which God personally entered in the Son, and which he is in the process of redeeming by the Spirit; and the vertical axis that connects our world, sometimes with God's spiritual enemies, but more and more with the unseen world of God's glory. Crossing these two axes, through his mastery of heaven and hell, and through his actions in history, the Son provides himself as a "ladder" and climbs himself with us, through the Spirit. The identity of God the Son, still mysterious in the heavens, but revealed in time and space, is the means by which our identity is restored and glorified. We are to be transformed, now that we have been rescued!

Sometimes drowning people do not recognize that they need to be rescued. And often people who are pursuing a certain course of action do not realize that it is leading them away from the goal. When the perspective, principle, and pattern are wrong, it is hard to respond to the Person who orders all things. So, then, we must not take lightly the misconceptions faced today, and should beware of these infecting our own thinking as we try to hold the course. However, the extreme rootlessness and the growing dangers of our unstable age may actually alert some, who become aware of their plight, preparing them for the reception of the good news and the healing work of the Spirit. Again, the confusion of the day is such as to keep us vigilant. We have been given the spirit of peace, not of fear, so we turn to compass and sheet (the creed and the Tradition) to help us, as we continue to follow the map (the Bible) and sail, with God's help. May we learn to sail not only to help those who are on board, but those overboard, and those who think they are mer-people!

Dealing with Distortion

This will require not simply thinking well, but worshiping with a whole heart, and living with a whole will, our faces and hearts turned both to the Lord and to others. It requires that we cultivate honesty and open hearts — Christ's own perspective. Like Reepicheep in Lewis's Chronicles of Narnia, we are sailing to water that is translucent and sweet, and away from the salty waters of death; so we need to match our final destination! Paul declares: "We have renounced underhanded ways, and refuse to practice cunning or to tamper with God's word . . . but commend ourselves to every person's conscience in the sight of God" (2 Corinthians 4:2). This is a harder thing to do than it might seem at first blush. Paul renounces deception and distortion, and resolves to handle the Scriptures with integrity and in charity. He commends this openness — towards God and towards others — to everyone. As Christians we all have "unveiled faces" before God: there is nothing to be hidden from the One who shines on us!

It is all too easy, when aware of danger from both outside and within our communities, to lose heart, and so to adopt strategies of secrecy and cunning. We may be tempted to envy the arsenal of others, who handle the Scriptures in order to score points, or to sway the listener with insubstantial rhetoric. So, for example, it would be easy to lose our bearings in the heat of debate, and grant ground to those who question the uniqueness of Jesus. It is hard to respond calmly to those who are decrying the theologically orthodox as "doctrinal terrorists" and who insinuate that we "have historically believed our religion to be superior to everyone else's." But to respond to this charge by launching into the glories of the Christian theological system would be wrong-headed. It would be to miss the point! For, as Christians, we do not *start* with doctrine or with a system of belief, though these are important. It is the Person Jesus and the personal God with whom we begin. We know of this Person from what God has shown us about himself — this we have learned in words, and also in less propositional ways, in the story of Israel and the Church, in the life of Jesus as mediated through others, in the lives of others, in our own hearts, and in the center of our communities. We begin with the particularity of a God who is Alpha and Omega, who led Israel, who revealed through Jesus that he is Father, Son, and Holy Spirit from and for all eternity. It is important, then, to listen carefully to the questions that are being posed, and to reshape these when they are misdirecting the questioner from the real issues.

Christians must not, then, begin with the maxim "I think, therefore I am." Rather, the Godhead is a source and pattern for us of being, truth, and love, and overflows in these good things to us. No, the Christian principle, derived from our personal God, and the salvation story, is "we are loved, therefore we are." We begin, so far as we are able, with the living God who shows himself to us in various ways, but most perfectly in and through his Son. It is not, then, that our "religion" is superior. Instead, we abide within the Christian story and so must affirm two "scandals," to use the words of the theologian Emil Brunner. The first offense is the scandal of particularity, because this living God has come to us among a particular people, the Jews, by acting in their midst and finally taking on human flesh in the particular man Jesus. The second, related offense is the scandal of universality, for from the beginning Christians have insisted that God's active revelation, or his revelatory action, is for all humanity — as Paul would say, to the Jew first, and also to the Gentile. We do not affirm these scandals in an attitude of triumphal imperialism, or because they are cherished intellectual constructs, nor out of arrogance. Rather, we affirm them because only Jesus is the God-Man who has lived, died, risen, and ascended on behalf of humankind.

We will need, then, to insist that Scripture be read honestly, and in context. Cleaving to the Person of God the Son, we learn from him the principle of authentic, God-initiated, and God-sustained love. We also discern, with delight, the pattern of the whole biblical narrative, and take on increasingly the perspective of openness to him and to others. Perhaps the most common response among those who strive for creedal fidelity is to forget that we are called, with open hearts, not only to tell the truth, but to re-present it in our beings: returning again to Paul, we find that the center of his hope, and his life, and his defense was Jesus himself. He had met the glory of God in the face of Christ, and continued to gaze steadfastly at that glory so that he would himself be changed. So Paul did not argue first for a system of belief, nor even primarily for the veracity of the Scriptures and the apostolic witness (though he believed in this): he concentrated upon the One who was the Word, preached Jesus Christ as Lord, sought to bring "every thought captive to Christ," and saw himself as the servant of others for Jesus' sake. This is all personal language, language which moves us into a deeper identity than being mere "people of the Book," wonderful though this is. For we are people of the One who is the Word, and called because of him, and in him, to be servants of others. Servanthood in the style and through the Spirit of the servant Jesus requires that we be open in heart to those whom we seek to help, even to those who do not accept our service, and to those who consider our service to be naive or destructive. Along with modeling an honest and whole reading of the Scriptures, with awareness of all that our brothers and sisters have seen there in the past, we must allow the Holy Spirit to make of *us* Bibles and icons of the God who reveals all truth — this requires concentrated effort and prayer on the personal, family, and corporate level. Much of the confusion we see in the Church today springs not from a desire to be unfaithful, but from a misplaced generosity of spirit, or a misconstrued sense of unity, which has become simply "tolerance."

Deadly Distortion

What some do not realize is that "tolerance" is cruel when it leaves the weak to their own devices, or when it does not curb disease and violence, when it is unprepared to heal for fear of offending those who will not own blindness. So then, to those who lay charges of "exclusivism" against the Church, we have only the straightforward answer that we are, rather, inclusive — inclusive of anyone who will take the medicine of repentance and discipline that God himself offers. (If our joy in the liberty of God has rendered us self-righteous, then we need a double-dose of the medicine ourselves!) Some may not fall prey to the silliness of Celestine Cyberspace or the esoterica of *Mansions of the Spirit*. These may find themselves caught up in even more dangerous and compelling spiritualities, such as the group-think spirituality fostered by the David Koreshes of the world, or the softer, more "Christian" individualist spiritualities that focus upon the *experience* of the "Christ of faith," separating this from what God has done in history in the human Jesus. Adherence to the wrong person or to the wrong principle can be particularly deadly, and are inevitably accompanied by a misunderstanding of the biblical pattern and the forging of a misguided perspective.

David Koresh, the leader of the cult that perished in a fire outside Waco, Texas, in 1992, intrigued his followers with his own charismatic personality and his claim to be a second Christ. In establishing his identity, he appealed to spiritual ideas, and biblical ones at that. He literalized the war imagery of the Apocalypse, stockpiling weapons and anticipating an Armageddon in which the death of him and his followers would bring about the spring of humanity, a rebirth. Styling himself "the sinful Lamb of God," Koresh justified his sexual intimacy with young virgins at the Branch Davidian compound at Waco as enacting a kind of sympathetic magic, as would their deaths, so that the springtime of the world would turn around, and the final consummation of all things would occur. This actually works in the opposite direction of the biblical picture of marriage and self-sacrifice, which are understood as mirroring, or pointing and giving glory to God himself, who loves the Church as a bride, and who gives *his* life for *her*. Where the Christian view is directed towards God's initiative, Koresh's view was that events could be manipulated so that God must act. Koresh's major problem was his inflated self-importance, and his reading of himself into the biblical story. However, the mode of his theological distortion may be instructive to us. For it is true that heresies are the unpaid debts of the Church. Did the version of Atonement that Koresh heard, and then accentuated in cult-like blindness, forget that God was the great initiator, that "*God* was in Christ reconciling the world to himself"? Did Koresh fall prey to a story that emphasized God as wrathful and vengeful against humankind, rather than as wrathful with our sin, and so open himself to this bizarre idea of forcing God's hand? In telling the story of God's drama, we must be sure to place God rightfully in the role of Subject, of Chief Actor, and never in the role of one who is worked upon. Koresh's version of the story appealed, it seems, to those with a need for a group marked by solidarity, purpose, and eccentric vision (crafted by their leader) — it is an extreme example of a group of simple people who looked to an idea, and a human leader, for the answer to the human dilemma. The result of their replacing the only true Christ with a charismatic manipulator was deadly.

Others are content to continue in the individualistic mindset that so marks our day, despite its attendant loneliness. Rightly discontent with the "cerebral" form of orthodox Christianity that they have encountered in various parts of the Church, they are pleased to hear from contemporary prophets how to rediscover, for example, *The Heart of Christianity* (the title of a 2003 book by Marcus Borg). The appeal to individual experience as a governing principle is so strong that a number of high-level popular books, followed by seminars aimed at fairly literate members and adherents to churches, have been devoted to helping Borg's lay students discover this dimension of Christianity. One of Borg's popular books, *Jesus: A New Vision*, speaks of an envisioning of Jesus in which room is made "for a dimension of reality beyond the visible world of our ordinary experience, a dimension charged with power, whose ultimate quality is compassion." Jesus is described by Borg as a unique person who brought together various traditions: he was a "holy-man" (healer and ecstatic) who healed and mediated holy reality; he was a sage who goaded his listeners so that their hearts could be transformed; he was a prophet vividly aware of the "nearness of the other world," not of the "end of the world." As such, his teaching has a "timeless" quality that speaks to us today and so he became the founder of a life-giving movement. Turned preacher himself, Borg calls on his readers to "give one's heart, one's self at its deepest level, to the post-Easter Jesus who is the living lord, the side of God turned toward us, the face of God, the Lord who is also the Spirit" (*Meeting Jesus Again for the First Time*, p. 137).

As those who are concerned with the Spirit, we will appreciate Borg's impulse to move beyond knowledge *of* God to knowing God. Borg, in his inimitable style, discloses his own unsatisfactory youthful experience, explaining that he was brought up in a doctrinally correct yet arid Christian context. His underlying premise that "dogma" blocks "authentic" faith, and that experience trumps religious doctrine, seems born of reaction to this past. But reaction does not always make for fruitful thinking. A long gaze at the incarnate Son and the Triune God (which revelations Borg humbly admits he "does not yet understand") confirms that classical Christianity directs us to the intimacy that Borg, like all of us, craves. It is helpful to recall the words of Dorothy Sayers: "It is the dogma that is the drama . . . there never was anything so exciting . . . [as the] orthodox creed of the church."

In reading Borg's work, we are hard-pressed to find a connection between the post-Easter and pre-Easter Jesus. Borg does not think that Jesus ever referred to himself as the center of the Kingdom, nor did he go to the cross deliberately. He does not believe that we should speak about resurrection in terms of the continuation (with transformation) of Jesus' human body. So, then, the Jesus of history was not God, nor did he refer to himself in any way so as to suggest this; but — as if by magic — the post-Easter Jesus becomes "the faith of God towards us." How? If the embodied Jesus and the spiritual post-Easter Jesus are not connected, if history is divided from theology in this way, how can full-blown faith live? The gospel becomes, despite the best efforts of those who preach it, thoroughly individualistic and moralistic. Borg looks for Spirit-filled individuals who will care about the world. The new community that he and those who follow him envisage must rest on the very slight branch of individual example. Unfortunately, the wedge that is driven between the Christ of faith and the Jesus of history, and the refocusing upon human experience and away from God's initiative, mean that the biblical story is strongly compromised. Enough of the trappings of Christianity, the lingo and the piety, are there to give it a sense of connection to the traditions; but the sheet is fraying, and may well be snapped, with the sail left to flap, or founder.

The Word Near Us

In our de-centered society, errors in perspective, pattern, principle, and person are legion. The weak-minded may be tempted towards the atrocities of groupthink, such as we have witnessed in Koresh's community; in contrast, the sophisticated may be attracted to the erudite arguments of those like Borg who retain some of the scriptural story, but jettison or re-interpret key moments of the creed for the sake of experience. The attraction in both routes is, it seems, the emphasis upon spirituality. Again, we are helped by Paul, who encountered similar distortions in his time. To those who would reshape God's story, or reform it around a different center, Paul spoke about our active God, who is the initiator, sustenance, and fulfillment of our creation, our redemption, and our re-creation. In Romans 9–11, the apostle criticizes any in Israel who thought that they were God's only concern, and that they had been able to establish their own way to God through the Law. In telling the story accurately, Paul shows how in Jesus, God moved beyond Israel to include all who name Jesus as Lord: but never once does he speak of this without reference to what God had already done in Israel, the final chapter of which was the sending of the Messiah, God's own Son. Paul sees a progression, but it is an active progression in history. Amidst Paul's discussion of God, righteousness, Israel, and the Gentiles, he sounds a clear caution about a path that ought never to be pursued — the dream that we can, by our own *experience,* do what God has done for us. To mystically search for further confirmation of our standing in Christ, or for further esoteric knowledge about God, is to forget that all our good gifts have one source — the Father — and that they have been made potentially available to all of us together in the Son, through the Spirit.

At the climax of this passage, Romans 10:6-8, Paul declares:

> And the Righteousness from faith speaks in this way: "Do not say in your heart, 'Who will ascend to heaven?' (that is, to bring Christ down) or, 'Who will descend into the abyss?'" (that is, to lead Christ up out of the dead). But what does Righteousness by faith say? — "Near to you is the word, in your mouth and in your heart" (that is, the word of faith that we proclaim).

Paul is completely clear that this "word of faith," centered on Jesus the Lord, is for *every* human creature. Our experience is never irrelevant to God: but he has himself entered our world, and this is the greatest experience that humanity has ever known. Human hope must not center on any other story, nor on personal spiritual exploits, nor on the hope for some new, transcendent understanding superseding what God has done in Jesus. For Jesus is the main actor in this drama that began with the stories of the Law, and it is by his Spirit that we are enabled to continue the drama with integrity and vitality.

Both the past acts of God and human mystical experiences pale beside the climax of God's drama — the coming of the only One who has soared to the heavens and plummeted to the abyss. The giving of the word, the making near of that One to our minds and our hearts, through the Spirit, means that the drama continues — but the shape is forever marked by the greatest gift of God, who cannot be surpassed, only known and loved more and more. Some contemporary mystics seek to bring down or up a new revelation that will comprehend all contradictions — but this cannot be done, for he has already come. We cannot go beyond the personal — that is what God gives to us when he gives himself. We cannot go beyond love to a deeper knowledge — for in the giving of Jesus love and knowledge meet. Our own living is not rendered by God's action a static thing, but is given shape when it enters this story of all stories that graciously enfolds us. Included here is not, indeed, simply humankind, but the whole cosmos, which is being and will be transformed as God's own people are brought to glory. We have what is necessary for a cosmic vision of peace and joy already — God's own magnetic mercy to draw us to himself.

FURTHER MEDITATION

> For the time is coming when people will not endure sound teaching, but having itching ears they will accumulate for themselves teachers to suit their own likings, and will turn away from listening to the truth and wander into myths. As for you, always be steady, endure suffering, do the work of an evangelist, fulfill your ministry. . . . Follow the pattern of the sound words which you have heard . . . in the faith and love which are in Christ Jesus; guard the truth that has been entrusted to you by the Holy Spirit who dwells within us. (2 Timothy 4:3-4; 1:13-14)

Footnote to All Prayers
He whom I bow to only knows to whom I bow
When I attempt the ineffable Name, murmuring *Thou*
And dream of Pheidian* fancies and embrace in heart
Symbols (I know) which cannot be the thing thou art . . .

And all men in their praying, self-deceived, address
The coinage of their own unquiet thoughts, unless
Thou in magnetic mercy to Thyself divert
Our arrows, aimed unskillfully, beyond desert.

C. S. Lewis, *Poems*†

* *Pheidias was a skilled sculptor of the fifth century* B.C. *who specialized in statuary representations of the Greek gods, sometimes using himself or other renowned men and women as his models. Lewis knows that all of us are prone — if only in the imagination — to "create God in our own image," however cunning our image-making.*

Lighten our darkness, we beseech thee, O Lord; and by thy great mercy defend us from all perils and dangers . . . for the love of thy only Son, our Saviour Jesus Christ. (Anglican Book of Common Prayer)

Most gracious God, we humbly beseech thee for thy holy catholic Church. Fill it with all truth; in all truth with all peace. Where it is corrupt, purify it; where it is in error, direct it; where any thing is amiss, reform it; where it is right, strengthen and confirm it; where it is in want, furnish it; where it is divided and rent asunder, make it whole again, through Jesus Christ our Lord. *Amen.* (Anglican Book of Common Prayer)

Almighty God, who art beyond the reach of our highest thought, and yet within the heart of the lowliest; come to us, we pray Thee, in all the beauty of light, in all the tenderness of love, in all the liberty of truth. Mercifully help us to do justly, to love mercy, and to walk humbly with Thee. Sanctify all our desires and purposes, and upon each of us let thy blessing rest, through Jesus Christ our Lord. (adapted from the Service Book of the Presbyterian Church of South Africa)

FURTHER READING

Bearse, Christine. "Archangel Metatron — The Christ Ray." Available on-line at http://www.awakeningrainbows.com/Metatron-The_Christ _Ray.htm.

Bibby, Reginald. *Fragmented Gods: Poverty and Potential of Religion in Canada.* Toronto: Irwin, 1987.

Borg, Marcus. *Meeting Jesus Again for the First Time: The Historical Jesus and the Heart of Contemporary Faith.* HarperSanFrancisco, 1994.

Borg, Marcus, and N. T. Wright. *The Meaning of Jesus: Two Visions.* HarperCollins, 1999.

Humphrey, Edith. "God's Treasure in Jars of Clay." Available online at http://www.edithhumphrey.net/god's_treasure_in_earthen_jars.htm. On the theology of Michael Ingham.

Koresh, David. "The Seven Seals of the Book of Revelation." In *Why Waco: Cults and the Battle for Religious Freedom in America.* Edited by James Tabor and Eugene Gallagher. Berkeley: University of California Press, 1995.

Lewis, C. S. *The Voyage of the Dawn Treader.* London: Geoffrey Bles, 1952; New York: Collier Books, 1970. See especially Reepicheep's voyage to "The World's End."

Lewis, C. S. *Poems.* Edited by Walter Hooper. London: Geoffrey Bles, 1964; New York: Harcourt Brace Jovanovich, 1977.

Tolkien, J. R. R. "On Fairy-Stories." In *Essays Presented to Charles Williams.* London: Oxford University Press, 1947.

FURTHER DISCUSSION

1. In which ways can art help and hinder our understanding the Christian life?
2. Do you agree that sins "of the flesh" are less dangerous than sins "of the spirit"? Why or why not?
3. If the center of Christianity is a Person, then what is the point of systematic theology or formulating a Christian system of belief?
4. Name and talk about some of the misshapen forms of Christianity, or alternative spiritualities that you have encountered. How can the full story of Christianity help in responding to these?

B

The Holy Spirit, Hope, and Healing

The Life-Giving Spirit

From the heart of Jesus flowing
Cometh Heaven's peace to me,
Ever deeper, richer growing
Through the Cross of Calvary
Passing mortal understanding,
Yet to seeking ones made known,
And for all the race expanding,
Gift of God unto his own.

(Charles Coller)

The above words, typically set to a traditional Scottish melody, were written by a nineteenth-century Christian not distinguished by any specialized education or position. A lay musician and clerk in the Salvation Army trade store for most of his life, Charles Coller also poured out his heart in memorable musical lyrics. Here he expresses the "gift of God" made possible to all God's own through Jesus: the song, though personal, is not individualistic.

"Gift of God": think for a moment about the implication of those words. Perhaps we most naturally assume that the phrase refers to a "gift" or "grace" that belongs to God and that he gives to us — grammar buffs would label this the "possessive" or "subjective genitive." In this case, we would be speaking of the *gift* that belongs to God, or that comes from God. Frequently in the west, Christians have objectified "grace" as though it were a "something" separate from God himself, a substance that can be given in measure, parceled out and sent to us. But the Incarnation astonishes us: God will not, in the end, allow us to divide "grace" from himself. God's greatest gift to us is *himself*. He *is* our salvation; he *is* our sanctification. And so we must acknowledge that other particularly Christian meaning of "Gift of God," the objective genitive — it is the Gift of *God*, that gift *who is God*. God-among-us, God-with-us, Immanuel!

"From the heart of Jesus flowing" comes the "gift of God," that gift who is God, coming unto "his own." Coller's hymn is based on a pervasive theme of Scripture — flowing water — that goes back at least to the time when the book of Isaiah was compiled. It would seem that the prophet himself hardly knew the full meaning of his words when God spoke that great invitation through him to the faithful in exile:

> Ho, every one who thirsts, come to the waters;
> And he who has no money, come, buy and eat!
> Come, buy wine and milk without money and without price . . .
> Incline your ear, and come to me;
> Hear, that your soul may live;
> And I will make with you an everlasting covenant,
> My steadfast, sure love for David . . .
> Behold you shall call nations that you know not . . .
> Because of the Lord your God . . .
> For he has glorified you.
>
> Seek the LORD while he may be found,
> Call upon him while he is near . . .
> For as the rain and the snow come down from heaven,
> And return not thither but water the earth,
> Making it bring forth and sprout,
> Giving seed to the sower and bread to the eater,
> So shall my word be that goes forth from my mouth.
>
> (Isaiah 55:1-11)

The prophetic plea is strong: come to the waters, live, receive a sure, loving covenant, become a light for others beyond the covenant family, seek the LORD, be inundated, inseminated and changed by God's living word. This invitation to the water is grounded in the LORD's promise regarding Judah's identity and renewal:

> Thus says the LORD who made you, who formed you from the womb and will help you. . . . I will pour water on the thirsty land, and streams on the dry ground; I will pour my Spirit upon your descendants. . . . They shall spring up like grass amid waters, like willows by flowing streams. This one will say, "I am the LORD's" . . . and another will write on his hand, "The LORD's." (Isaiah 44:2-5)

God's word is to come as water on thirsty ground, his Spirit poured upon and among them, bringing life: so God's people are to be confirmed in their identity, their close communion with him. The prophets glimpsed from afar what the eyes of "renewed Israel," God's own (you and me!), have seen. They glimpsed, and so hoped for, a new creation made possible by the intimate presence of God among his own sons and daughters. The prophets spoke about the Spirit and the Word of God coming among God's people, and so renewing them and the face of the earth. What they glimpsed from afar, we have seen — "From the heart *of Jesus* flowing" is God's peace, God's *shalom*, the "Gift of God" himself. As St. Paul puts it, "God, who said, 'let there be light,' has shone in our hearts to show us the light of the knowledge of the glory of God in the face of Jesus" (2 Corinthians 4:6).

With God there are frequently surprises. When one considers the brokenness and waywardness of humanity, and the majesty of God, one could hardly have anticipated how God would restore humanity to himself, so that we could once more, like the Edenic couple, "walk" with him. It seems that our Sovereign, in reclaiming what had become "enemy" territory, adopted a two-pronged attack — or rather, a two-pronged method of healing. The Incarnation, by which we are gathered up to God, followed by the full gift of the Holy Spirit to work within us, are the two major movements. In both of these, God gives us himself. Hints of these actions greet us throughout the books of the prophets, not least in the passages that we have just considered. Yet God's plan was so bold, so beyond our human imagining, that it needed not simply to be accomplished, but *interpreted* to us. Jesus, in the most intimate of Gospels, the Fourth, exegetes or explains these prophetic passages of invitation and promise, passages that we read not only in Isaiah but in Zechariah and the other prophets. The Son's personal and exhilarating instruction is part and parcel of that role which John the evangelist ascribes to him: "the only Son, who is in the bosom of the Father, has exegeted him." (This is the word used in the Greek, most often translated "made him known," 1:18.) Jesus' express purpose was to "exegete" God, "to make him known," to "interpret" him in life, deed, and word. In John 4, John 7, and John 19, Jesus explains the mystery and wonder of God's life among and in us through his words — God's life comes to us as living water, he says. We are called to drink, and to be filled.

Jesus' invitation to living water is both surprisingly specific and general. Jesus matches his offer to whomever he happens to be speaking, whether that person is caught up in distorted religion or following the little that they know to be true. Jesus intends to move both the confused and the dutifully religious to a place of hope and healing: for the human heart cries out for *living* water. To the Samaritan woman, an outsider to Israel whose people had been theologically and culturally syncretistic for centuries, he explains, "If you knew the gift of God, and who it is that is saying to you, 'Give me a drink,' you would have asked him, and he would have given you living water. . . . [W]hoever drinks of the water that I give him will never thirst; the water that I shall give him will become in him a spring of water welling up to eternal life" (John 4:10, 14). To the loyal worshiping pilgrims on the last day of the feast of booths, Jews seeking light and life, Jesus proclaims, "If any one is thirsty, let him come to me, and let the one who believes in me drink. As the scripture has said, 'Out of his heart shall flow rivers of living water'" (7:37-38). Notice, however, that even here where Jesus' words are addressed specifically to those gathered in Jerusalem, they issue a general invitation: "If *any one* is thirsty, let him come to me, and *let the one who believes in me* drink" (my emphasis).

We have to work a little bit to understand the Master's mind here. In his homily upon this passage, St. John Chrysostom queries, "But where has Scripture said, that 'rivers of living water shall flow from his belly'? Nowhere!" We need, then, to search the Scriptures, to understand their pattern in fullness, so as to make sense of Jesus' words. There is no "proof text" in the Old Testament that corresponds to Jesus' words. Rather, he is calling to mind the entire great story of God, a story that looks forward to God's promised living water that will never cease to run, and that directs us to worship that One who is the source of that stream. Throughout the ancient Scriptures and writings we hear about the living water *from* God, flowing perennially to east and west from Jerusalem in Zechariah's vision (Zechariah 14:8), flowing from the eschatological temple (Ezekiel 47), coming from the Wisdom of God (Baruch 3:12). But from time to time in the Old Testament, we encounter the suggestion that God *himself* is this stream, as in Jeremiah 2:13, where the compassionate God complains, "My people have committed two evils: they have forsaken me, the fountain of living waters, and hewed out cisterns for themselves, broken cisterns that can hold no water."

It is in the Person of Jesus that these two ideas come together — the stream will come *from* God; the fountain of living waters is to be identified *with* God. John, with the other Gospel writers, sees that Jesus is in continuity with the Hebrew Scriptures, yet he also declares that through his coming into the world, something absolutely new has happened. Jesus is not simply an interpreter, not simply one who draws from the well for us, though this he is. Rather, something definitive happened with Jesus, so that God's people may go beyond simply understanding *about* God's living water, to an intimate communion with the One who is life itself. We see the great sign of this in the description of Jesus' death in John 19:34-35. "One of the soldiers pierced his side with a spear, and at once blood and water came out. He who saw this has testified so that you also may believe. His testimony is true, and he knows that he tells the truth." Consider the solemn way that this is both described and attested. The flow of blood and water is very important to the evangelist, because it both testifies to Jesus' humanity and actual death, and also hints at God's provision for humanity. In commenting about these things, the First Epistle of John says, "This is he who came by water and blood, Jesus Christ. . . . And the Spirit is the witness, because the Spirit is the truth. There are three witnesses, the Spirit, the water, and the blood, and these three agree" (1 John 5:6-8).

This is the gospel: God sends to us no life-force, no substitute fountain, but offers himself as our life, our refreshment, our water of life. The events set in motion in the first century were the cosmic turning point. There, in Galilee and in Judea walked One who was truly the representative of God's chosen people, Israel, and truly the representative of humanity. His life was in itself God's great offer of water, and became, says the evangelist, a living, life-giving river. In this offer, Father, Son, and Spirit act together. For, in the Father's will, and through the events of Jesus' death, resurrection, and glorification, this river, outpoured in the Holy Spirit, is flowing in a dramatic and intimate way with the people of God.

Living water, that is, water which moves rather than sitting in stagnation, has the property of nurturing and sustaining life. So, then, after the drama of the cross and that first Sunday morning, Jesus appears to his disciples, shows them his hands and his side, whence the blood and water had come, and says to them, "Peace be with you. As the Father has sent me, so I send you." The solemn words are accompanied by a great sign. "When he had said this, he breathed on them and said to them, "Receive the Holy Spirit." In John's Gospel, of course, all the images come together. We have moved from a living spring to a re-creating breath. We are reminded of that other time when a human being was breathed upon by God. There, in the garden, the first human received "the breath of life" by the intimate touch of God. Here, in the upper room, the new community receives something more — not simply a breath of life, but the very Spirit of God himself.

God's people have been marked by and will be inundated with the very Spirit of God. From this point on, they are not simply nourished, or sustained in life; they have the wherewithal to become, themselves, those from whom God's life flows. Once Jesus had come into his glory, by the way of the cross and resurrection, the living water could be unleashed upon God's people, placed within them, so that the river would become a flood. As the Gospel narrator interprets Jesus' earlier words about this flowing water, "Now Jesus said this [regarding living water] *about the Spirit,* which believers in him were to receive; for as yet, there was no Spirit, because Jesus was not yet glorified" (John 7:39).

In considering our separation from God, and the monstrosities of spirituality gone wrong, we have seen the dire need of humankind for the true and life-giving water — both inside and outside of the Church. Concentration upon those things that are deadly to humanity makes us all too aware of our need for healing. However, in this sober assessment of our situation, we do not want to forget the complete drama that has been revealed to us, promised in the New Testament, and glimpsed by those closest to God's heart. Here is the marvel! God aims to do more than to wash, refresh, and heal us. God intends to make of us new creatures who have within them the source of refreshment spilling out into a brand new creation. This is not a promise only for the St. Gregorys, Teresas, and Evelyns of our Church. He aims to dignify and transfigure the whole of human life, and all who belong to him — in fact, Paul tells us that our transformation will herald the rebirth of the entire created order (Romans 8:19-21).

God's healing and enlivening activity, encompassing us, both comes from without, when the Son entered our world, and works deep within, for the Church has received God's own, particular Spirit. God's waters are deep, strong, and overwhelming. He speaks a word that is at once iconoclastic and confirming. Nothing in our history or in the created order can fill the place of God's gift of himself in Jesus; yet our history and God's entire world are utterly significant, for God has entered them. The point at which the Son assumes humanity is a vital center that questions, illuminates, and transforms all that came before and all that comes after. He calls us into his own life, indwelling us personally and together by his Spirit, and calling us to put on the mind of Christ.

The Two Hopes: Healing and Glory

St. Paul speaks about the magnitude of the hope to which we have been called, in the same breath as he appeals to the life of the Holy Spirit. In Romans 5, he sums up the implications of the gospel in this way:

> Therefore, since we are justified by faith/fullness, we have peace with God through our Lord Jesus Christ. Through him we have obtained access to this grace in which we stand. Let us rejoice in the hope of sharing the glory of God. More than that, let us rejoice in our sufferings, knowing that suffering produces endurance, and endurance produces character, and character produces hope, and hope does not disappoint us, because God's love has been poured into our hearts through the Holy Spirit who has been given to us. (Romans 5:1-5)

The gospel has a past, present, and future aspect: Jesus *has* justified us through his faithfulness; we *have* peace with God as the result of this; and we *hope* to share, through God's outworking energy, in his glory. *Hope*, then, provides us with the context in which to rejoice. Yet that joy is not automatic: for Christian hope remains mindful of the real world, in which suffering, endurance, and character-building play their distinct and inter-related parts. The gift of the Holy Spirit to those who are in Christ is a link between past, present, and future: through the Holy Spirit, Jesus lived and died faithfully, and rose again for us; in the Holy Spirit, we participate in Christ, experiencing joy even while things are not yet fully accomplished; because of the Holy Spirit, who is our living sign, the seal of God's promise (Ephesians 1:14; 4:30), we are assured of God's ongoing work in us and for us. As Paul encourages the Philippians, "I am sure that he who began a good work in you will carry it on to completion until the day of Christ Jesus" (1:6).

In order for "hope" to make any sense, it needs to be exercised in the context of the world in which we live. We may be tempted to think of hope as related to fantasy and unreal expectations, as in the expression "hoping against hope." Yet in fact the Christian virtue of hope is utterly realistic, because it matches the "in-between" place in which we find ourselves. We are *in medias res,* as the Greek dramatists put it, "in the middle of things." Much has been done already, for we have a true status in Christ (or if we are not believers, there is the provision for this); but all has not yet unfolded, even for those in God's family. As the elder John reminded his congregants, "Beloved, we are God's children now; it does not yet appear what we shall be, but we know that when he appears we shall be like him, for we shall see him as he is. And every one who thus hopes in him purifies himself, as he is pure" (1 John 3:2).

The last sentence should give us pause! First, hope is realistic, for we are hoping on the basis of promises made by a trustworthy God, One whose purity has been expressed fully in the human being Jesus: "he *is* pure." Second, our hope itself is *active,* it *accomplishes* our purification — for, after all, hope comes from God, whose gifts are effective. Interestingly, hope is spoken about a disproportionate number of times, negatively and positively, in what is arguably the darkest of the Old Testament books: Job. Again, Jeremiah, the weeping prophet, gives to the Lord the titles "the hope of Israel" and "the hope of the fathers." Job, though he considered himself in worse shape than a dead tree (14:7, 19), was surprised to learn that God can answer even the hopeless. Even at the critical moment of Israel's history, when she was on the verge of exile, Jeremiah reminded those with ears to hear that God's word and work cannot fail, and that he is the source of all hope.

Hope, then, matches our current situation of being "passers-by," on the way, pilgrims. Hope is not simply a matching or reactive mood, not simply a response, though true hope must answer to reality; hope also has its own vibrant role to play in our wholeness, for, when authentic, hope is from the lively and life-giving God. Biblical hope, though it can contemplate resurrection, is never unrealistic, for it comes on the heels of the crucifixion, and is offered to those who have a sober assessment of their deadly situation. The prophet Ezekiel, for example, offers his vision of the resurrected dry bones to those who said, "our hope is lost; we are clean cut off" (Ezekiel 37:11).

In dealing with hope, one of the three "theological virtues" (along with faith and love), Peter Kreeft speaks of the uncanny way that this virtue matches the greater reality revealed in the scriptural drama. Like faith, which lays hold of God's true actions in the past, hope is also a response to God's initiative, to his "very definite, specific, and verbal Word to us" (*Back to Virtue*, p. 75). But full-blown hope goes beyond a response to God's spoken word, and answers, even more deeply, to God's character or being:

> Hope means that my deepest values, wants, demands, longings, and ideals are not meaningless subjective blips on my inner mental sea but are like radar, an indication of objective reality. Hope means that when I must choose life, the reason is that at the heart of reality, life is chosen. Hope means that when I say that it is better to be than not to be, my very existence and the existence of anything that is joins me in a great universal chorus of approval. Hope means that my implicit desire for God is God's own trace in my being. Hope means that my agony and ecstasy of longing for a joy this world can never give is a sure sign that I was made for him who is Joy, and him alone. (*Back to Virtue*, p. 76)

At the tail end of "Christendom," however, authentic Christian "hope" may easily be confused for the facsimiles of hope that have been parasitic on the real thing, found wanting, and discarded. Many who cannot distinguish between hope and wishful thinking, or fond optimism, are in our day reacting, with reason, to what passed for hope during the heyday of Christianity's social acceptance. The optimisms of humanism, or socialism, or scientism, or capitalism, are passé. Since these were bound up with a certain version of the Christian metanarrative, either as spinoffs, or as reactions to the holy story, many have assumed that the Christian narrative, with its characteristic check-mark contour, ought also to be put on the junk-heap. The decline of these various myths of progress that followed the two world wars, and the pessimism that was clinched in the decades following the sixties, has given birth to the postmodern "incredulity towards metanarratives" (Jean-François Lyotard, *The Postmodern Condition*, p. xxiv). There is probably not one person from the Baby Boom Generation and younger that has not been touched by this phenomenon: "hope" frequently conjures up images of a pollyanna attitude that can never and should never again be recovered.

But this would be to mistake human-made stories for the living story of the living God. It would be to ignore the profundity of the biblical narrative, in which the peculiar ending of the story (resurrection and glory) follows the deep plunge of the passion and crucifixion, and our difficult echo of this in human death. What if the human drive to find meaning in our world, the story-making capacity of human beings, is there because there is, in fact, a promised (though unexpected!) ending? (On this human desire for a satisfying ending, see the work of the theologian Wolfhart Pannenberg.) Yet there is no denying that in our declining society, "hope" is on trial. In a way, this very skepticism can provide an opportunity for our generation to see true Christian hope in all its strangeness and countercultural glory. In their very helpful book, *Hope against Hope*, Richard Bauckham and Trevor Hart picture our human location as caught between Good Friday and Easter:

> We must suppose ourselves as people of hope to be located on that day of which Scripture tells us nothing whatsoever: Easter Saturday. This day is bounded on the one side by all the horror of history symbolically concluded in the events of Good Friday, and on the other by the open future of God who raises the dead to life on the dawn of Easter Sunday. In the meanwhile we live and travel in hope, able to face squarely and in all their awfulness the horrific aspects of that history within whose temporal boundaries we actually still live precisely and only because the terror of history no longer haunts us. Instead, through the captivity of our imagination, God's Spirit draws us forward into the reality of his own future, a future the openness of which is no longer a threat, therefore, but a source of that joyful energy under the influence of which God calls us, for now, to live and labour in the world. (*Hope against Hope*, p. 71)

Actually, our brothers may not be entirely right that the Scriptures are mute on the mystery of Easter Saturday. The creeds, for example, seem to think that we can speak, on the basis of such obscure passages as 1 Peter 3:19 and 4:6, of Jesus' rescue attempt of "the dead" during this time. From the perspective of the living, however, this was a time of stasis; indeed, from the perspective of the dead there may have been no perceived activity either, for the dead cannot watch what is happening. Likewise, in the Easter Saturday of our daily existence, we may not always be aware of the Vital One who is now rescuing us, pulling us through the cross, out of the grave, like Lord Adam and Lady Eve in Orthodox iconography.

We are, however, grasped by the hand of the living Christ, and drawn by the magnetism of the Spirit, to dwell within this Story that is so contrary to the haphazard skepticism and fancies of our age. Christian faith and hope "will be shaped from first to last by the call to 'be holy', to be different" (*Hope Against Hope*, p. 82). This marked difference applies to our story as well as to our life choices:

> To the extent that Christians are at all 'holy', set apart, different from others, this will be due in large measure to the apparent oddity of the fact that they are looking and moving towards an alternative ending to the human story. To be a Christian . . . is precisely to live as a person for whom God's future shapes the present. (p. 83)

Insofar as Christians attend to the complete story of the Scriptures, meditating upon these together, they will encounter the Person of Jesus as One who lives truly, dies deeply, rises for us, and ascends to bring us glory. In the strength of these actions, which embrace us, we may hope to be increasingly set apart by the enlivening Spirit. Colossians 1:27 refers to God's "mystery, which is Christ in you, the hope of glory."

Let us not suppose that this "mysterious indwelling" will exclude the darker shadows of life, of which many lovers of God become increasingly aware: for suffering, endurance, and the hard work of building character are intertwined with the hope that will not, in the end, disappoint. Josef Pieper (*On Hope*) commends to the Christian the accepting submission of Job, so that we learn with him to say, "Although he should slay me, yet will I trust him." We have, after all, not only the example of Father Abraham, who offered his son, but also the wonder of God's very own love, which does not, in the end, exact that ultimate sacrifice from any but himself. Indeed, Josef Pieper has taught with great insight that Christ is the embodiment, foundation, and actual fulfillment of our hope, a hope that through the Spirit guards us against both despair and presumption. What we anticipate is shaped by the scriptural story, and reinforced by the Spirit, who reminds us that we are pilgrims who must continue to "pray and not lose heart" (Luke 18:1). Hope, then, steers the course between despair, which "assumes that . . . prayer will not be granted" and presumption, which cannot genuinely *pray*, because the presumptuous person "fully anticipates . . . fulfillment," even without the request (Pieper, *On Hope*, p. 70). Hope is both confident in the Lord and sober regarding our human condition; between the fading old order and the coming new world hope is the bridge "by which we *were* saved" (Romans 8:24).

In the Spirit-cultivated perspective of hope, then, come together all the terror and all the joy of the ages. Hope requires both an expense of energy, the walk of the pilgrim, and a trust in the One who has both forged and lit our way. Hope is directed both towards our present healing (and the healing of this world) and towards a multi-faceted glory that we can scarcely imagine. In hope, our God-desiring brothers and sisters went out of themselves, running toward the goal, for the sake of joy — and found themselves met by a God who has run the course for us, and now indwells us, giving us the second breath that we need to finish the course.

Healing

For the present, though there may be glimpses of glory, we are, along with God's world, in the mode of being healed. It is interesting to note that because of its association among the Hebrew people with divining and idolatry, it would not be until about the time of the New Testament that the profession of physician, and the metaphor for God as Physician, would be recognized among God's people. However, by the first century A.D., the healing activity of the physician was becoming more accepted, and made its mark upon the New Testament, especially in Luke's works. It is interesting to notice that, in the first place, the Gospels are concerned about actual physical healing, and do not inevitably present these as mere ciphers for the process of spiritual healing. There is no playoff of body and soul, but the entire person is of concern to Jesus, as well as to the evangelists who narrate the stories of his healings.

The Third Gospel, in particular, shows remarkable knowledge

throughout its narrative concerning contemporary medical issues, especially those that affected women, presenting Jesus himself as the healer *par excellence*. Jesus' mission is described in Luke's Gospel, during the episode when the Lord visits the Nazareth synagogue, as the means by which God will accomplish "recovery of sight for the blind." Over against Mark's Gospel, which presents Jesus as healing authoritatively by word alone (evidence of his divinity to create *ex nihilo*, "out of nothing"), Luke highlights Jesus' healing method as that of using touch and objects. It is in Luke's Gospel that Jesus quotes the secular proverb, "Physician, heal yourself!" (4:23) when he remarks that he cannot be honored in his hometown. It is in Luke's Gospel that Jesus, at the climactic point in Gethsemane, touches the ear of the high priest's servant (22:51) so that it is healed. In the parable of the good Samaritan, the would-be amateur healer puts wine and oil on the wound of the waylaid man (10:29-37). Again, it is in Luke's Gospel that we hear Jesus say, "Those who are well have no need of a physician" (5:31-32). Throughout, it is clear that Luke sees the healing of illness as an indication that God's rule is coming in a vital way upon his people. At the same time, illness and natural disaster are not to be facilely interpreted as God's direct punishment; this is made clear in Jesus' words in Luke 13:2. These are part of the difficult human condition, for which God has pity.

Moreover, the portrayal of Jesus as healer is found not simply in Luke. Indeed, in the concise Gospel of Mark, 47% of the material is concerned with accounts of healing! Here Jesus explains his activity among the riffraff of society by remarking, "Those who are well have no need of a physician, but those who are sick; I came not to call the righteous, but sinners" (Mark 2:17). The most obvious point made in Mark's Gospel is that healing establishes the authority of Jesus, who works by "the finger of God." But it also establishes God's character, as we watch One who has "compassion for the people" and seeks to do them good. Throughout the Gospels, we find a carefully-tuned view concerning the cause of illness, one that aims to correct those who have a mechanistic view of the relationship between sin and illness, and that offers an explanation of suffering which admits the extraordinary healing power of God. At times, Jesus links the forgiveness of sins to healing:

> And they came, bringing to him a paralytic carried by four men. And when they could not get near him because of the crowd, they removed the roof above him; and when they had made an opening, they let

down the pallet on which the paralytic lay. And when Jesus saw their faith, he said to the paralytic, "My son, your sins are forgiven." Now some of the scribes were sitting there, questioning in their hearts, "Why does this man speak thus? It is blasphemy! Who can forgive sins but God alone?" And immediately Jesus, perceiving in his spirit that they thus questioned within themselves, said to them, "Why do you question thus in your hearts? Which is easier, to say to the paralytic, 'Your sins are forgiven,' or to say, 'Rise, take up your pallet and walk'? But that you may know that the Son of man has authority on earth to forgive sins" — he said to the paralytic — "I say to you, rise, take up your pallet and go home." And he rose, and immediately took up the pallet and went out before them all; so that they were all amazed and glorified God, saying, "We never saw anything like this!" (Mark 2:3-12)

A similar story is told in the Fourth Gospel, of a paralytic by the Sheep Gate whom Jesus heals (John 5:8) and then warns "Sin no more, that nothing worse befall you" (5:14). Lest this be misunderstood, however, John also tells the story of the man born blind in John 9, where Jesus makes it clear that the man is in misfortunate circumstances not because of direct relationship to sin. Through his healing, God's glory — that is, both his power and his compassion — will be made evident!

The Gospel writers are clearly interested in Jesus' concern for the physical, but also direct us to perceive the tragedy of spiritual blindness (John 9:39-41), and the necessity of recognizing this malady, so that the great Physician can heal. This connection with spiritual illness, however, does not lead us to think that physical illness is insignificant. So, Jesus weeps for his dead friend, Lazarus, and for the predicament of humanity, so marked by death (John 11:33). Jesus' grief is no mere stage show, designed to give a flashy "honor" to God. Rather, God's glory is revealed in the compassionate Jesus, who has the power to give life. The condition of Lazarus, and of humanity, gives our Lord pain, and he is determined to do something about this. The Gospel writer is also concerned to make a distinct separation between Jesus the great Healer, and the theurgist, or God-manipulator. This we see in 11:41-42, where Jesus prays, and explains the rationale for his prayer. Jesus is not one who needs to implore God to act, for he is in communion with the Father and knows his very will. Jesus' personhood is defined in terms of his relationship *toward* the Father (1:1); it is out of this communion that he acts and offers life.

It is because of this central picture of Jesus the Physician that the early Church Fathers frequently used this metaphor for Jesus, and indeed, for the ministry of the Church itself. By the fourth century, St. John Chrysostom speaks this way about our role in the church:

> The school of the church is an admirable surgery — a surgery not for bodies, but for souls. For it is spiritual, and sets right, not fleshly wounds, but errors of the mind, and of these errors and wounds the medicine is the word. This medicine is compounded not from the herbs growing on the earth, but from the words proceeding from heaven — this no hands of physicians, but tongues of preachers have dispensed. On this account it lasts right through; and neither is its virtue impaired by length of time, nor defeated by any strength of diseases. For certainly the medicines of physicians have both these defects; for while they are fresh they display their proper strength, but when much time has passed, they become weaker. . . . Whereas the divine medicine is not such as this, but still retains all its inherent value. . . . ("Against Publishing," p. 234)

Chrysostom uses the "not this, but rather that" polemic not to downplay the importance of bodily healing and medicine, but to talk about the deeper medicine of the Word of God. Here he does not disparage the use of medicine for the body; elsewhere in his homilies, he calls upon his listeners to show mercy and to do physical good to those in need. He speaks in harmony with other ancient Christians, for example, Irenaeus and Athanasios, who both spoke about miraculous healing as something that went on in their own time, and saw this activity as part and parcel of God's renewal of the creation. Chrysostom's passage, reminiscent of many others, shows that the healing ministry was considered so significant in the Church that it could be used as an image of inner healing. Similarly, in the writers of that time, the Eucharist is spoken of as a heavenly medicine, whereby our divine Physician heals those who have come to the "surgery" or "care-facility" of the Church.

Physical healing, then, takes its place in the Christian family as part of a larger picture. The natural work of doctors and the surprising work of miraculous healers under Christ all mirror what God is accomplishing through the Holy Spirit in our world, and hints toward what God plans to do when all is fulfilled in the New Jerusalem. We must remember that our gospel is as much concerned with Jesus' victory over death as it is with his victory over sin: "As one man's trespass led to condemnation for all people, so one man's act of righteousness leads to *acquittal* and *life* for all people" (Romans 5:18). Christians in the healing profession, or who care for the body, are expressing God's rule over the world every bit as much as preachers who deal with sin and repentance. In the Gospels, in the letters of Paul, there are two enemies that Jesus has come to vanquish: Sin and Death. (See especially Romans 5.) God has of course acted decisively in Jesus' Incarnation, death, resurrection, and ascension. Yet, as we have seen in the vibrant witness of those who have come before us, the faithful have a very real role to play as we await God's finale when what Jesus has accomplished comes to fulfillment. Let us recall the concentric circles (Romans 8:18-28) through which the Holy Spirit is acting, working within Christians who cry within fallen humanity, and on behalf of a broken world.

Within the New Testament, the healing miracles of Jesus, visionary passages about the renewal of the whole cosmos, and explicit teaching on the resurrection show the material world and the body to be of utter importance to God, the Healer. There is an ease with which the early Christian Fathers speak of Jesus as the Physician of both body and spirit, and of the Church's role in playing out this healing in their own day. Our imaginations must be fired by the physicality of baptism and Eucharist, by the opportunities given to the Church for the healing of the world, and ultimately by the luminous vision of a New Jerusalem. There is to be an utter concern for the whole person, and for God's whole universe. He has made us, as we are, after his image, and of the same stuff as the created order, for a purpose. Our position is, in every respect, "priestly" — we are in a bridge position, and have been called to give thanksgiving for what God has made, to bless and use it, to heal and nurture it. We have been given "time to redeem" and God's created material to organize and to enhance. We look forward to a timeful rather than a timeless existence and to a new Jerusalem, in which heaven and earth meet, where God dwells with us permanently!

And meanwhile? We are in the midst of Act V, called (quite surprisingly!) to participate in the healing of this world. The healing goes on in different ways, with many different players, and is directed towards body, mind, spirit, the environment, society, nations, the cosmos. It comes through direct graces such as a surprising prophetic word or an unexpected healing, and through other types of human mediation, including (I hope!) theological teaching and the medical arts. It comes through Bible study, where God's refreshing and healing word meets us, and through the Eucharist. Indeed, both the study of Scriptures and celebration of the Lord's Supper provide places in which direct divine action and human action meet: our feeding upon the Word is attended by both the action of the Spirit and the human actions of translation, paper-making, book-binding, type-setting, and reading; our feeding upon the Supper is attended by the Spirit who meets with our human gifts of wine and bread, spoken prayer and dramatic action, activated memories and kindled hearts. In both the reading of the Word and the breaking of the bread, Christ is present.

Paradoxically, healing comes even through that dreaded visitor, death, whose teeth have now been removed. In that dark context of physical death, the palliative work of the medical profession and the work of a Mother Teresa take on great dignity. How can it be that God can use even our most savage enemy to our good? C. S. Lewis gives an answer:

> Our enemy . . . becomes our servant: bodily Death, the monster, becomes blessed spiritual Death to self, if the spirit so wills — or rather if it allows the Spirit of the willingly dying God so to will in it. . . . Humanity must embrace death freely, submit to it with total humility, drink it to the dregs, and so convert it into that mystical death which is the secret of life. But only a Man who did not need to have been a Man at all unless He had chosen . . . could perform this perfect dying; and thus . . . either defeat Death or redeem it. . . . He is the representative "Die-er" of the universe. . . . Because the higher can descend into the lower He . . . can also most fully descend into the horrible and (for us) involuntary death of the body. . . . His death can become ours. (*Miracles,* pp. 156-57)

For those who have not been "up close and personal" with one who is dying "in the Lord," Lewis's evocative words concerning this "great exchange" may seem theologically orthodox, while remaining abstract and remote. We may find particularly perplexing his call to willing abandon and submission, so caught up are we in the "interior noise" of our unsettled hearts and in the frenetic, ambitious rhythms of contemporary Western life. It may be, however, that our restlessness is not merely a symptom of our social context. Could it be that we actually *welcome* the besieging activity and clamor because it keeps us from coming face to face with our fallen reality, with ourselves, with others, and with God? Even as we conspire with the world to keep ourselves distracted, however, life forces us (from time to time) to stop. God has, of course, given to us the graces of sleep, and of the Sabbath day. But when we are heedless of these built-in times of peace, we cannot escape the severe mercies that come to everyone — uncertainty, illness, and even death. Only a moment's reflection will show us the potential nightmare of living *forever* in our current state — left to their own ends, even the strengths of fallen humanity, without the chastening effect of death, might easily devolve into strong evil! And so it is that God takes even these, our dread enemies of corruption and death, and by them provides for us a space, a place of quiet, a window by which we can see and be seen.

I have been honored to learn about death, by proxy and by communion, through a master teacher who has been in my life from the beginning — my own father. My father's last seven years, in which he was besieged on all fronts by a neurological disease, were hard on the entire family. The two most obvious natural gifts that God had amply bestowed on my father — his articulate tongue and his agility of thought — were, little by little, suppressed. As Christians know from Jesus' stance toward illness and death, the loss of such abilities cannot be designated the "express" will of the creating God, whose first words concerning humanity were "It is very good." At evening, and throughout the day, Jesus healed those afflicted in body and mind; at the tomb of Lazarus, he cried, moved by the tragedy and indignity of death. In our weak fallen condition, these beautiful yet fragile bodies are assaulted by corruption and death — yet God still is at work in us. "We have these treasures in jars of clay." So it is that I learned from my father's final years as I also learned from his more robust days. For in the days when his tongue was halting, his mind disjointed, and his limbs hampered, he came to show forth a serenity of spirit and a depth of devotion to the Lord that was palpable. When he was weak, then God was strong.

My father, student of poetry and of the Scriptures, recognized and eventually embraced the power of this paradox. The glory of God shone forth unexpectedly in Dad's spontaneous prayers, and in his afternoon hymns — these prayed and sung in a tongue known only to himself and to the Holy Spirit! When at last he could not even be physically active, and stopped restlessly urging us to push him around in his wheelchair (with the constant plea, "Let's go!"), then God gave to him *time* — time to commune with the heavenly Father, time to remind those around him of God's intimate dwelling among those who are called by his name.

Nothing is wasted with God — not even our seasons of frailty and impotence. The same man who delighted me with numerous books, who entertained a carfull with songs and quips on long summer drives to the beach, who frolicked in the waves of the Atlantic, who laughed at a dripping dog who had plunged into a pond after ducks, who challenged his high-school students to reason with integrity and to love words, who played a bass line in the church (Salvation Army) band with gusto, who was moved by a lyrical hymn-tune, who was exuberant in verbal debate at table and Bible study, who was the life of the New Year's Eve party, who engaged many (including my own young fiancé) in deep discussion about the Christian faith, who lived and played hard, and who had the grace to admit his failings — this dear one now made another mark upon those who surrounded him in death. In his last years, he impressed upon us the significance of simplicity and trust — trust in others who cared for him, and trust in the God-Man who gave up all, even to the point of death.

In being with him, and waiting with him, I learned how to hear God speak in a deeper way, in the moments of stillness. I participated, with him, in the gift of communion — the joy of presence with each other and with our heavenly Father. In his last few days, though there was nothing left to be said, we remembered hymns together, and were simply *with* each other in silence. The time was hard, but pregnant, for it pulled together a lifetime of activity, ideas, words, emotions, struggle, and sheer fun. Jesus was with us. His presence, through the Holy Spirit, conjoined all those whose lives were linked with my father, even when not all of us were physically present in the same room. Because he is a child of God, because we are joined together in love, and in Christ, we were together even while physically apart. The epistle of Hebrews tells us that this communion does not cease with death, but that we continue through Christ to live a common life. In the case of my father, the Great Lent of life's waning and end made a palpable and remarkable impact, not only upon him but on us: he was stripped of many things we hold dear, and yet (and so?) his communion with the Lord grew more intimate. In Christ, he was given the grace to be "ecstatic," to go out of himself and embrace what came to him, a situation both at one time feared and certainly unsought.

And so, Lent gave way to Eastertide — an Easter that he now celebrates, and for which we wait. Watching God's severe and tender mercies with my father has made a mark upon my imagination, so that I have at least a glimpse of what it means to die in Christ and so to live. Death remains a dark mystery, and a source of sorrow, yet the sting is indeed removed, for it is evident that death itself may be co-opted, by God, for our healing.

Sometimes the various ways in which healing occurs seem to collide with each other: yet our understanding is limited, and we have only part of the picture. Physical death and physical healing continue to strike us, with our limited understanding, as polar opposites, even though we know that God has worked, and continues to work through both in order to reclaim the world. It is difficult to weigh all these different aspects of living properly, as we engage in our several vocations as followers of Christ. However, the five acts of our story give us a solid framework, as well as the knowledge that the Holy Spirit is working in us to accomplish his healing purposes. As we live, serving each other and others, we will at times find it difficult to come to terms to with life, health, disease, and death. This may be particularly difficult when we are called to act prophetically, and not simply supportively, in the lives of those who are close to us. Is it time to remind a gravely ill brother and sister of the health-giving God or of the importance of dying faithfully? Is it time to plead with a faithless spouse to repent, and renew the marriage bond, or to allow the dear transgressor "freedom" so that God can deal with him or her? Is it time to continue working from within a spiritually-ill church community that continues to turn its back on the central truths of the faith, or to shake off the dust, freeing ourselves for active ministry in a new context? There are times when the answers do not come easily. But we have the One who is Life and Truth itself, and we have the whole Body of Christ, those present with us physically, and those joined with us in mystery. Together, God will guide us through such ambiguous situations to the place where all is light, life, health, and *shalom*.

Made Worthy of the Blessed Hope

It may be helpful, in the ambiguity, to remember how, in John 14–17, the inner mystery of the trinitarian fellowship was revealed in the holy context of Jesus' own agony. The coming together of fellowship and suffering reveals to us a way to live, a way to be with God and with each other in the present.

This is a way that affirms God's sovereignty over the whole of life, and his promise to enlighten our shadow-land. This is a way that affirms compassion, authority, and unity — surely the answer to that very crisis in which we find ourselves, whether we look at the sickness of society, of the family, or of the Church. In Jesus we have seen a personhood that is not expressed by defining itself off against others, yet in which there is no confusion of identity. It is neither a matter of "the I versus the not-I" nor of merely different *modes* of being. Rather, the Person of the Son is understood as eternally being towards the Father, and as ever in relation to the Holy Spirit. In Jesus' suffering, and in his life among us, we see the divine ecstasy and intimacy by which God also touches us — a going out to the extreme point, and a dwelling among us that is nearer than our own breath. The mystery of the Incarnation is that God has assumed human nature, taking it up into himself so that it may be both healed and glorified: body and soul, we have been visited by our Creator, and we see the location of this mystery in Jesus himself. All those things that are out of joint — our spirit, will, heart, mind, passions and body which tend to war against each other, our inter-personal relationships, our relationship with the other parts of creation — all these things find their healing because of the initiative of God. Further, because our nature has been taken up into God the Son, a new potential for intimate fellowship with the Father, and the glory of the Spirit that accompanies this, has now been forged. God's own actions of deep ecstasy and utter intimacy are being fostered in us. Our very sacraments proclaim the rhythm — in baptism we go out of ourselves as we are immersed in Christ's death and sealed by his Spirit. In the Eucharist, we commune with him and with each other, in growing intimacy.

All this begins with the act of God, continues through the wooing of God's Spirit, and issues in the willing turn of the human spirit to him. "Turn us again, O God. Show the light of your countenance and we shall be whole." What happens when we set our face steadfastly towards this light? When we acknowledge clearly our neediness as creatures in his hands, creatures that have been given the present time in which to meet with him? When we quiet ourselves before the living God and allow him daily, moment by moment, to speak into our clamor and anguish? When we cease to fuss about the past and worry about the future, knowing that these are God's prerogative, and that for now, we are "children of the day," of the *present*. Surely then we hear the divine voice directing us to heed his Son. The Holy Spirit forms Christ in us, granting us liberty to be transformed together, even through suffering, as we live in the world that God is reclaiming, and that he promises to renew.

Bless us, O Lord,
Whom you have brought through a holy calling
To the wonderful light of knowing you:
Help us to know
The sure foundation of your word
On which our instruction rests.

Pour your Holy Spirit upon us
That we may live
As little sheep of the one true shepherd,
Signed with the seal of the Holy Spirit
And precious members
Of the body of your Church;
And in the world to come
Make us worthy
Of the real and blessed hope
Of the kingdom of heaven,

That with all the saints
We too may glorify your Name
Which is worthy of all honour and majesty,
Father, Son and Holy Spirit, now and forever, Amen.

(adapted from an Eastern Orthodox
prayer for catechumens)

FURTHER MEDITATION

Reading the Holy Scriptures is like a treasure. With a treasure, you see, anyone able to find a tiny nugget gains for himself great wealth; likewise in the case of Sacred Scripture, you can get from a small phrase a great wealth of thought and immense riches. The Word of God is not only like a treasure, but is also like a spring gushing with ever-flowing waters in a mighty flood. . . . Great is the yield of this treasure and the flow of this spiritual fountain. Don't be surprised if we have experienced this:

our forebears drank from these waters to the limit of their capacity, and those who come after us will try to do likewise, without risk of exhausting them; instead the flood will increase and the streams will be multiplied. (St. John Chrysostom, Homily *III*, *Homilies on Genesis 1-17*)

The glorious fount of him Who was sitting
at the well as Giver of drink to all,
flows to each according to his will:
different springs according to those who drink.
From the well a single undifferentiated drink
Came up each time for those who drank.
The Living Fount lets distinct blessings
Flow to distinct people.

(St. Ephrem the Syrian, *Hymns on Virginity* 23.3)

Brother, let me be your servant, let me be as Christ to you.
Pray that I might have the grace to let you be my servant too.

We are pilgrims on a journey, we are [travelers] on the road.
We are here to help each other walk the mile and bear the load.

I will hold the Christ-light for you, in the night-time of your fear,
I will hold my hand out to you, speak the peace you long to hear.

I will weep when you are weeping, when you laugh, I'll laugh
    with you.
I will share your joy and sorrow till we've seen this journey through.

When we sing to God in heaven, we shall find such harmony.
Born of all we've known together of Christ's love and agony.

[Sister,] let me be your servant, let me be as Christ to you,
Pray that I might have the grace to let you be my servant too.

Richard Gillard [adapted]
© 1977 Scripture In Song.
c/o Integrity Media, Inc.,
1000 Cody Road, Mobile, AL 36695.
Used by permission

Hope means that our heads do not bump up against the low ceiling of this world; hope means that the exhilarating, wonderful, and terrifying winds of Heaven blow in our ears. (Peter Kreeft, *Back to Virtue*, p. 74)

Look upon Zion, the city of our appointed feasts. Your eyes will see Jerusalem, a quiet habitation, an immovable tent, whose stakes will never be plucked up, nor will any of its cords be broken. But there the Lord in majesty will be for us a place of broad rivers and streams.... The Lord is our king; he will save us.... Then ... no inhabitant will say, "I am sick"; the people who dwell there will be forgiven their iniquity. (Isaiah 33:20-24)

FURTHER STUDY

A. On Hope

Bauckham, Richard, and Trevor Hart. *Hope against Hope: Christian Eschatology at the Turn of the Millennium.* Grand Rapids: Eerdmans, 1999.

Kreeft, Peter. *Back to Virtue: Traditional Moral Wisdom for Modern Moral Confusion.* San Francisco: Ignatius Press, 1992.

Lyotard, Jean François. *The Postmodern Condition.* Translated by Geoff Bennington and Bryan Massumi. Minneapolis: University of Minnesota Press, 1984.

Pannenberg, Wolfhart. "Eschatology and the Experience of Meaning." In *Basic Questions in Theology III,* translated by R. A. Wilson, pp. 192-210. London: SCM Press, 1974.

Pieper, Josef. *On Hope.* Translated by Sr. Mary Frances McCarthy. San Francisco: Ignatius Press, 1986.

B. On Healing

Avalos, Hector. *Health Care and the Rise of Christianity.* Peabody, Mass.: Hendrickson, 1999.

Bergner, Mario. "Redeemed Lives," "Alive Again," "Returning Sons." Material for a course on healing, available online at http://www.redeemedlives.org and P.O. Box 1211, Wheaton IL 60187.

Chrysostom, St. John. "Homily LI on John vii.37, 38." In *Nicene and Post-Nicene Fathers,* 14:183-86. Edited by Philip Schaff. Peabody, Mass.: Hendrickson, 1889, 1994.

————. "Homily III" in *Homilies on Genesis 1–17*. In *The Fathers of the Church* 74:34-50. Translated by Robert C. Hill. Washington: Catholic University of America Press, 1986.

————. "Against Publishing the Errors of the Brethren." In *Nicene and Post-Nicene Fathers* 9:235-42. Edited by Philip Schaff. Peabody, Mass.: Hendrickson, 1889, 1994.

Coyle, J., and Steven Muir. *Healing in Religion and Society from Hippocrates to the Puritans*. Lewiston, N.Y.: Mellen, 1999.

Ephrem the Syrian, St. *Hymns on Virginity*. Translated by Kathleen E. McVey. In *Ephrem the Syrian: Hymns*. Classics of Western Spirituality. New York: Paulist, 1989.

Lewis, C. S. *Miracles: A Preliminary Study*. New York: Macmillan, 1947.

Martin, Dale. *The Corinthian Body*. New Haven: Yale University Press, 1995.

Wilkinson, John, M.D. *The Bible and Healing: A Medical and Theological Commentary*. Grand Rapids: Eerdmans, 1998.

FURTHER DISCUSSION

1. Consider the images of water and breath as complementary expressions of God's life given to us. What are the drawbacks of only using these organic pictures?

2. Why is it common, in Christian practice and liturgy, to bless physical things that God uses for our benefit — e.g. the Bible before it is read, the elements of the Lord's Supper? Is this simply a reminder to those involved that God requires our watchfulness in these actions, or does the blessing make an actual impact upon what is heard and what is ingested? Is it superstitious to bless "things"?

3. If Jesus is the substitute and perfect "Die-er," why are human beings still (for the most part) required to travel through death to God's new life?

4. What direct actions and programs could your church or small group implement in order to foster hope in those who are tempted to despair? Which groups in society today are the least effectively served by the church, and would most benefit from such programs?

C

Suffering, Transformation, and New Creation

It is a pity that Steve Martin's hilarious film L.A. Story was relatively un-successful. Perhaps it was too subtle for the average American viewer — playful references to Hamlet, The Tempest, popular hymns, and the Bible interweave its lines and stud its zany plot. At one point the two main characters, on the verge of love, enter a courtyard garden between two city buildings. As they enter its gates, we go into "slow-mo," and the two stone lions at the entrance pillars turn their heads to gaze on the couple. Around them the garden bursts into bloom, reminiscent of the luxurious growth of Eden. They continue walking together, hand in hand, and the camera pans down to their feet, where we notice, with a smile, that their adult shoes do not fit them anymore. The lovers walk out of them into bareness, and have become innocents in paradise, leaving behind all the complexity of their urban, jaded, postmodern lives. This theme of a re-turn to innocence is the controlling one for the film, and seems to reflect Martin's wistful longing for simplicity, as does the climactic musical mo-ment, in which a lone bagpipe intones "Amazing Grace."

The yearning to return to Eden has been an insistent theme for cen-turies, especially since the West's movement into "modernity" and indus-trialization. This yearning speaks both of our sense that things are not as they should be — we know suffering and disorientation — and of our de-sire that God (or someone!) should reverse the destructive patterns of our world. The "problem of pain" is felt by every human being who has not abandoned himself or herself to fatalism, and may even be amplified for the Christian. Christians, after all, must hold together three seemingly ir-reconcilable precepts:

247

1. God is perfectly loving.
2. God is all-powerful.
3. Evil is real.

To let go of any one of these three statements is to adopt a different story from that told in the Scriptures. The creation and salvation story both presuppose and exhibit God's love. The doctrine of creation *ex nihilo*, the practice of prayer, the prophetic announcements regarding God's historical actions, the awe-inspiring signs of the prophets and Jesus, the resurrection, and our anticipation of the story's end are all bound up with God's omnipotence. The drama and conflict of our metanarrative, the serious statements regarding God's hatred of sin, the universal fact of death, the grave act of the atonement, and the references to an adversary forbid us from thinking that evil (or suffering) is simply a construct of the human mind in the way that some Buddhist or Gnostic thinkers have suggested. The Christian simply is not at liberty to radically question any one of these statements and still remain connected with the Christian story. Typically, of course, professional and amateur theologians alike qualify one of these in their attempt to cope with the problem. They will say, "Ah, but God's goodness is not of the human sort — it is beyond our comprehension." They will suggest, "But human freedom, chosen by God, is in contest with God's power, and so we see many problems." They will mutter, "Well, evil's reality is not of the same sort as that of God and goodness — its 'reality' is only parasitic upon what is truly real, and so need not concern us."

Each of these explanations no doubt goes some way in helping us to manage in difficult situations. Moreover, the final suggestion, that evil is a "privation" of good, has a long and august history, and will, we believe, be borne out at the end, when God is all in all. But if we press any one of these qualifications to the extreme, we have lost the game. For if God is truly "beyond good and evil" as some have declared, if he has tied his own hands in an "open-ness" to the creation that critically mitigates his power, if evil is, indeed, nothing at all, there remains no Christian story, and the revelation of God and this world that we have been given must be mistaken. Our very difficulty in holding together the three statements witnesses to the depth of disjointedness and pain that racks this world at every level. God is not dismissive of suffering; nor must we be.

However, the shape of the biblical story, and the sharing of God the Son and Spirit in human pain mean that suffering is not absurd or meaningless. To the contrary, the passion of Christ and the birth-giving cries of the Spirit (Romans 8) are both effective and critical elements of our story. Though our formal intellectual grasp of suffering's meaning remains elusive, suffering comes to be understood in our living, for we are bound up with Jesus, who plumbed the depths of this dark mystery, and with the Spirit, who brings life out of unpromising darkness. Seen in the light of God's work in the world, even natural and political turmoil are interpreted as the "birth-pangs" heralding God's new creation:

> For nation will rise against nation, and kingdom against kingdom; there will be earthquakes in various places, there will be famines; this is but the beginning of the birth-pangs. (Mark 13:8)

> But as to the times and the seasons, brethren, you have no need to have anything written to you. For you yourselves know well that the day of the Lord will come like a thief in the night. When people say, "There is peace and security," then sudden destruction will come upon them as travail comes upon a woman with child, and there will be no escape. (1 Thessalonians 5:1-3)

In particular, God's suffering people play a role in God's plan for the world, for we are strengthened by the Spirit, who groans alongside us (and within us) as a kind of midwife to the new creation. Our prayers, given purpose and force by the Holy Spirit, have a role to play as God brings about a new birth of the whole of creation: all that he has made "will obtain the freedom of the glory of the sons of God" (Romans 8:21). Thus the salvation that has come into our world in Jesus now is directed from the inside out, through the Spirit. Though (or *because*) like Jesus we taste suffering, we "boast in the hope of sharing the glory of God" (Romans 5:2), assured that the suffering of God's people will affect the entire creation! This hope does not render suffering any less painful.

Suffering that Transforms

The Christian story, then, is world-affirming, not world-denying. Paradoxically, part of its affirmation of life includes the dignity that suffering is afforded. Paul assures the Corinthians,

But we have this treasure in clay jars, so that it may be made clear that this extraordinary power belongs to God and does not come from us. We are afflicted in every way, but not crushed; perplexed, but not driven to despair; persecuted, but not forsaken; struck down, but not destroyed; always carrying in the body the death of Jesus, so that the life of Jesus may also be made visible in our bodies. . . . So we do not lose heart. Even though our outer nature is wasting away, our inner nature is being renewed day by day. For this slight momentary affliction is preparing us for an eternal weight of glory beyond all measure. . . . (2 Corinthians 4:7-10, 16-17)

How could it be otherwise? After all, we must take our lives as they are, and Act II (the Fall) has occurred. Moreover, Paul patterns his life after that of Act IV's Jesus, and so understands the calling of the apostle to be cruciform. His "we" in 2 Corinthians refers specifically to those with an apostolic calling, but by extension embraces all who understand the Christian way. Paul's insight has been grasped on a personal level by many of the mystics or spiritual theologians whose work we have tasted: they learned, in the times of seeming desolation, that God was at work, forging a deeper intimacy with them than before. However, the transformative use to which God puts our necessary suffering has a larger dimension, that goes beyond the development of our own personal character. Suffering, though not God's first choice for the cosmos, and a clear source of pain for the One who is touched by our infirmities, has been embraced and redirected towards transformation. The paradox of Paul, that life can be held within death, is also expressed in the visions of the seer John. In his visions unveiled for us in the book of Revelation, John described this mystery as embedded within the complexities of our world. Buried within the central part of the book of Revelation, at 12:1-18, we find two conjoined stories that portray the present ambiguous identity of God's people. Consider the scene: in this section, John is looking at things from the vantage point of earth, gazing up into the heavens, where he sees, cast upon the dark screen of the heavenlies human shadows, projected big, and merged with the cosmic drama. The drama has its heights and depths, its moments of danger and rescue, its points of hope deferred and hope enjoined.

There are three main parts to the chapter. In the first part, verses 1-6, John introduces two luminous signs in heaven. The first is a great and wondrous portent of a woman "clothed with the sun, with the moon under her feet and a crown of twelve stars on her head." She is a queen, and is about to give birth. Then begins the drama. John says, "I saw another sign, and behold, a great red dragon" — an enormous red dragon with seven heads, ten horns, and seven crowns. The monster sweeps a third of the stars out of heaven, and blocks the woman, in an attempt to devour her child. The child is a son "who will rule all the nations," and so is snatched out of harm's way, up to God's throne, while the woman flees to a special place in the desert.

John then introduces a parallel scene, a scene of war in heaven (verses 7-12). In this vignette, Michael and his angels are in combat with the dragon and his angels, and are finally victorious, casting the evil crew down to earth. At this point we are told the identity of the symbolic dragon — "the ancient serpent, or Satan, who leads the whole world astray." After his expulsion from heaven, we hear a confident declaration from the loud voice in heaven:

> Now have come the salvation and the power and the kingdom of our God and the authority of his Christ, for the accuser of our comrades has been thrown down, who accuses them day and night before our God. But they have conquered him by the blood of the Lamb and by the word of their testimony [or "martyrdom"], for they did not cling to life, even in the face of death. Rejoice then, you heavens and those who dwell in them! But woe to the earth and the sea, for the devil has come down to you with great wrath, because he knows that his time is short! (12:10-12)

Notice that through this declaration, we are given a further insight into the battle. According to the conjoined two visions, the male child was rescued, while Michael and his angels fought against the dragon; but in the declaration we hear that the dragon has been overcome *by the blood of the Lamb,* and by the word of the martyr-witnesses. We may have thought that the first story concerned the earthly nativity of the Messiah. Rather, we now learn, the Messiah (now called the Lamb) did not escape death. (Was that "birth" actually a "new birth," that is, his resurrection after death, followed by exaltation to heaven?) At any rate, he has spilled blood, and is declared the real victor. The Lamb's death is the means by which Satan has been cast down. Yet there is something to make us uneasy. What does the

casting down of Satan mean for those on earth? — it means suffering, because the dragon is livid at his expulsion, and is out for more blood.

The combined effect of victory and danger is intriguing: it is also helpful, if read with care and with sensitivity. The accuser of God's people, the
one who wants to devour the child and hurt the woman, is God's enemy.
In one sense, he has been conquered. The decisive battle has been fought
through the death of Jesus, the Lamb. *Now* has come the authority of
God's Messiah, the Lion of Judah who is also a Lamb. No longer will God
listen to the accusations of the adversary; no longer does Satan have access to the throne, because of what Jesus has done. *Now* have come God's
power and kingdom and salvation. Yet this very conquest means the un-
leashing of Satan upon the world — like a doomed man, the adversary
will fight against anyone associated with the woman, against her family.
Suffering is a necessary *result* of the conquest of Satan — it is also a *means*
to his defeat: "They overcame him by the blood of the Lamb, and the word
of their martyrdom." This is not strict logic, but can be communicated
within the kaleidoscopic reality of the vision. From one perspective, the
enemy is conquered by suffering; in another odd way, that very conquest
of Satan entails the suffering of God's people here and now on earth.

After this astonishing revelation, John returns in verses 13-17 to the
conflict between the dragon and the woman. The dragon is no longer
able to devour the child, and so pursues the woman. And she is given
help, both from the earth and by God. Like Israel of old, she is given eagle's wings to rescue her. Twice in the Hebrew Scriptures, the flight of Israel from Egypt to the promised land is described in these terms:

> You have seen what I did to the Egyptians, and how I bore you on ea-
> gles' wings and brought you to myself. (Exodus 19:4)

> Like an eagle that stirs up its nest, that flutters over its young, spread-
> ing out its wings, catching them, bearing them on its pinions, the
> LORD alone did lead him, and there was no foreign god with him. He
> made him ride on the high places of the earth, and he ate the produce
> of the field; and he made him suck honey out of the rock, and oil out of
> the flinty rock. (Deuteronomy 32:11-13)

The God-given wings in the Old Testament spirit the Hebrew people
away from danger, through the desert, and *into* a land of plenty. In John's

vision, however, the woman is rescued on eagle's wings, but taken *to the desert,* to a place prepared for her by God.

So the seer John speaks in harmony with what the spiritual theologians have learned from their own harsh experience. The desert also is included in God's design. It is a place of preparation. Our mysterious symbolic woman, clothed with the twelve stars, reminds us of Israel, with her twelve tribes; but she is also the mother of other offspring who "obey God's commandments and hold to the testimony of Jesus" (12:17). So this heavenly woman must stand for the entire people of God, both the original race that brought forth the Messiah, and the new congregation, against whom the adversary fights. Insofar as she is linked with the Christ, the One who suffered, she must taste suffering. In the desert, however, there is still God's protection.

The refugee queen, then, is a sign that does double duty, reminding us that those who belong to the Messiah are marked both by humility and nobility. Her two places of residence — heaven and the desert — are pictures of her identity. She is born to glory, but for the meantime must abide in a marginal, "liminal" place, the desert. The symbol of the desert, and her sojourn there for "time, times and half a time" (that is, three and a half) are significant. Far too much fruitless speculation has been published in certain North American circles about the significance of this number for the timing of the "tribulation" and the "rapture." We should consider the number within the context of the Revelation rather than in terms of an eschatological time-table made up by human beings. The time period of three and a half is seen throughout the Apocalypse: it is the length of time that the holy city will be trampled upon (chapter 11); this is the space of time during which the demonic beast, who deceives the world, will be allowed to blaspheme and exercise authority (chapter 13). During the very time of their shame and persecution, God's noble people, in a desert place, will be cared for and prepared. John's visions pile image upon image, showing us that suffering and the seeming victory of evil are temporary, but allowed by God. The desolation, the humiliation, the oppression are being used by the Lord to his glory — they are part of the care of his people, they are a prepared time. The seer's vision confirms Paul's statement: "For this slight momentary affliction is preparing us for an eternal weight of glory beyond all measure."

But sometimes the affliction does not seem so very *slight.* It is hard to put the desert together with the hope of glory; it is harder to juxtapose a bewildering battle with the hymns of joy. John's vision brings us to a point of inner conflict, insisting that we see things in ways that are counter-intuitive. Although war is being waged on earth by the dragon, God is still sovereign. We are encouraged by John to adopt a sobriety concerning evil, even while we insist upon the ultimate authority of the Almighty. Thus, in the midst of all these visions of strife, there is placed a great declaration of present victory: "*Now* has come the salvation." God's people are in the midst of all this, yet they hear from the voice of heaven that victory is secured. The time of suffering is real, it is potent, but it is limited. The number of suffering, humiliation, and exile, three and a half, is only half of seven, the number of fullness or perfection. So then, the time in the desert is, if you like, only half the story; and even this difficult time is superintended by God.

In the Apocalypse, God's people are pictured as the Queen of Heaven, a woman in exile, who is in the midst of her transformation by God. Yet she has not fully come into that inheritance. Like the scroll that John has eaten, her life retains a bittersweet quality. Reality is complex, and must be seen from different perspectives. The casting down of the dragon means both joy and woe. God reaches into the situation of the woman, calling out in assurance, giving her eagle's wings, keeping her safe, making her time of exile a time of maturation. From the perspective of one who is embroiled in the battle, suffering is the lot of God's people. Yet that "witness" or "martyrdom" has its own strong effect, and is joined with the sacrifice of the Lamb (12:7).

By tracing this cosmic drama of which we have become a part, John shows us that suffering is part of something larger and more important than we can imagine. We are given comfort in this, even while the darkness, the shadow of reality, remains. Called to praise, we know that the desert is still a reality. John's words may strike those of us who live in comfort as bizarre. Yet we must stop and think: If the Church at the dawn of the third millennium is unaware of this tension, this great drama of the heavens and the desert, then perhaps we require a revolution of the imagination, so that we identify more strongly with the persecuted queen, with those in trouble, and with the martyrdom of Jesus.

The Lamb and Suffering

The ambiguity of the current age is further explained by another scene in the Apocalypse, the vision of Revelation 4–5. Here John has been invited, and we through him, through an open door, to "come up here" into the throne room of heaven. What he beholds is not, at first, drama, but worship:

> After this I looked, and lo, in heaven an open door! And the first voice, which I had heard speaking to me like a trumpet, said, "Come up hither, and I will show you what must take place after this." At once I was in the Spirit, and lo, a throne stood in heaven, with one seated on the throne! And he who sat there appeared like jasper and carnelian, and round the throne was a rainbow that looked like an emerald. Round the throne were twenty-four thrones, and seated on the thrones were twenty-four elders, clad in white garments, with golden crowns upon their heads. From the throne issue flashes of lightning, and voices and peals of thunder, and before the throne burn seven torches of fire, which are the seven spirits of God; and before the throne there is as it were a sea of glass, like crystal.
>
> And round the throne, on each side of the throne, are four living creatures, full of eyes in front and behind: the first living creature like a lion, the second living creature like an ox, the third living creature with the face of a man, and the fourth living creature like a flying eagle. And the four living creatures, each of them with six wings, are full of eyes all round and within, and day and night they never cease to sing, "Holy, holy, holy is the Lord God Almighty, who was and is and is to come!"
>
> And whenever the living creatures give glory and honor and thanks to him who is seated on the throne, who lives for ever and ever, the twenty-four elders fall down before him who is seated on the throne and worship him who lives for ever and ever; they cast their crowns before the throne, singing, "Worthy art thou, our Lord and God, to receive glory and honor and power, for thou didst create all things, and by thy will they existed and were created." (Revelation 4:1-11)

In full knowledge of our present human condition, how do we respond to such solemnity and joy? Here is a scene of mystery: the Holy One, attended by twenty-four noble elders — perhaps our representatives, the

prophets and apostles. The worship is led by strange angelic living creatures who never cease their praises; even the noble faithful fall down before the One on the throne, because he is worthy of all honor. He is the
Creator, and they are his creation. In this chapter there is a sense of timelessness, of ongoing and uninterrupted praise, of continual joy before the
Creator for his mighty acts. The whole of creation is represented by those
four strange beings, who are pictured like various animals, and yet have a
foreign quality. The churches of God are represented there, too, by the elders, and by the seven lamps blazing before God's throne.

Yet perhaps this scene seems too lofty, too removed, too strange for
us to enter. We look, via John, through a window in heaven, at a vivid
scene that can hardly seem permanent, at least from our perspective.
What do we know of such uninterrupted sight of God? John, too, feels
the separation. As he gazes at the One on the throne, he becomes aware
of a problem:

> And I saw in the right hand of him who was seated on the throne a
> scroll written within and on the back, sealed with seven seals; and I
> saw a strong angel proclaiming with a loud voice, "Who is worthy to
> open the scroll and break its seals?" And no one in heaven or on earth
> or under the earth was able to open the scroll or to look into it, and I
> wept much that no one was found worthy to open the scroll or to look
> into it. (Revelation 5:1-4)

There is an unread scroll, an unopened book of complete and utter
importance, and no one is able to open it. Here is the whole cosmos before God, and a book that will explain all things: all the pieces of the puz-
zle are there, but John doesn't know what to do with them. No one can
open the sealed scroll, he thinks, no one can make sense of the strange
and puzzling events of our world; no one can put all this together so that
it fits in with the grand scene he is viewing.

This matters so much to John that he weeps and sobs, unable to contain himself despite the scene of praise. Here is a blot on the perfect
praise of God. But is John whisked away so that he does not spoil the
scene? Perhaps we imagine that such perfection would be jealous of its
own calm, and reject, ignore, or drown out a discordant voice. Instead,
the weeping one is embraced by the worshipers, and drawn into their act
of worship. Our sense of dissonance, of not belonging, may or may not

be so intense, but there are many human reasons to feel out of step with the universal chorus.

Yet John is taken seriously. One who is intimate with God, an elder, responds to his grief, and says, "Don't weep!" This is not a dismissal, however, for he gives John *a reason!* It is not that John's sense of confusion and pain are unimportant, or unfounded — it is that there is a solution to them. The answer the elder gives is our Lord Jesus himself — "Behold, the Lion of Judah" — the One who is a majestic Lion and who became for us the meek Lamb of sacrifice (5:5-6). The elder's words are an answer to John's mourning and unspoken prayer. The answer comes in the Person of Jesus himself, not in words of instruction or exhortation. John sees through his vision that the Lion is the Lamb of God, the One who died and yet who stands. The elder directs John to look upon the One who loves him, and who has assumed human suffering: this is the answer to his prayer.

Notice also that the role of the elders (v. 8) is to present the prayers of believers before the Almighty. The prayers, joyful or fearful, confident or tearful, are important to the Lord, and like an offering to him. Perhaps we may feel at times that our prayers are aimless, unfocused, flying around randomly. There is, lost somewhere in my children's library, but enshrined in the memory of a mother reading to her five-year-old, a book about a little Buddhist child who visits a monastery for the first time. In the story, a priest runs along a wall fitted with prayer wheels — as he runs by, he sets the cylinders flying around, and the prayers fly out everywhere, set loose by the motion. But this is not the picture of prayers that we receive in the book of Revelation. There, the prayers of God's people, the saints, are collected by angels in vials or bowls: they are not randomly let loose, but offered up as incense in a worship service as a sweet smell of praise to the Lord. So, John's yearning to have the scroll opened, and our yearning to understand God's will for us, for the Church, for the world, are honored. They are honored by a sight of the Lion-Lamb himself, who has plumbed the depth of grief and suffering for our sake.

We know from experience that tears are ambiguous, springing from causes both superficial and profound. Sometimes the expression or evocation of tears in Christian gatherings says less about the worship than about artificially heightened emotion or undisciplined passion. However, both Eastern and Western Christianity have recognized authentic sorrow, both for personal sin, and for the state of others or the world, as a gift of

God — they speak of "the gift of tears" and of "godly grief." John's actions in the Apocalypse surely fall into this category as a sacrificial expression of tears. His lament in the throne room is a true response to which the God of truth can, in turn, truly answer. If we have never come to John's point of weeping before God, we have just not been around long enough, or we have found a good way to insulate ourselves against reality. Perhaps we have deadened ourselves to suffering, saying "this is just life" and not expecting too much any more. The Apocalypse assures us, to the contrary, that weeping is neither faithless or futile. John pictures a transformation of our weeping, a turning of our prayers of pain, into incense:

> And when he had taken the scroll, the four living creatures and the twenty-four elders fell down before the Lamb, each holding a harp, and with golden bowls full of incense, which are the prayers of the saints; and they sang a new song, saying, "Worthy art thou to take the scroll and to open its seals, for thou wast slain and by thy blood didst ransom men for God from every tribe and tongue and people and nation, and hast made them a kingdom and priests to our God, and they shall reign on earth." (5:8-10)

The twenty-four elders, as representatives of our world, hold before God bowls of incense, bowls brimming with our prayers — and the perfume and smoke of the incense goes up to God along with the songs of the saints. They pray and they sing. And what do they sing to the Lion-Lamb?

> You are worthy to take the scroll and to open its seals, because you were slain, and with your blood you purchased humans for God from every tribe and language and people and nation. You have made them to be a kingdom and priests to serve our God, and they will reign on earth.

If we follow the lead of the beasts and the elders, we undertake two actions at once: we pray and we sing. Our prayers will sometimes be prayers of tears, prayers of struggle, of reality, of pain. And why not? The Lamb cried tears too, tears of blood. He delights to share our lot, to assume our identity, and so to heal us. John, and with him, we ourselves, are told, by the voice of the elder, "Behold the Lion of Judah!" So, we turn, and see the fulfillment of his weeping — the Lion-Lamb, the One who knows all too well what it is to suffer, what it is to weep, what it is to live in a confusing and complicated world that is still in the process of becoming. John finds that his tears have been added to the bowls of prayers being offered up before the Lamb, the Lamb who is being crowned Lord of all, and to whom a new song can be sung: he has triumphed, he is worthy, he is able. Even John's tears of longing make harmony with the new song, in which they find their hope and their fulfillment. He is part of a kingdom, part of a priesthood, and his tears, with his prayers, have their place (5:10).

John's vision was twenty centuries ago, but it expresses what is true of all times and places. Our near contemporary Evelyn Underhill challenges those of us who crave intimacy with God, and who desire his new creation, without entering into suffering ourselves —

> Prayer is the substance of life. It gives back to man, insofar as he is willing *to live to capacity* — that is to say, to *give love* and to *suffer pain* — the beatitude without which he is incomplete; for it sets going, deepens and at last perfects that mutual indwelling of two orders which redeems us from unreality, and in which the creative purpose reaches its goal. (*An Anthology of the Love of God*, p. 127)

Here, then, are two amazing things: that the worship of heaven should be interrupted by us in our suffering, and that our interruption should be naturalized so as to become part of a new song! This amazement is matched by the vision we are offered by the One who has healed us — he is both a Lion and a Lamb, both the Lord on the throne and the One among us. Revelation 5:6 declares that he is both in the midst of the worshipers and in the center of the throne — not "*between* the throne and the elders," as most versions wrongly translate, but in both places at once! He has conquered — but in a way that we never could have expected. He rules from his throne, and invites us into the worship that brings life to our dry and thirsty hearts.

New Creation

In our place in Act V, then, we find ourselves at a point of nexus. For us, life is bound up with suffering, yet as we look at suffering more closely, in the light of the Incarnation, we see that this is true because the One who is Love has expressed himself through his willingness to give, and to suffer pain. This could only be glimpsed from afar by those who did not know what God's Son would accomplish. The new state of affairs ushered in by Jesus was startling, even to those who knew the promises of the old covenant; however, God's plans were not entirely undisclosed prior to his coming. The prophets Isaiah, Jeremiah, and Ezekiel had, by God, intuited that suffering was not simply a punishment for the disobedience of Israel, but that it would finally issue in glory, and thus could be accepted with hope. Thus the three great prophetic books move back and forth between suffering and glimpses of hope, until each of them makes the grand crescendo — as readers, we are propelled forward from the plight of God's people to anticipate the new creation. Isaiah 40–66 envisions the "regathering" of the chosen people whom the Lord "created" (43:1-7), and their new state of blessing. In the final chapter, God's people emerge through a "new birth" as a joyful nation, nurtured in the holy city, whose number is swelled by foreigners (66:18-21). There will be "a new heaven and a new earth" in which "all flesh" will continually worship him. Jeremiah's vision is less sweeping, but every bit as profound. This prophet glimpses a time when "they shall be radiant over the goodness of the LORD" (31:12), when a new covenant will be forged (31:31-34) and when God will create "a new thing" (31:22). Ezekiel pictures the new creation in terms of purity: the people are re-gathered under the true divine Shepherd (34:1-31), renewed by washing and the gift of a new heart (36:16-37), brought back to life "out of the grave," "inbreathed" by God's Spirit (37:1-28), and placed within an immense temple-garden filled with the divine glory (43:1–47:23).

In this way, the Hebrew prophets portrayed the new creation as the prerogative of God's chosen people, a hope offered specifically to those who were suffering at the hands of Gentile superpowers, and who were longing for an end to earthly exile. However, the prophetic vision of the new creation could not be contained. Though directed to the faithful in Israel, the prophecies and the hope overreach themselves, going beyond the boundaries of the Holy Land: the glory and life-giving power of the LORD will shine, we are told, even upon the "alien" (Ezekiel 47:22). Ezekiel's two rivers join to form a huge freshwater sea, adorned with "trees for healing" (47:12), and Isaiah's Zion envisages a remade cosmos. Jeremiah, though not aware of the *extent* of the re-creation, knows of its *depths:* God intends to place his will within his people, so they will know innately his plans for this world.

It is not expected that they would have understood, prior to the unveiling of God's secret, the shape that the new creation would assume. Similarly, though we have the pattern of Jesus' own resurrection and ascension, we do not yet see our hope clearly. We look for "what no . . . human heart conceived, what God has prepared for those who love him" (1 Corinthians 2:9). God has something new in store for us. Though it is beyond our ken, we can be assured that this new thing has a deep connection with this present world, since God himself has entered our physical world in the Incarnation, renewed it in the resurrection, and glorified it by the ascension. The Lion-Lamb stands both "in the center of the throne" and "in the center of the elders." He has full right to the heavenly throne, and a legitimate place in the midst of the people. Like the Lamb, the new creation of the Lamb partakes of the glorious realm of God, as well as of the wonderful creation that is presently our home.

Our understanding of the new creation, then, must be informed by a thorough understanding of the Incarnation, for God the Son assumed humanity, body and all, not simply to redeem, but also to heal and glorify. In the course of his fiery letter to the Galatians, that letter in which Paul reaffirms what it means to be joined to God through the new covenant, the apostle exclaims, *"But a new creation [is everything]!"* (Galatians 6:15b). Paul's outburst makes it clear that we can hardly over-emphasize the importance of God's gift of new life to us, his "new creation." In terms of our great metanarrative, we see that the "new creation" (or at the very least, the seed of that creation) was established in Act IV, through the Son's Incarnation, human life, death, resurrection, and ascension. Though this creation is "new," there is an unbroken connection between Act IV and the three preceding Acts. Jesus summed up and corrected all that went before; again, Jesus undid the effects of Act II, showing what God intended both Adam and Israel to be. Act IV, then, is quite literally, "crucial," and through its grand action, Christians in the new covenant are presently given new eyes through which to interpret the world.

For those of us who live now in Act V, there is a new way of being: "If anyone is in Christ, behold — new creation!" (2 Corinthians 5:17; my translation). This new creation is present to us, though still hidden in some respects: the foretaste that we have been given in the Holy Spirit points forward to the final completion of all things. Yet in the New Human, Jesus, the new creation has already begun. Through his actions in Act IV, God's new creation is presently bequeathed to those Act V players who are *in Christ*, and it will come to fruition in Act V, when we behold, with transformed eyes, the new heavens and new earth. We can, indeed, see the "newness" implied in the Gospel narratives about this Son of Man. There, Jesus is portrayed as that new human being who re-tread the road of humanity, but this time in a new mode, without sin and so as to conquer death. So Luke introduces Jesus as "son of Adam, son of God" (3:38) and then proceeds to show his triumph over the tempter in the temptation story. Again, as we have seen, at the climax of the Fourth Gospel, Jesus "breathes" upon the apostles. His action follows the motif of the creating God who breathed upon the Edenic couple, replaying it in a higher key — the followers of Jesus receive the Spirit, not simply the gift of life. Even while Paul recognizes that corruptible "flesh and blood" cannot inherit the full gift of God, he looks for us not to be disembodied, but to be "re-clothed" more gloriously (2 Corinthians 5:1-5). We expect neither a "resuscitation" into the same fallible bodies that we now possess, nor a spiritualized existence that is void of the joy of the senses. When that time comes, we will have bodies vivified by the very Spirit of God, rather than simply animated by the breath of life. In 1 Corinthians 15:44, Paul says that in the New Cosmos we will have "en-Spirited bodies" *(soma pneumatikon)* rather than "en-souled" or "animated bodies" *(soma psychikon)*. So then, in our final home, all of us, including our bodies, will have been transfigured completely by the tryst of the human spirit with the Holy Spirit.

We conclude our discussion of Christian spirituality, then, by wondering again at the shape of the biblical story — that unique shape, which must never be graphed as a "v" but always as a check-mark. Some still yearn for a return to Eden. The biblical narrative ends differently. Although the first human couple begins in Paradise, the final scene is that of an enfoliated, fruitful city, inhabited — or perhaps identified with — a multitude (Revelation 21–22). Its scope is immense and inclusive of the entire people of God, built with twelve gates named for the Old Testament tribes, and upon twelve foundations named for the new covenant apostles.

It is important that we read these final chapters of Revelation (which are, of course, the closing pages of our canonical story) in close connection with the first five acts. To detach them from the rest of the story would be like looking to the back of the math book without working through the problems, or turning to the dénouement of a novel before we have experienced all the twists and turns of the plot. Revelation 21 is no wishful glance forward to the future: it is a chapter that sums up all the hopes and fears of Israel and of all humanity, while celebrating and bringing to completion the intimate and magnificent acts of the God who is strong on our behalf. Throughout the book, John has been the reader's "tour guide" to disorienting but telling mysteries of the past, present, and future, the abyss and the heavenly abode. In the final chapters, the veil is lifted again, and we are given a glimpse of something completely new (22:5). John's final vision is that of marriage, including a new earth (which we might have expected) and a new heaven (which is somewhat of a surprise!). On the cosmic level, we find the same pattern that we have seen imprinted upon our smaller human lives, as we have learned from entering more and more into the mystery who is Christ. God is both the fulfiller of our dreams and the great iconoclast of our unworthy idols. He is "of old" and yet forever new.

In Revelation 21:1-2, this newness is signaled both positively and negatively: negatively by the absence of "the sea" and positively by the spectacle of "the new Jerusalem, coming down from heaven . . . as a bride." The reader of the entire Apocalypse has met the sea twice already in John's vision: first, as the crystal sea in the heavenly throne room (4:6), which corresponds to the bronze sea or basin for purification found in the Jerusalem Temple; and then, as the standing place of the adversary of God, and the birthplace of his human ally, whose role is to deceive and destroy humanity (12:18–13:1). The sea thus evokes two contrasting themes: the necessity for purification before a holy God and the uncomfortable presence of chaotic forces which compete with God's order, and which leave humankind and nature in disarray. In the new creation of God, there will be no need for purification, nor will there be any further tendency to anarchy.

But there *will* be a new human community, which John sees coming from God's own presence, prepared, as it were, by him and for him. The figure is both a city and a bride and its meaning is interpreted by the heavenly voice — "God's dwelling will be with humankind" (21:3). Part of the "newness," then, is an astonishing order of intimacy between God and the "peoples" or "nations" (note the plural in the best manuscripts!). God's people together are conjoined to make a new dwelling place for the Alpha and the Omega, the first and the last. Totally new, too, is the triumph over the pain and death common to every member of the first created order (21:4; 22:3). The curse of Eden has been reversed.

Of real importance is the interplay between the communal and the personal. The vision shows a community, a re-created order, and emphasizes the identity of God's people *together*. Yet it goes on to appeal to each hearer: "I will give *to the thirsting one* [grace] to drink from the water of life. *The one who* overcomes will inherit all these things . . ." (21:6-7). We have a clue as to how these corporate and personal emphases are harmonized in the second half of verse 21:7. There we hear the promise: "I will be his God, and he will be my son." Let us remember that the title "son" is by no means intended to exclude the female believer, for we have already read that God's dwelling is with "humankind." (The Greek word *anthropoi* in 21:3 is deliberately inclusive.) Rather, language about "God's Son" recalls the traditional pictures of Israel (Jeremiah 31:20) and of the Messiah, the anointed representative of God's people (Psalm 2:7; John 1:14; Galatians 4:4; Hebrews 1:2). So, then, it is through our participation in Christ that we are, each personally, and all together, confirmed in our doing and our being. Who each of us is as a child of God, and who we are as humanity together, are all reclaimed by the re-creating God. We are again reminded of our calling to be "small-c" christs, participants in the anointing of the Messiah, the One who is both our representative and God's unique Son. It may be an imaginative stretch for women to use the language of "son" about themselves: yet men are surprised by the vision to picture themselves in feminine metaphor, as making up the "bride" of the Lamb. Challenges are issued, in the spiritual life, for all of God's children!

In John's picture of the descending city, he describes it in continuity with Israel (21:12) and the apostles (21:14), in its protection by celestial beings (21:12), and its measurements as a perfect cube (21:16-17). The appearance of the city-bride recalls that other mysterious female symbol in Revelation, the refugee woman of chapter 12, who was harassed by the serpent in the desert and "prepared" for a certain time while kept safe in her ordeal of persecution. That woman was crowned with twelve stars, surrounded by the glory of the sun and moon, and crying in childbirth (12:1). Surely she reappears *transformed* here in our final chapters, with all mourning gone, with the battlemented crown of a city, and with "no need of the sun . . . or moon" since she is surrounded by the glory of God and the Lamb. Here is the ultimate affirmation that suffering has meaning in the lives of God's faithful: their time of ordeal has not gone unheeded by God, but is transformed into a time of preparation. This word offered hope in a first-century time of terror for the earliest Christians. It can equally sustain those who suffer today at the hands of temporal rulers, even as it confronts those of us for whom suffering in Christ seems odd.

Certainly the magnitude and splendor of the city are not unimportant. Its proportions are so vast that only a heavenly being can measure them (15); it is made up of precious stones (17-21) that by their nature reflect the glory that illumines it. The image of God is fully restored in God's people. John's vision recalls the visionary chapters of Ezekiel 41–48 and Isaiah 65:17–66:24, but there is both more glory and more intimacy here. Here is also a rejuvenated garden, a dwelling for God's new creation in which all fit harmoniously together. Here is a vast city, in which the best of humanity's fruits are included (21:24, 26). Here is the bride of the Lamb, the one who shares in the glory of God because she has suffered and overcome in him. Here is the fulfillment of God's promises, promises that include not only a *return* to bliss, but a creative *remaking* in which we participate together. Chapter 21 does not promise "pie in the sky, by and by" but the dwelling of God *with* a re-created and glorified (21:8, 27) humanity. It is the promise of a new identity, together and personally, as we share in the glory of the Lamb. This transformation of ourselves and of our world — for which we yearn (22:27) — is sure to be fulfilled, because victory has been already accomplished through the mighty Lion (11:15), who is indeed a humble and slaughtered Lamb (5:5-6, 12:11, 19:13). It is he himself who has called us into the cosmic drama. It is through his world-overturning reign of vulnerability that the water of life flows (22:1), with future healing for all the nations (22:2), and with present sustenance for whoever will come and drink (21:6).

Despite its condemnation of Babylon, the Apocalypse does not bring its seer or its reader back to an un-retouched Eden. The final answer to godless or god-defying society is not a razing of that city, but a new city, the New Jerusalem. The situation is truly "new" and yet it has been prepared both in time and in space: events have occurred during the temporary "time, times and half-time" that is spoken of throughout the dramatic passages of the book of Revelation; God's people have been prepared in the ascetic place of the desert, but also, mysteriously, in the heavens, whence she appears, "from God." In past years, much emphasis was placed in the Church's preaching upon the final judgment, and preparation for the end of things. It is more common today to overlook this dark prelude to the new world of God. Some, indeed, imply that the current situation of suffering in which we find ourselves is the only purgation that we and this world require, and that the present time will issue

final created order is seen in all *fullness* and fecundity as *united* in common life and worship (22:3). The irrigating effect of the divine fountain will be complete! Just as God is revealed in the story of Israel and of Jesus to be Trinity and not a simple "monad," so here the created order, and redeemed humanity within her, are seen in glorious diversity as united in common and mutually interconnected worship of the One from whom comes all love, light, and life (22:3). Human culture is bound for transformation so as to share in the glory of God himself; all that we call nature is no mere backdrop for our life, but a reality of which we are, and will remain, a part. We will not become disembodied spirits, but will retain that link with the material world that God has declared to be "good" — though there will be more substance and glory to ourselves and to God's world than we can now imagine.

In all this, we see that our God who creates *ex nihilo* and who resurrects also intends to redeem and glorify his whole world. A firm attachment to the new creation will instruct us not to disparage the body, not to leash the Spirit of God, and not to despise the world that God has created. Instead, we learn to see with new eyes the beauty and final end of all God has made. Ecology is given a strong basis, healing is naturalized as part of God's purpose, and salvation is recognized as having an immensely broad scope. Thus, we are taught to be grateful not simply for our rescue from sin, but for the shining hope of a new creation, embedded already in this bittersweet world: everything around us, but especially the worship of Christ's gathered people in the Spirit, becomes the gift and sign of the Father's promise. As Alexander Schmemann puts it:

> The world . . . becomes an *epiphany* of God, a means of his revelation, presence, and power. . . . We *need* water and oil, bread and wine, in order to be in communion with God and to know him. . . . There is no worship without the participation of the [human] body . . . because the Holy Spirit "makes all things new." (*For the Life of the World*, pp. 120-22)

FURTHER MEDITATION

Glorious things of thee are spoken,
Zion, city of our God;
he whose word cannot be broken
formed thee for his own abode;

on the Rock of Ages founded,
what can shake thy sure repose?
With salvation's walls surrounded,
thou may'st smile at all thy foes.

See! the streams of living waters,
springing from eternal love,
well supply thy sons and daughters
and all fear of want remove.
Who can faint, when such a river
ever flows their thirst to assuage?
Grace which, like the Lord, the Giver,
never fails from age to age.

Round each habitation hovering,
see the cloud and fire appear
for a glory and a covering,
showing that the Lord is near.
Thus they march, their pillar leading,
light by night, and shade by day;
daily on the manna feeding
which he gives them when they pray.

Blest inhabitants of Zion,
washed in the Redeemer's blood!
Jesus, whom their souls rely on,
makes them kings and priests to God.
'Tis his love his people raises
over self to reign as kings:
and as priests, his solemn praises
each for a thank-offering brings.

Savior, if of Zion's city,
I through grace a member am,
let the world deride or pity,
I will glory in thy Name.
Fading is the worldling's pleasure,
all his boasted pomp and show;

solid joys and lasting treasure
none but Zion's children know.

(John Newton, 1779)

Who walks as One
And dance as Three
And reigns as glorious Trinity
O Father take;
O Son renew;
O Spirit make our feet praise You!

Who shaped the stars
And formed the earth,
Who sculpted life, and casts new birth;
O Father take;
O Son renew;
O Spirit make our hands praise you!

Who darkness slays
With Holy Light
Who shines mid dayspring and thru night:
O Father take;
O Son renew;
O Spirit make our eyes praise you!

Who hears the cries
Of poor and weak,
Who heeds the prayers the voiceless speak,
O Father take;
O Son renew;
O Spirit make our ears praise you!

Whose thunderous roar
Splits rocks and trees,
Whose still, small voice calms wave and breeze;
O Father take;
O Son renew;
O Spirit make our tongues praise you!

Whose love was borne
Upon the Cross,
Who death endured to save the lost:
O Father take;
O Son renew;
O Spirit make our hearts love you!

(© Kris Michaelson, used by permission)

FURTHER READING

Lewis, C. S. *The Problem of Pain*. New York: Macmillan, 1944.

Gorman, Michael J. *Cruciformity: Paul's Narrative Spirituality of the Cross*. Grand Rapids: Eerdmans, 2001.

Schmemann, Alexander. *For the Life of the World: Sacraments and Orthodoxy*. Crestwood, N.Y.: St. Vladimir's Seminary Press, 1973.

Underhill, Evelyn. *An Anthology of the Love of God*. London: Mowbray and Co., 1953.

FURTHER DISCUSSION

1. What difference does it make to speak about the blessed hope as "going to heaven" or as "participating in the New Heaven and Earth"?
2. How can we avoid opening God to charges of cruelty when we speak of the transformative power of suffering, both on a personal and cosmic scale?
3. How important is it for us to think and teach about judgment and death, as penultimate to the final victory? How do we reconcile this with the knowledge that Jesus has died *for* us?
4. What are the various ways in which redeemed human beings can cooperate in sanctifying the created order for God? Which specific callings are most urgent in today's context as we prepare for the return of Christ, the final judgment, and the New Jerusalem?

Generic Spirituality — Abomination or Open Door?

For the most part, these triads concerning Christian spirituality have taken the form of a family discussion, the musing of one Christian among brothers and sisters, past and present. Yet the nature of love is to be expansive, the nature of light is to shine in darkness, the nature of life is to bring forth more life. If authentic spirituality begins with the particulars of the Christian story, and is shaped by the love, light, and life that originate in the Trinity, this is of importance not only to us but to anyone with ears to hear and eyes to see. Many today complain that in the twenty-first century the work of evangelism is particularly difficult, because we share so little foundational ground with those outside of the Church. Certainly it is true that there are impediments particular to our time, including the very widespread assumptions that spirituality is an individual thing, and that "truths" are individual. The movement away from linear thinking, the inroads made by irrationality, the lack of historical memory that prevents many from recognizing that they have already made significant (and perhaps unhelpful) philosophical decisions — all these are troubling. Added to this is the vague impression in the West that Christianity is already well known, and that it has had its day.

From one perspective, these tendencies block our generation from hearing the gospel, as it has been proclaimed in the past few centuries. It is unlikely that traditional apologetics as practiced since the Enlightenment will make much impact on younger minds, for their imaginations are elsewhere than those of their forebears. From another perspective, the tone-deafness of the early twenty-first century to linear logic and its openness to personal stories provides an entrée. After all, it is the personal God who is wooing his own: when they will not hear arguments or words, his arsenal is not exhausted. The Son, in the days of his earthly life, was well known himself not only for debate, but also for disarming his listeners by telling stories, and so drawing them in. The Holy Spirit, as we have discovered, frequently works through means that are not precisely cognitional, in the center of the being (though God's goal is to integrate each of us, so that heart, mind, will, and body are not at odds with each other). The Scriptures themselves provide a number of different genres, any one of which can communicate, and on different levels of the person — warming the heart, firing the imagination, stirring the conscience, drawing the initially unwilling. Michael Wilcock, in his commentary on the book of Revelation, comments on the peculiar power of that spiritual book to inform God's people in a different manner than the other, more doctrinal sections of the New Testament:

> The conviction that Revelation really is meant to *reveal* truth, and not to obscure it, and that its treasures really do lie on the surface if one looks for them in the right light, is by no means the same as a belief that its meaning will be spelt out for us verbally, with logic and precision. Of course God does not despise verbal communication; after all, 'the Word' was the name he gave to his own Son. But his words, his declarations, and arguments and reasonings, have all been spoken by the time he brings John to Patmos. What he has in store for his last unveiling is a word of a different sort: an acted word, a word dramatized, painted, set to music — a word you can see and feel and taste. In fact, it is a sacrament.
>
> It is no use reading Revelation as though it were a Paul-type theological treatise in a slightly different idiom, or a Luke-style history projected into the future. You might as well analyze the rainbow — or the wine of communion or the water of baptism. Logical analysis is not what they are for. They are meant to be used and enjoyed.
>
> We . . . of all people, should understand this. We live in a post-literate age, which, tiring of words, is beginning to talk again in pictures. So television replaces radio, and the noun 'image' comes back into use with a dozen connotations. Well, God knew about it long ago and when his children have had enough of reciting systematic theology, he gives them a gorgeous picture-book to look at, which is in a different way just as educational.

Pictures, potent images of Christian truth, to use as we use the sacraments — that is what we are given in Revelation. . . . It is the images that stick. John's pages are studded with them . . . that our imagination, as well as our mind, should grasp the key concepts of the faith. So, till the bridegroom returns — till the city descends from the sky, and the day of the wedding-feast dawns — we do this, in remembrance of him. (*The Message of Revelation*, pp. 24-25)

Since God uses different means to transform us, then it must be the case that there is no locked and barred door today where those outside the Church are concerned. It may well be that our own thirst to know God, something we thought was only a matter of our personal growth, or of the corporate strengthening of the Church, can be turned to the help of others who do not yet believe. Indeed, the very disciplines connected with spiritual ecstasy and intimacy, commended to us by those who have become intimate with God, are "transferable": that is, to be in the process of becoming friends of God places us in a situation of potential friendship with the others that he loves, who do not yet name him. Concentration upon God's word, attentiveness in prayer towards him, diligence as we discipline the unruly body and passions, the cultivation of hope as an informed decision when we are tempted to despair, delight in the stories and strengths of others who know him, concerted effort in worship even when our imaginations will not cooperate, working through the problems and wonders of the creeds as we have ability and time, bearing with the irritations that come our way within the Church, returning good for evil, learning the proper and timely use of words and silence — all these practices, enjoined by the Scriptures and the Church's teaching, will be honored by the One who has practiced them perfectly. In following this route, we will come more and more to share in him and to see him.

In seeing him, we find ourselves in a place where we can see others. (God is reversing the great tragedy outlined in Romans 1:21-32, where the primal refusal by humans to honor and give thanks to God issued in blindness concerning the cosmos and the general disruption of human nature). Such godly practices (worship, correction, watchfulness, love, restraint, and delight in the other) all lead to the cultivation of honest hearts. We have forged within us centers of integrity, by which we have the strength to truly understand another's problem in understanding, or seeing, or trusting. Out of that still place of security, we can offer a response that is matched to the day, and to the specific person whom we are learning to love. If we find ourselves questioned by someone who is not interested in complex theology, we have, after all, a Person to offer, and a story about that Person that has beckoned to human beings for centuries. We need not, in the beginning, even attempt to argue that this is a "meta-story" — the Person has the wherewithal to speak through his very own story, even as we tell it! We can rest assured that his purpose with whom we are engaged is to make them whole on every level, including the level of the intellect. It is not necessarily our job to do everything. If, however, we know that we are loved, then it is that Person whom we will put in the center of our action, or conversation: other things will fall into place. If we are worshipers, and have caught even a glimpse of the One who is both seated on the throne and standing among us, it will change us, and folks will be asking why.

Even the greatest difficulty that we face as Christians can be turned to direct our potential brothers and sisters to the One who is truth. It may be shocking for a twenty-first-century "free spirit" to hear us call Jesus the Lord of all. Yet this is a statement about him, not about our religion, or our own clever thinking. If we honor him, we can count on the Holy Spirit to work out the scandal that such "exclusion" (which is really the only means of "inclusion") initially causes. It is helpful in all this to remember that the work has already been done, and is being worked through, by God himself, who is the great Initiator, Pilgrim, and Fulfiller of the human way. Because he has come in history to reside with us in Jesus, because sin has been dealt with on the cross, and because death has been conquered through the resurrection and ascension, we know that God has taken humanity up into himself; yet his Spirit is now most specially within his living Temple, the ones "called out" to worship him and to minister within the human sphere and within his creation, until everything is liberated from its bondage, along with all the children of God. In the Christian story, particularity and universality, past action, present life and future hope, come together in a marvelous way. All of this is a seamless robe, and if we can entice our friends to grasp just one thread — through our joyful report of Jesus, through our evident love for our church community, through our admiring narrative of a holy brother or sister in the faith, through tasting worship, or art, or song with us — they may get more than they bargained for. Our God specializes in raising the dead and in creating out of nothing. He works from many angles, for he knows them all. Nor are the "angles" dishonest ploys: they are all part of the same reality, which he knows better than any of us.

It is probably not true that the greatest barrier to effective evangelism is the erring philosophy and predisposition of the world. It is as it ever was — that the words and life of God's people do not always match. We continue to talk *about* God without allowing God's Word and Wisdom to change us in any substantive way. We want a "quick fix" for others (and for ourselves) when we have been presented with a lifetime and "eternity-full" of re-orientation and transformation in the God-ward direction. We end where we began our quest for authentic Christian spirituality — challenged by one of the earliest hymns of the Church. Through it, Paul encouraged his friends to allow the Holy Spirit to form within them "the mind of Christ." His exhortation was styled as an awestruck rehearsal of God's living drama, in which Jesus is both our salvation and our example. Here is strong medicine not only for Paul's friends in the first century, but also for our individualistic, relativistic, and flatly egalitarian age:

Let the same mind be in you, the one in Christ Jesus,
Who, though he was in the form of God,
Did not regard equality with God something to be seized,
But emptied himself,
Taking the form of a slave,
Being born in human likeness,
And being found in human form,
He humbled himself and became obedient to the point of death —
That is, the death of the cross!

Therefore God also highly exalted him, and gave him the name
    that is above every name,
So that at the name of Jesus, every knee should bow,
Heavenly, earthly, or under the earth,
And every tongue should confess that Jesus Christ is Lord
To the glory of God the Father. (Philippians 2:5-11)

Paul recites these words to the Philippians, explaining that these will help them with the problem of mindset that they are having — a problem of ambition, pride, and disunity. He says, consider for a moment the grandeur of who God the Son is, and what God the Son did — let it fill your hearts, your minds, your spirits. Let this hymn seize you and change you: what God offers you is the mind of Christ. That same mind which is in Christ Jesus is yours, for you are in him. Look: Jesus had the highest status imaginable, and he gave it up, completely, to become one of us, to become a man who died on a *cross*. Down to humanity and death, and the grave, and up to the highest place, to be worshiped by every creature everywhere! Learn, mark, inwardly digest, let this invade your imaginations — then you will shine, you will no longer complain and argue, you will look out for each other, and be completely loving, just as Jesus was and is and will always be. Let the Lord of Glory change you as you praise him!

To say, "Jesus is the LORD" is not a matter of exclusivism nor arrogant imperialism. We have to do with the living God who commanded light to shine out of darkness and who has given us the light of the knowledge of his glory in the face of Christ. We have to do with the Son, Jesus himself, the One in whom God's promises were fulfilled and the One by whom our hopes will be answered. Our answer to those of other faiths can only be to tell, in utter humility, the story of Jesus in our corporate and personal lives. We tell this story in who we are, and also in word, but always making sure that it is Jesus whom we are proclaiming, and not our own cultural baggage. As Paul puts it, "we have this treasure in clay vessels to show that this all-surpassing power is from God and not from us" (2 Corinthians 4:7).

Our answer to today's seeker after spiritual truth and excitement need not be, in the first place, to speak of the dangers and absurdity of pluralism, nor to dwell on the securities of orthodoxy — though we must understand these things, and may indeed come to speak of them with our friends in time, as we note them among ourselves. Our first answer will be to respect the image of our God in the face of the one with whom we speak, and like Paul, to "proclaim that Jesus is Lord" because he was a servant! It is not ourselves, nor our systems, that we commend, but Jesus himself, who is the Truth, and who is (through the Spirit) capable of moving the heart and removing the veil that is over the eyes of the blind. "Not losing heart" will mean that we seek to understand the complex problem of our confused culture, and our implicated churches, and that we will speak and live in the light of the only real solution we have — our true Father God, interpreted to us by Jesus, the Son and known in increasing measure through the indwelling Holy Spirit. So, we pray, along with St. Thomas Aquinas, for the Christ-like ordering of our minds, hearts, wills, and bodies, knowing that every effort made by us is possible only because we are in Christ, and because the Spirit is at work within us:

> Grant, O merciful God,
> Concerning those things which are pleasing to you —
> that I desire ardently,
> search prudently,
> acknowledge truly,
> and bring them to perfect completion,
> for the praise and glory of your name.

We began this study by considering Christian spirituality to be the study of what happens when the human spirit and the Holy Spirit meet. Perhaps our carefully tuned definition of spirituality is still a little skewed. In talking about spirituality as a study, we risk making the great Initiator, the Alpha, the One who is "for us" and "in us," the *object* of our study; or, we may turn our attention away from him to an experience. Better, I think, for us to take seriously the saying, "a theologian is one who prays" and to take as our closing symbol of Christian spirituality the well-known figure of the woman praying in the catacombs, the *Orans*, or "Praying One." She gazes towards heaven, her open hands raised with palms upwards, aware of human need. She provides for us a powerful picture of the soul at prayer, or the Church at prayer, or both together at prayer. With her open hands she says to the Lord, "Come!" "Turn us again, O God. Show the light of your countenance and we shall be whole." And yet we only invite him to fill what is already his: for in him we live and move and have our being, and indeed, in him and through him, we pray. "The Spirit and the Bride say, 'Come!'" A full-bodied Christian spirituality, then, will lead us at every moment to invite God's Spirit to make a personal dwelling in our lives, knowing that we do this together, as the body of Christ. It is out of God's own ecstasy towards us that the intimacy for which we yearn comes. This is the gift of God unto his own.

> Be Thou my Vision, O Lord of my heart;
> Naught be all else to me, save that Thou art;
> Thou my best Thought, by day or by night,
> Waking or sleeping, Thy presence my light.

This female figure, from the catacombs, is known as the "Orans" (literally, the "Praying One"). She is understood by many to be a symbol of the praying Church.   Scala / Art Resource, NY

Be Thou my Wisdom, and Thou my true Word;
I ever with Thee and Thou with me, Lord;
Thou my great Father, I Thy true son;
Thou in me dwelling, and I with Thee one.

Be Thou my battle Shield, Sword for the fight;
Be Thou my Dignity, Thou my Delight;
Thou my soul's Shelter, Thou my high Tower:
Raise Thou me heavenward, O Power of my power.

Riches I heed not, nor man's empty praise,
Thou mine Inheritance, now and always:
Thou and Thou only, first in my heart,
High King of heaven, my Treasure Thou art.

High King of heaven, my victory won,
May I reach heaven's joys, O bright Heaven's Sun!
Heart of my own heart, whatever befall,
Still be my Vision, O Ruler of all.

(Attributed to Dallan Forgaill,
8th c., tr. Mary E. Byrne, 1905)

FURTHER READING

Aquinas, St. Thomas. "Prayer for Ordering a Life Wisely." Available online at http://home.earthlink.net/~thesaurus/thesaurus/Varia/Concede.html. My own translation is offered above.

Michael Wilcock. *The Message of Revelation: I Saw Heaven Opened*. Downers Grove, Ill.: InterVarsity Press, 1975.

Bibliography

Ancient and Liturgical Texts

I Enoch. Translated by E. Isaac. In *The Old Testament Pseudepigrapha* I, edited by James A. Charlesworth, pp. 5-89. Garden City, N.Y.: Doubleday, 1983.

Joseph and Aseneth. Translated by C. Burchard. In *The Old Testament Pseudepigrapha* II, edited by James A. Charlesworth, pp. 177-247. Garden City, N.Y.: Doubleday, 1985.

St. Thomas Aquinas. "Prayer for Ordering a Life Wisely." Available online at http://home.earthlink.net/~thesaurus/thesaurus/Varia/Concede.html.

St. Augustine of Hippo. *The Confessions*. In *Augustine of Hippo — Selected Writings*, translated by Mary T. Clark. Mahwah, N.J.: Paulist Press, 1984.

St. John Chrysostom (attributed). *The Divine Liturgy of St. John Chrysostom*. Available online at http://www.ewtn.com/library/LITURGY/DILITSJC.TXT.

—————. *Commentary on St. John the Apostle and Evangelist*, Homilies 48-88. Translated by Sr. Thomas Aquinas Goggin. In *The Fathers of the Church: A New Translation*. Washington: Catholic University of America Press, 1960.

—————. "Homily LI on John vii.37, 38." In *Nicene and Post-Nicene Fathers*, Volume 14, edited by Philip Schaff. Peabody, Mass.: Hendrickson Publishers, 1889, 1994.

—————. "Homily III on Genesis 1–17." Translated by Robert C. Hill. In *The Fathers of the Church: A New Translation*. Washington: Catholic University of America Press, 1986.

———. "Against Publishing the Errors of the Brethren." In *Nicene and Post-Nicene Fathers*, Volume 9, edited by Philip Schaff. Peabody, Mass.: Hendrickson Publishers, 1889, rpt. 1994.

St. Ephrem the Syrian. *Hymns on Virginity*. Translated by Kathleen E. McVey. In *Ephrem the Syrian: Hymns*, Classics of Western Spirituality. New York: Paulist, 1989.

———. *Hymns on the Church*. Translated by Sebastian Brock in "The Holy Spirit as Feminine in Early Syriac Literature" in *After Eve: Women, Theology and the Christian Tradition*, ed. J. M. Soskice. London: Marshall Pickering Collins, 1990.

St. Gregory of Nyssa. "Sermon Six on the Beatitudes." In *The Lord's Prayer; The Beatitudes*. Translated by Hilda C. Graef. Ancient Christian Writers. Westminster, Md.: Newman, 1954.

———. *Life of Moses*. In *Gregory of Nyssa: The Life of Moses*, translated by A. Malherbe and E. Ferguson. Mahwah, N.J.: Paulist, 1978.

———. *Commentary on the Song of Songs*. In *From Glory to Glory: Texts from Gregory of Nyssa's Mystical Writings*. Translated by H. Musurillo. Crestwood, N.Y.: St. Vladimir's Seminary Press, 1979.

St. Gregory Palamas. *The Triads*. Edited by J. Meyendorff. New York: Paulist, 1983.

Herbert, George. *The Complete English Poems*. London: Penguin, 1991.

St. John Climacus. *The Ladder of Divine Ascent*. Translated by Colm Luibheid. New York: Paulist, 1982.

St. John of the Cross. *The Dark Night of the Soul*. In *The Collected Works of St. John of the Cross*, translated by K. Cavanaugh. Washington, D.C.: Institute of Carmelite Studies, 1976.

Julian of Norwich. *Showings*. Translated by E. Walsh. Mahwah, N.J.: Paulist Press, 1978.

(Pseudo-) Macarius. *Pseudo-Macarius: The Fifty Spiritual Homilies and the Great Letter*. In *Collection II of Pseudo-Macarius*, translated by G. Malone. Mahwah, N.J.: Paulist Press, 1992.

St. Maximos the Confessor. "Chapters on Knowledge" and "The Church's Mystagogy." In *Maximus Confessor: Selected Writings*, translated by G. Berthold, pp. 150-67, 203. Mahwah, N.J.: Paulist Press, 1985.

St. Symeon the New Theologian. *Hymns of Divine Love by Symeon the New Theologian*. Translated by G. A. Maloney. Denville, N.J.: Dimension, 1976.

St. Teresa of Ávila. *The Interior Castle*. In *the Collected Works of St. Teresa of*

Ávila, II. Translated by K. Cavanaugh. Washington, D.C.: Institute of Carmelite Studies, 1980.

The Cloud of Unknowing. Edited by James Walsh. New York: Paulist, 1981.

Thomas à Kempis. *My Imitation of Christ.* Translated by J. J. Gorman. Brooklyn, N.Y.: Confraternity of the Precious Blood, 1982.

Wesley, John and Charles. "A Plain Account of Genuine Christianity," and "Wrestling Jacob." In *Selected Prayers, Hymns, Journal Notes, Sermons, Letters, and Treatises,* edited by F. Whaling. Mahwah, N.J.: Paulist, 1981.

Contemporary Texts

Achtemeier, Elizabeth. "Female Language for God: Should the Church Adopt it?" In *The Hermeneutical Quest.* Allison Park, Pa.: Pickwick, 1986.

Artress, Lauren. *Walking a Sacred Path: Rediscovering the Labyrinth as a Spiritual Tool.* New York: Riverhead Books, 1996.

Avalos, Hector. *Health Care and the Rise of Christianity.* Peabody, Mass.: Hendrickson, 1999.

Barth, Karl. *Church Dogmatics* III and IV. Edinburgh: T&T Clark, 1957.

Bauckham, Richard, and Trevor Hart. *Hope against Hope: Christian Eschatology at the Turn of the Millennium.* Grand Rapids: Eerdmans, 1999.

Bearse, Christine. "Archangel Metatron — The Christ Ray." Available online at http://www.awakeningrainbows.com/Metatron-The_Christ_Ray.htm.

Bergner, Mario. "Redeemed Lives," "Alive Again," "Returning Sons." Available online at http://www.redeemedlives.org.

Bibby, Reginald. *Fragmented Gods: Poverty and Potential of Religion in Canada.* Toronto: Irwin, 1987.

Black, Hugh. *Friendship.* Chicago: Revell, 1903.

Borg, Marcus. *Meeting Jesus Again for the First Time: The Historical Jesus and the Heart of Contemporary Faith.* San Francisco: HarperSanFrancisco, 1994.

Borg, Marcus, and N. T. Wright. *The Meaning of Jesus: Two Visions.* New York: HarperCollins, 1999.

Brock, Sebastian. "The Holy Spirit as Feminine in Early Syriac Literature." In *After Eve: Women, Theology and the Christian Tradition,* edited by J. M. Soskice. London: Marshall Pickering Collins, 1990.

Bultmann, Rudolf. *The New Testament and Mythology.* In *The New Testament and Mythology and Other Basic Writings by Rudolf Bultmann.* Selected, edited, and translated by Schubert M. Ogden. Philadelphia: Fortress Press, 1984.

Clément, Olivier. *The Roots of Christian Mysticism: Texts from the Patristic Era with Commentary*. Translated by Theodore Berkeley. New York: New City Press, 1993.

Coller, Charles. "From the Heart of Jesus Flowing." In *The Song Book of the Salvation Army*, Song 490. London: Salvationist Publishing and Supplies, 1955.

Coyle, J., and Steven Muir. *Healing in Religion and Society from Hippocrates to the Puritans*. Lewiston, N.Y.: Mellen, 1999.

Downey, Michael. *Understanding Christian Spirituality*. New York: Paulist Press, 1997.

Dupré, Louis, and James A. Wiseman, O.S.B. *Light from Light: An Anthology of Christian Mysticism*. Mahwah, N.J.: Paulist Press, 1988.

Egan, Harvey D. *An Anthology of Christian Mysticism*. Second edition. Collegeville, Minn.: The Liturgical Press, 1996.

Evdokimov, Paul. *The Sacrament of Love: The Nuptial Mystery in the Light of the Orthodox Tradition*. Translated by Gythiel Steadman. Crestwood, N.Y.: St. Vladimir's Seminary Press, 1985.

Fieguth, Debra. "Whose Footprints?" *Christian Week* 14, Issue 9, August 2000.

Fiske, Adele M. *Friends and Friendship in the Monastic Tradition*. Cuernavaca, Mexico: CIDOC Cuaderno, 1970.

Florensky, Pavel. *The Pillar and Ground of the Truth: An Essay on Orthodox Theodicy in Twelve Letters*. Translated by Boris Jakim. Princeton, N.J.: Princeton University Press, 1997.

Gorman, Michael J. *Cruciformity: Paul's Narrative Spirituality of the Cross*. Grand Rapids: Eerdmans, 2001.

Harper, Tom. *The Spirituality of Wine*. Kelowna: Northstone, 2004.

Hays, Richard B. "Awaiting the Redemption of Our Bodies." In *Homosexuality in the Church: Both Sides of the Debate*, edited by J. S. Siker. Louisville: Ky.: Westminster/John Knox, 1994.

———. *The Faith of Jesus Christ: The Narrative Substructure of Galatians 3:1–4:11*. Grand Rapids: Eerdmans, 2002.

Humphrey, Edith M. "God's Treasure in Jars of Clay." Available online at http://www.edithhumphrey.net/god's_treasure_in_earthen_jars.htm

———. "Called to Be One: Worshiping the Triune God Together." In *The*

Trinity: An Essential for Faith in Our Time, edited by Andrew Stirling. Nappanee, Ind.: Evangel Publishing House, 2002.

———. "Same Sex Eroticism and the Church: Classical Approaches and Responses." In *The Homosexuality Debate: Faith Seeking Understanding,* edited by Catherine Sider Hamilton. Toronto: Anglican Book Centre, 2003.

———. *Joseph and Aseneth.* Guide to Apocrypha and Pseudepigrapha 8. Sheffield: Sheffield Academic Press, 2000.

———. *The Ladies and the Cities: Transformation and Apocalyptic Identity in Joseph and Aseneth, 4 Ezra, the Apocalypse, and The Shepherd of Hermas.* JSP Supplements 18. Sheffield: JSOT Press, 1995.

Ingham, Michael. *Mansions of the Spirit: The Gospel in a Multi-Faith World.* Toronto: Anglican Book Centre, 1997.

James, Steve. "Christ Your Glory." Song 272 in *Sing Glory.* Chelston, Torquay: Jubilate Hymns, 1999.

Fr. John of Kronstadt. *Spiritual Counsels: Select Passages from* My Life in Christ. Edited by W. J. Grisbrooke. Crestwood, N.Y.: St. Vladimir's Seminary Press, 1967.

Just, Arthur A., Jr., ed. *Ancient Christian Commentary on Scripture: New Testament 3: Luke.* Downers Grove, Ill.: InterVarsity Press, 2003.

Kimbrough, S. T., Jr. *Orthodox and Wesleyan Spirituality.* Crestwood, N.Y.: St. Vladimir's Seminary Press, 2002.

Koresh, David. "The Seven Seals of the Book of Revelation." In *Why Waco: Cults and the Battle for Religious Freedom in America,* edited by James Taylor and Eugene Gallagher. Berkeley: University of California Press, 1995.

Kreeft, Peter. *Back to Virtue: Traditional Moral Wisdom for Modern Moral Confusion.* San Francisco: Ignatius Press, 1992.

Lewis, C. S. *The Four Loves.* London: Geoffrey Bles, 1960.

———. *Miracles: A Preliminary Study.* New York: Macmillan, 1947.

———. *Poems.* Edited by Walter Hooper. London: Geoffrey Bles, 1964; New York: Harcourt Brace Jovanovich, 1977.

———. *The Problem of Pain.* New York: Macmillan, 1944.

———. *The Voyage of the Dawn Treader.* London: Geoffrey Bles, 1952; New York: Collier Books, 1970.

Lossky, Vladimir. *The Vision of God.* Translated by Asheleigh Moorhouse. Crestwood, N.Y.: St. Vladimir's Seminary Press, 1983.

Lyotard, Jean François. *The Postmodern Condition.* Translated by G.

Bennington and B. Massumi. Minneapolis: University of Minnesota Press, 1984.

Martin, Dale. *The Corinthian Body.* New Haven: Yale University Press, 1995.

Meilaender, Gilbert. *Friendship: A Study in Theological Ethics.* Notre Dame: University of Notre Dame Press, 1981.

Merton, Thomas. *New Seeds of Contemplation.* New York: New Directions, 1962.

————. *Contemplation in a World of Action.* Garden City: Doubleday, 1973.

Pannenberg, Wolfhart. "Eschatology and the Experience of Meaning." In *Basic Questions in Theology, III,* translated by R. A. Wilson. London: SCM Press, 1974.

Peterson, Eugene H. *A Long Obedience in the Same Direction: Discipleship in an Instant Society.* Downers Grove, Ill.: InterVarsity Press, 1980, second ed. 2000.

Pieper, Josef. *On Hope.* Translated by Sr. Mary Frances McCarthy. San Francisco: Ignatius Press, 1986.

Schmemann, Alexander. *For the Life of the World: Sacraments and Orthodoxy.* Crestwood, N.Y.: St. Vladimir's Seminary Press, 1973.

Schumacher, Michele M., ed. *Women in Christ: Towards a New Feminism.* Grand Rapids: Eerdmans, 2003.

Stevenson, Mary. "Footprints in the Sand." Available online at http://footprints-inthe-sand.com.

Tolkien, J. R. R. "On Fairy-Stories." In *Essays Presented to Charles Williams.* London: Oxford University Press, 1947.

Underhill, Evelyn. *The Spiritual Life.* New York: Harper and Bros., 1936.

————. *The Ways of the Spirit.* New York: Crossroad, 1993.

————. *An Anthology of the Love of God.* Edited by L. Barkway and L. Menzies. London: Mowbray and Co., 1953.

Van Leeuwen, Mary Stewart. *Gender and Grace: Love, Work and Parenting in a Changing World.* Downers Grove, Ill.: InterVarsity Press, 1990.

Von Speyr, Adrienne. *The Farewell Discourses; Meditations on John 13–17.* Translated by E. A. Nelson. San Francisco: Ignatius Press, 1987.

Walsh, Brian J., and J. Richard Middleton. *The Transforming Vision: Shaping a Christian World-View.* Downers Grove, Ill.: InterVarsity Press, 1984.

Ware, Kallistos. *The Orthodox Way.* Crestwood, N.Y.: St. Vladimir's Seminary Press, 1995.

————. *The Orthodox Church.* Second revised edition. London: Penguin, 1993.

—————. "Approaching Christ the Physician: the True Meaning of Confession and Anointing." Lecture given at Sacraments of Healing: the OPF Retreat in Vézelay, France (April, 1999). Available online at http://www.incommunion.org/kal3.htm.

Wilcock, Michael. *The Message of Revelation: I Saw Heaven Opened.* Downers Grove, Ill.: InterVarsity Press, 1975.

Wilkinson, John. *The Bible and Healing: A Medical and Theological Commentary.* Grand Rapids: Eerdmans, 1998.

Wright, N. T. *The New Testament and the People of God.* Minneapolis: Fortress Press, 1992.

—————. *What St. Paul Really Said.* Grand Rapids: Eerdmans, 1997.

Zizioulas, John D. *Being as Communion: Studies in Personhood and the Church.* Crestwood, N.Y.: St. Vladimir's Seminary Press, 1993.

Index of Subjects and Names

287

Index of Scripture and Other Ancient Sources

p. 46 in X neither "gay" nor "straight" – on homosexuality